TACTICAL CIVICS™

High School Edition

A Popular Constitutionalism Tutorial for Homeschooling Christians

Second Edition

David M. Zuniga
Founder, TACTICAL CIVICS™

Copyright © 2022 by David M. Zuniga

TACTICAL CIVICS™ High School Edition: A Popular Constitutionalism Tutorial for Homeschooling Christians (2nd Edition; paperback)

by David M. Zuniga

Printed in the United States of America

All rights reserved solely by the author, who warrants that other than American founding documents in the public domain and noted quotations, all contents are original and do not infringe on legal rights of any other person or work.

Tactical Civics™, TACTICAL CIVICS™, AmericaAgain!™, the Constitution and quill logo, and Indictment Engine™ are trademarks of AmericaAgain! Trust Foundation and AmericaAgain!, LLC.

This book may not be reproduced in any form without prior written approval of the author.

Paperback ISBN 979-8-4265-3322-6

March 5, 2022

Dedication

I dedicate this tutorial course for homeschoolers to all you mothers who are tenaciously rebuilding our civilization – one diaper, one research project, and one tearful prayer at a time.

Like the countless unsung women on the American frontier, if true greatness is yet found in America today, it is in your lioness Proverbs 31 hearts.

:::

Oh you great ones! I dedicate this work to you.

May God bless your children and grandchildren

to replenish our desolate land,

and to do great exploits,

that your hearts may be lifted up in joy.

Table of Contents

Note to Parents 1

To the Student 3

Lesson 1: Overview of federal government 5

Lesson 2: Tactical Civics™ Introduction 13

Lesson 3: Applying Romans 13 in America 25

Lesson 4: Dishonest Abe, American Idol 31

Lesson 5: Split Them Up 35

Lesson 6: Bring Them Home 39

Lesson 7: True Law Enforcement 45

Lesson 8: Nineteen Steps to America Again 55

Lesson 9: Granite Dome Syndrome 59

Lesson 10: What's Under the Hood 67

Lesson 11: The People Themselves 73

Lesson 12: Republic, Republic, Republic! 77

Lesson 13: Our First Right 81

Lesson 14: The Last D.C. Congress 91

Lesson 15: Our Job, Not Trump's 95

Lesson 16: Cabbages, Kings, and Tactical Civics™ 97

Lesson 17: The Fear Porn Industry 99

Lesson 18: The Founders, Right Again 105

Lesson 19: The ConCon Come-On 111

Lesson 20: Allegiance to What?..113

Lesson 21: Culturism is Not Racism..115

Lesson 22: Support Our Troops?..121

Lesson 23: Shooting Second Amendment Blanks.....................................129

Lesson 24: Fake History = Fake News..135

Lesson 25: 'Rights' is Wrong...139

Lesson 26: The Greater Magistrate (Part I)..141

Lesson 27: The Greater Magistrate (Part II)..147

Lesson 28: The Greater Magistrate (Part III)..151

Lesson 29: Some Days, the World Just Changes.....................................157

Lesson 30: Follow the Money..161

Lesson 31: A New Way of Life Begins...167

Appendix A: Recommended Reading – A Liberty Library....................171

Appendix B: 28th Amendment Fact Sheet...191

Appendix C: Ratification Vote Model Resolution...................................195

Appendix D: Declaration of Independence...199

Appendix E: U.S. Constitution..203

Appendix F: AmericaAgain! Declaration...227

Appendix G: Tactical Civics™ Declaration..255

Note to Parents

We are living in the most exciting time in American history since our ancestors took up arms against their own government, seeking independence.

As a second-generation homeschooler who designed curriculum and planted four school boards and their K-12 classical Christian schools in Iowa, North Carolina, and Texas three decades ago, I can confidently assert that this tutorial is unique in the history of American education, and is most fit for a homeschool setting.

This 31-unit tutorial [in the free PDF the links are live] constantly reiterates key principles to teach the precepts, principles, and norms of the historic mission, TACTICAL CIVICS™, a new way of life for the responsible remnant.

It is a criminal shame that history and civics are not taught truthfully in America. Human nature and God's providence are nowhere more clearly illustrated than in accurate history. This is what your child will receive in this course. *So beware! Review this text. Are you willing to engage your child in these hard, true things?*

In the 1750s and beyond, the ruthless tyrant over Americans was based across the Atlantic; the world's most powerful government. Today, we face no tyrant; merely our servants operating organized crime since Lincoln's administration.

Using Congress as its game-pieces based in the most powerful, ruthless city-state in history, evil men and their corporations first used our servants as minions to conquer the lands and natural resources of these sovereign States. Then they turned their insatiable lust on the rest of the world, beginning with the theft of Hawaii, then Teddy Roosevelt's "splendid little war", when he bought foreign countries in arrogant violation of our Constitution. Over the past 130 years, the D.C.-based Military Industrial Complex *invaded over 115 sovereign countries.*

Yet, I assert that this is the most exciting time since our War for Independence because since our sovereign States, lawful U.S. Dollar, and constitutional Militias were hijacked by Lincoln and the 37th Congress to benefit globalists, We The People never had a way to arrest the criminals. *Now we do!*

Some may consider this tutorial too advanced for undergraduate Political Science courses; but any 15-18 year-old of average intelligence who is passionate about ethics and government will breeze through it and go on to *Recommended Reading.*

This tutorial is designed to require no *teaching* by you, but parents should read the text, provide an audience for your child's essays and oratorical presentations, and answer at least one question at the end of each lesson. *Dad: Showing sincere interest in your child's work for this tutorial can truly change everything.*

Unlike graduation speakers' blithe assertions, your child will become America's hope for the future by completing this tutorial and taking it to heart.

So should you.

To the Student

This will be the *strangest* course you will have taken or likely ever take. Honestly. There has never been anything like this tutorial in any homeschool, private school, undergraduate or graduate program of which we are aware.

In this tutorial you will learn the following facts and precepts and be able to inform other Americans of any age, of them:

- The vital importance of repentance (actions, not words) in our time
- Why elections are irrelevant in failed systems
- American government's design as we stipulate in the Constitution
- The purpose and key stipulations of our highest human law
- Who 'We The People' actually refers to
- The People's two ancient law enforcement institutions
- America was hijacked in the generation of Lincoln, Marx, and Darwin
- Modern politics is *organized crime* in state and D.C. palaces
- Corollary A: Parties and electoral politics are *not* law enforcement
- Corollary B: It is *absurd* to look to our servants as saviors
- Why this is *potentially* the most blessed time in 200 years
- How TACTICAL CIVICS™ is God's gift to the repentant remnant
- How just half of 1% of the population can maintain rule of law

Tutorial Requirements

Complete one or two lessons weekly. *We reiterate key concepts many times.* At the end of each lesson: 1) write Lesson #, date, and a 250-300 word essay in your own words, on the key ideas; 2) deliver an oration of about five minutes based on your essay, to an adult audience which can be Dad (Mom will have already heard it), one or more of your grandparents, a neighbor, pastor, family friends, civic club…even in a mall or town square; and 3) get one of your parents to answer <u>*at least one*</u> of the *Questions for Parents* at each lesson's end.

Do not deliver orations to a TACTICAL CIVICS™ chapter or your homeschool co-op. Even if others do not cheat off of your superb work, the presentations will become much too repetitive.

Think outside the box.

Lesson 1
Overview of federal government

The government of these fifty United States is based on a written Constitution which is only 4,400 words long; the shortest national constitution in the world. It is also the oldest written national constitution in effect in the world today.

After the Constitutional Convention in Philadelphia, held from May-September 1787, the final Constitution was sent to the 13 states for ratification.

Supreme Law, Not a 'Compact'

Many textbooks claim that our Constitution for the United States was a 'compact' or a contract and the States were the parties to that contract. That is false, as evidenced by Article VI, Section 2 of the law itself, which states,

This Constitution, and the Laws of the United States which shall be made in Pursuance thereof; and all Treaties made, or which shall be made, under the Authority of the United States, shall be the supreme Law of the Land; and the Judges in every State shall be bound thereby, any Thing in the Constitution or Laws of any State to the Contrary notwithstanding.

Thus, the U.S. Constitution is not a compact or a contract. It is the highest and most authoritative *law* in these united States, by which We The People created, defined, and *severely limited* our federal servants in three branches.

In Article I, we create and define the legislative branch (Congress; U.S. House and U.S. Senate). In Article II, we create and define the executive branch (presidency). In Article III, we create and define the U.S. supreme Court, and authorize our Article I creature to create its own inferior federal courts.

On June 21, 1788, New Hampshire ratified the Constitution giving it the necessary nine out of 13 votes needed for the Constitution to become law. It officially went into effect on March 4, 1789. It consists of a Preamble, seven Articles, and 27 Amendments thus far.

From this one law, the federal government was created and supposed to be severely limited, as We The People stipulate in Amendments IX and X.

But using the excuse, *"the Constitution is a living document whose interpretation changes over time"*, criminal minds in Congress have used the interstate commerce and 'necessary and proper' clauses to embezzle trillions of dollars and perpetrate racketeering under color of government agencies. Our federal servants and supposed representatives violate the highest law with utter impunity all the way over in D.C., far from their collective sovereign We The People.

The only human power with authority to stop this crime spree is *We The People*.

Three Branches of Our federal Servant

In the U.S. Constitution, We The People created three branches of government to serve us in particular ways, each branch having its own functions.

Legislative: This branch, Congress, is *supposed* to make federal laws. It consists of two houses, the Senate and the House of Representatives.

Executive: We grant the executive power to the president, who is given the job to execute and administer the laws and government. The *massive* bureaucracy is part of the executive branch, and We The People plan to seriously reduce it, as you will learn in this tutorial.

Judicial: The federal judicial power is vested in the U.S. supreme Court and inferior federal courts. Their job is to interpret and apply federal laws through cases brought before them. While judges can issue their *opinions,* as we will explain, *We The People have the final decision on what the Constitution says.*

Five Principles of American Civics

The Constitution's five basic principles were once deeply ingrained in the minds of Americans but today have all given way to D.C. organized crime:

Popular Sovereignty: This principle states that the source of governmental power lies with the People; we are collectively the sovereign over all government. We establish government for our own benefit; when any government starts doing the opposite, in the Declaration of Independence we told the world that such a government should be changed or dissolved by the People.

Limited Government: We The People create, define, and severely limit the powers and functions of our servants. So, despite what you see it claiming every day in every way, the U.S. government does not derive its power from itself. It must obey its own laws and especially must only do the things that We The People authorize it to do, in the U.S. Constitution.

Separation of Powers: Our federal servant is divided into three branches so that no one branch has too much power. *Theoretically,* each branch has its own purpose: to make laws, execute laws, and interpret laws.

Checks and Balances: To protect ourselves against corrupt servants, We The People establish *horizontal* checks and balances; each branch of our federal servant keeping the other two from becoming too powerful. The president can veto legislation, the supreme Court can declare acts of Congress unconstitutional, and the Senate must approve treaties and presidential appointments. Then, our own *vertical* checks, We The People in Grand Jury and Militia, superintending them.

Federalism: This is the principle that federal servants have *only* the 17 powers granted to them by We The People, who reserve *all other conceivable powers* for ourselves and our state servants. Presently, federalism is hijacked by organized crime, as you will soon read.

Napoleon in a Black Dress? No!

Civics and government courses include another supposed basic principle of federal government, *judicial review,* but misrepresent it as judicial *supremacy,* making the supreme Court more authoritative than the legislative or executive branches. Yes, the power of 'judicial review' was created by chief justice John Marshall in a side note to his opinion in *Marbury v. Madison* in 1803. But law schools teach that Marshall created a new governing power over presidents and Congress; yet that is not at all what Marshall wrote, viz:

[T]*he Constitution of the United States confirms and strengthens the principle…that a law repugnant to the constitution is void; and that courts, as well as other departments, are bound by that instrument.*

[T]*he framers of the Constitution contemplated that instrument as a rule for the government of courts, as well as of the legislature.*

The legal industry and schools have been lying. We The People, the sovereign in our Republic (far above federal judges!) must restore rule of law, including putting lawless judges back in their place.

Our Hijacked Political Process

Many countries have political *coalition governments;* factions who join together to cut deals, to win political power and control. While We The People in the U.S. Constitution stipulate and limit the powers of our servants, our highest law is *daily violated* by a massive, corrupt machine, the *Deep Axis,* described on page 17.

The Democrat and Republican machines are actors in theater to keep the People entertained as the politics industry cuts deals, trades favors, and *passes laws written by industry lawyers, not by legislators.* Yes: for generations, laws have been written by industry lawyers and only *sponsored* by legislators.

We *supposedly* elect a president via the Electoral College, one elector for each member of Congress. But in most states, Electoral College votes are 'thrown' by the dominant political machine to the candidate with the most votes; corrupt state legislatures and party machines destroyed the Electoral College.

The corrupt party machines have been operating for generations. Fraudulent electronic voting has been going on for decades. Nobody knows how many politicians are in office legitimately. As long as Dominion Voting Systems and other criminal enterprises are counting electronically, turnout will continue to drop in elections and the criminal fraud will repeat as in 2020, perpetrated by countless Democrat counties that installed Biden as 'president' and several senators and congressmen who did not actually win.

Yet, despite the rampant corruption, *this is the most exciting time in two centuries of American history*. Why? Because elections and constitutional rule of law can be restored by an informed sovereign, We The People. We only need to *repent*.

Living Above The Line

This is the first infographic accurately depicting the unique system of government and hierarchy stipulated by We The People in our U.S. Constitution.

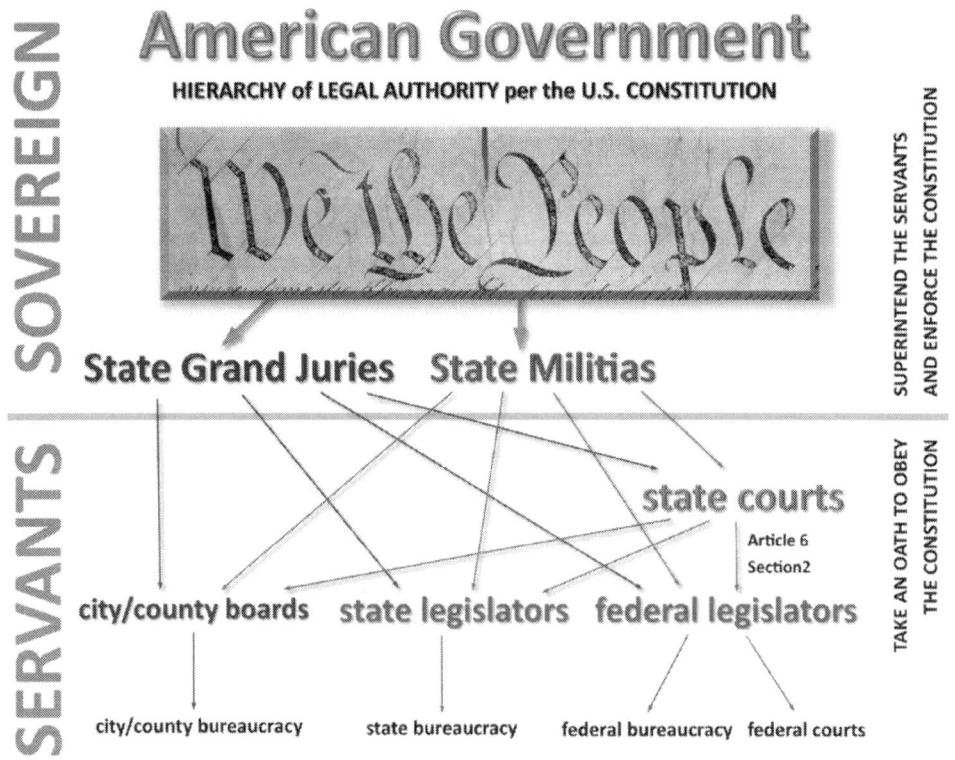

Our Founding Fathers had learned the hard way in England that any government with too much power will plunder and oppress people. They distrusted the power of monarchs and knew that *servant* government was key to liberty. They felt that separation of powers, *horizontal* checks and balances, and the People's *vertical* checks would best prevent tyranny. James Madison said, *"In framing a government which is to be administered by men over men, the great difficulty lies in this: you must first enable the government to control the governed; and in the next place oblige it to control itself."*

That was much easier in 1787 than today. The *horizontal* checks depend on godly, principled men in all servant branches so that no branch gained too much power. With sin now rampant in every level of public life, it is imperative that a critical mass of the People (we think half of 1% is enough) must do our duties 'above the line'. The *vertical* check; We The People, in Grand Jury and Militia. Imagine, in 1787 those duties were already 790 years old in English Common Law!

Legislative Branch

The structure of the houses of Congress was the greatest debate during the Constitutional Convention. By dividing representatives equally and based on size, the Founding Fathers ensured that small states had a voice in federal government. The Senate has two senators per state, and the House of Representatives is based on population. It should have about 6,600+ members at present, but only has 435. Why? Because, beginning in 1890, Congress illegally limited the number of U.S. House districts to increase the power held by each congressman and assuring that powerful men and industries had fewer politicians to pay off.

Then in 1929, while the People struggled to survive the Great Depression, Congress limited the number of U.S. House districts to 435; a power which We The People never gave them. This one crime had amazing corrupting influence, as George Washington feared in the 1787 convention. In later lessons we will further discuss *The Crime of '29* and 'Our First Right'. But back to basic civics.

In Article I, Section 8 of the U.S. Constitution, We The People *explicitly* list the legislative powers of Congress. Besides the power to make laws, the most significant of the 17 *specifically enumerated* powers of Congress are:

- Declaring war
- Levying taxes (must be apportioned among the States, and uniform)
- Overseeing expenditure of public funds
- Borrowing money
- Coining money from silver and gold
- Regulating commerce between states, other countries, and Indian tribes
- Impeaching and trying federal officers
- Approving treaties negotiated by the executive branch
- Approving presidential appointments

But instead of limiting itself to the lawful functions that we gave it in Article I, Section 8, Congress increasingly grows cancerous 'implied' powers not even *remotely* authorized by us in the Constitution, simply lumping them under the 'necessary and proper' or interstate commerce clauses.

It's also insane that our servants set their own salaries and benefits. In this course, you will learn how We The People can arrest further attempts to add unlawful powers to their existing snake's nest, and how we can scrape back all the powers conjured up by our criminal servants.

But now, let's see why the People's *vertical* check, law enforcement, is the key.

Fascism (a.k.a., 'Deep Capture')

Given man's sin nature, every society needs laws. In these united States, We The People authorize Congress to write federal laws. In Article I, Section I of the U.S. Constitution, we state in part, *"All legislative Powers herein granted shall be vested in a Congress of the United States, which shall consist of a Senate and House of Representatives".*

But in fact, since the Lincoln administration, federal laws have been written by law firms working for powerful industries, corporations, and lobbying groups. As mentioned above, members of Congress merely *sponsor,* they do not write, laws!

Italian dictator Benito Mussolini defined Fascism as *the alliance of strong central government with the corporations, to control the people in the service of the State.* Fascism in Washington D.C., control of government by industry, is called *Deep Capture.*

Not only are most federal laws not written by legislators under the supervision of We The People, as our system was designed…

Not only do legislators get to cash in on buying or 'shorting' stock of companies in industries that they are about to greatly affect via legislation; a federal crime when the People do it…

Not only when legislators are voted out for doing a terrible job, do they continue to receive taxpayer checks until death…

But they often go to work for industries whose laws they sponsored!

Obviously, these crimes must be stopped. But who will do that, *Congress itself? Or the federal courts, which exist and serve at the pleasure of Congress?* (See Constitution, Article III, Section 1.) Now you see why most civics and government courses are *fantasy?* Our servants have been running organized crime for generations. But Americans don't sense God's judgment, refusing to repent and continuing to play electoral politics rather than perform our duties: oversight and law enforcement.

Executive Branch

The executive branch is headed by the president, who acts as the head of state in diplomatic relations and as commander-in-chief for all U.S. branches of the war industry, even those branches that are not constitutionally authorized to exist.

The president is responsible for implementing the laws written by Congress. He appoints the heads of federal agencies including the cabinet, which was originally very small. Now, the president is chief bureaucrat over the Deep State that serves itself and has grown to control as many aspects of our lives as possible.

The vice president is next in line of succession, becoming acting president should the current president die or become incapacitated while in office, or is impeached and removed from office. Impeachment has largely been ceremonial. Not all impeachments remove the officeholder from office, most corrupt judges are never impeached, and the impeachment of Trump was a transparent, blatant political attack as part of a larger gaslighting operation.

The 15 federal bureaucratic 'departments' create, oversee, and enforce the massive reams of rules and regulations currently in force in America. As the administrative tentacles of the president, these departments serve as his advisory cabinet. The head of each executive department, called a 'secretary', is appointed by the president and takes office after confirmation by the Senate.

The heads of executive departments are included in the line of succession to the president, after the vice president, speaker of the House, and president *pro tempore* of the Senate, in the event of a vacancy in the presidency.

Judicial Branch

The federal laws are a Byzantine mishmash that has grown like a cancer through American history. Some federal laws are vague and others very specific. Many are confusing as well as unconstitutional. Supposedly, the federal judicial system sorts through this mountain of laws and regulations to decide what is constitutional and what is not. But it is the People's authority and not that of the courts, to determine this. How can the People do so? We explain in detail, in this course.

The judicial branch is made up of the supreme Court of the United States (SCOTUS). It is made up of nine members, with the highest-ranking given the title of 'chief justice'. Each judge serves 'for life', but when one retires, resigns, is impeached, becomes incapacitated, or dies, a replacement is appointed by the president. A majority of the Senate must approve the nominee.

While SCOTUS is the highest court in the republic, the judicial branch also includes lower courts that We The People in Article III, Section 1, authorize Congress to create. Thus, federal courts are creatures of Congress. *Remember this!*

The federal court system is divided into twelve judicial districts, or 'circuits'. If a case is appealed beyond a district court, it moves to a federal appeals court, and then possibly to the U.S. supreme Court for a final decision.

Federalism in these United States

As shown in the page 8 infographic, We The People through our Constitution establish a servant government based on *federalism;* the antithesis of central power. We The People are the highest layer; under us are our state servants, and under them are our federal servants. In the Tenth Amendment to the Constitution, we stipulate: *The powers not delegated to the United States by the Constitution, nor prohibited by it to the States, are reserved to the States respectively, or to the people.*

Thus, the 17 functions ('powers') enumerated by us in Article I, Section 8 are granted to Congress, and *we reserve all others to ourselves*! All functions that Congress is currently exercising that are *not* specifically enumerated by us to Congress, *are being exercised illegally*. As criminal as fraud or embezzlement.

Some actions, such as printing money and declaring war, are exclusive to the federal government. Others, like conducting elections and issuing marriage licenses, are responsibilities of the individual states. Both the states and federal servants can do things like establish courts and collect taxes.

But here is the key point in this lesson: our servant governments at all levels have only those powers that We The People grant to them in our written Constitutions. Anything else they do – no matter how long they have been getting away with it unchallenged – is organized crime. *Period.* No qualifications.

We should not have to find ourselves like so many Russians or Chinese, powerless and under lawless government commands, before We The People, the collective sovereign *over* the Constitution, start enforcing it!

Lesson 1 Questions for Parents

1. Which fact of American civics in this lesson most shocks or surprises you?

2. Can you name an attitude or practice that most contributes to the steady decline of our Republic, by which we individually and collectively enable and encourage the staggering criminality in Washington D.C.?

Lesson 2

Tactical Civics™ Introduction

To control the Supreme Court we must first lay claim to the Constitution ourselves. That means publicly repudiating justices who say that they, not we, possess ultimate authority to say what the Constitution means…It means refusing to be deflected by arguments that constitutional law is too complex or difficult for ordinary citizens…the Supreme Court is not the highest authority in the land on constitutional law. We are.[1]

– **Larry D. Kramer**

Amen. This is the *best* time to be alive in American history. And this tutorial can be the most important thing you have ever done for the future. It will debunk lies and teach you vital civics that schools leave out, giving you all you need to live a new way of life as we repair America's fallen walls, end D.C. organized crime, and begin to restore our civilization.

Many excellent organizations *teach* the U.S. Constitution. This course trains you to *enforce* the Constitution and teach future generations to do the same. A whole new way of life. Yes, we have a lot to repair. But America was not destroyed in a year and it won't be restored overnight. As you learn how our government is designed to work and how simple it is to take responsibility, you'll wonder why it took us so long to do this.

We will astound ourselves (and the world) over the next generation if we can realize this is not about presidents. This restoration project is, and always has been, *up to us*. And as you will see, this is not politics. *It's life.*

Our Mission to America

We thought that Donald Trump was crucial to We the People ending the control of the Deep State that our ancestors allowed. His unlikely victory over 16 primary candidates; his team's shrewd social media campaign; his tireless cross-country rally schedule; the massive throngs of normal Americans; his saying that his was *our* victory – all were God's answer to millions who prayed, worked and voted. But Trump was only step one. And of course, *the Deep Axis struck back!*

In this lesson, you learn that We the People alone have the authority to restore our rule of law. Born into this uniquely blessed civilization, our ancestors let it collapse. Not *once* have they ever *enforced* the Constitution.

---

[1] Dr. Kramer, at that time dean of Stanford Law School, on pages 247-248 of his groundbreaking book, *The People Themselves: Popular Constitutionalism and Judicial Review.*

This lesson first presents seven TACTICAL CIVICS™ principles; then it debunks nine proposed 'solutions' that have never worked; finally, it detoxes you from insidious propaganda in the civics vocabulary we take for granted.

After the COVID hoax and Election Steal 2020, can we end today's hijacking? Absolutely. In the Constitution, We the People create, define, and limit our federal servant, give them 17 duties, and give ourselves only one: *enforce it.*

'We the People' means only those Americans who choose to perform the duties that we confer on ourselves in our highest law. This remnant can do what a president cannot dream of doing. We must only graduate from fear, cynicism, Facebook rants, pointless rallies, and Fear Porn.

This is not theory; it's a boot camp for the repentant remnant who are ready to take responsibility and teach our children and grandchildren a new way of life. It requires only dedication, very little time, and $5 monthly member dues.

AmericaAgain! is a charitable trust and member organization whose mission was developed by 44 volunteers: professional engineers, a former U.S. Secret Service agent, a Fortune 500 tech manager, a former naval medic and helicopter instructor, a former missionary, authors, software designers, and others who have invested over 60,000 hours in R&D since early 2008, and now run the TACTICAL CIVICS™ Training Center – not a social media hangout, but *action.*

After reading 'restore America' books for decades, I found no solution so in 2008, we published the AmericaAgain! Declaration; in 2010, *This Bloodless Liberty;* in 2015, Fear The People; and in 2020, *A Republic to Save.* These and other titles are available as free PDF books when you join us. To restore America, our objectives in order are:

- Launch & build a TACTICAL CIVICS™ chapter in every county
- Support true county Grand Juries via our county ordinance
- Restore constitutional Militia via our county ordinance
- Finish ratifying the original First Right in our Bill of Rights
- Take Congress out of Washington D.C. forever
- Force through 18 other reform laws over time
- Launch the AmericaAgain! Indictment Engine™

Countless books, conferences, blogs, podcasts, radio shows, videos and declarations rehash the problem. But as you now see, Washington D.C. is earth's most corrupt city-state and federal judges will not help. We The People, through Grand Jury, Militia, and our State courts are *the only constitutional means* to finally end the hijacking that began with Lincoln.

It takes time to learn what Americans have not been taught for five generations. While these materials are written at 10th grade comprehension level, Americans need to re-learn how to live a responsible new way of life, and that includes many aspects. Teaching this and executing it, is the mission of TACTICAL CIVICS™.

You Have What It Takes

Retired Americans have the most free time, and military and 'law enforcement' veterans have the most training, but if you are 18 or older, you can formally be a 'missionary to America', and in fact, any American who can grasp the concepts in this tutorial is old enough to inform others.

Remember, TACTICAL CIVICS™ is not politics but *responsible* life in America. Learning basic civics and teaching it to others, you break the downward spiral of hopelessness leading to apathy. That is service to your country!

Politicians, Bureaucrats and the Deep State

We can never convert the masses, but as Margaret Meade said, *"Never doubt that a small group of thoughtful, committed citizens can change the world. Indeed, it is the only thing that ever has."* Most people are apathetic and will not change. That is no problem; as noted earlier, we only need about half of 1% of America to do this.

In the next lesson, we deprogram you from absurd Roman civics that churches teach. Our system of government is *popular constitutionalism,* meaning that We the People have power and authority like no other population on earth.

Politics cannot arrest crime cartels; politics and Big Tech are the Deep State's PR machine. George Washington said of political parties:

"However they may now and then answer popular ends, they are likely in the course of time and things, to become potent engines by which cunning, ambitious, and unprincipled men will be enabled to subvert the power of the people and to usurp for themselves the reins of government, destroying afterwards the very engines which have lifted them to unjust dominion."

That was what Trump said to all the squirming politicians at his inauguration. See how they retaliated?

Elites buy politicians like pets; just a business expense. No political party will ever restore rule of law because the Deep State invented two-party theater. Remember the reality of D.C.: industry writes federal laws and gives large donations to politicians, engaging in *deep capture,* hiring former members of Congress, federal regulators, and staffers. In turn, regulatory agencies hire former industry employees. Using these tactics, the Deep State controls all three branches of federal government and the regulatory agencies that supposedly keep industry honest. For a deeper dive, research the most blatant industry moles in D.C., called the 'Senior Executive Service'.

After 150 years of Deep State hijacking, our constitutional crisis is as precipitous as that faced by the Mexican people. But unlike them, we have the power to *arrest* this nonsense.

As Mexicans 'expatriate' in hordes to our republic, many Americans are also expatriating to every paradise and backwater on earth, seeking to escape the fascist Leviathan with its tentacles in every toilet flush, light bulb, medical exam room, browsing session, phone call, text, and email communication, now demanding that citizens be jabbed with toxins or lose their jobs!

Most Americans still refuse to flee our great republic. Instead, they stay to live out the Orwellian nightmare, complaining daily but doing nothing to end the hijacking. Only posting social media rants, they meet Einstein's definition of insanity: *"repeatedly doing the same thing and always expecting a different result".*

As he walked out of the 1787 convention, Ben Franklin was asked by Lady Powell of Philadelphia, *"Doctor Franklin, what kind of government have you given us?"* He replied, *"A Republic, Madam, if you can keep it."*

Obviously, we haven't kept it. Our employees are embezzling us blind, doing things every day that we never authorized. Not only do they arrogantly violate the law, but the *very existence* of 75% of federal agencies, bureaus, offices, programs and regulations violate the Constitution. By definition, criminals don't play by rules; they *break* them.

Seneca the Younger said *"He who does not prevent a crime when he can, encourages it".* We *encourage* criminals when we merely attend rallies with posters and colonial costumes. We *encourage* criminals when we only send powerless emails to them for amassing $22 trillion in debt and over $170 trillion in unfunded liabilities.

We *encourage* criminals when we give them 9% approval rating yet allow them to set their own salaries, staffing levels, opulent offices – and pay them lifelong benefits *even after we have fired them!*

We *encourage* criminals when we send busloads of kids to gawk at 535 politicians who *each* spend $11 million annually… who each have as many as *eight* offices and staffs… whose palace is as opulent as those of kings: white-glove gilded dining rooms and gold-plated china… who hire limousines, spas, and private jets… who incite parasites against producers… who arrange for the top 1% of 1% to feed on the productive middle class… who enable the Sodom Confederacy, militant Islam and a flood of illegal aliens to destroy our culture and break our state, city, hospital, and school district budgets… who conducted gaslighting for five years: Russiagate, Shampeachment, the Bat Scamdemic, and Election Steal 2020 to literally *overthrow* our government! Washington D.C. arrogantly violates our Constitution and perpetrates *massive* crimes, while all 'patriots' do is keep studying the Constitution and *making posters!*

When we think that elections can arrest the hijacking, we encourage criminals. In <u>AmericaAgain!- The Movie</u>, we survey seven categories of felony crimes that our federal servants have been committing. Over 20 years ago in <u>The Sovereign Individual</u>, James Davidson and William Rees-Mogg described how the Internet would challenge bloated governments. It's happening. *Opportunity faces us.*

Trump's Missed Chance

His populist style was Andrew Jackson or Teddy Roosevelt; his hard-nosed business sense, Calvin Coolidge. His PR strategy and vocabulary were Cassius Clay, like a force of nature. Yet Donald Trump was only one *effect* of the movement in America's heartland that included Moral Majority, Christian Coalition, the Constitution and Libertarian parties, Ron Paul Revolution, and the TEA Party. *The Deep Axis beat them all.*

The Deep Axis

By *Deep Axis,* I am referring to a massive coalition consisting of:

- Hundreds of thousands of federal bureaucrats *including career military*

- Big Tech (who control what Americans see and think)

- Media (all major media, owned by a handful of corporations)

- Big Banking (they finance all American wars)

- Big Oil (gets Big War as mercenary security force, free of charge)

- Big Law (firms who *write* America's laws; legislators only *sponsor* them)

- Big War (global corporations who control the Pentagon and much of D.C.)

- Big Pharma (who keep America sick, and Trump praises them)

- Most universities and colleges; government K-12 schools

- Communist Party USA, Chinese Communist Party, and Democrat Party

- Hollywood (programs American sensibilities, perversions, and desires)

- Millions of state, county, city, and school district bureaucrats and politicians

This is the predator-and-parasite force that has overspread and feeds off the American heartland's production.

With his huge ego and opulent lifestyle, Mr. Trump never appreciated that he was our *servant,* whose job was to serve us by obeying the Constitution. Still, when heartland America elected him, we did more than cast a ballot in one more election; we crossed partisan lines in 2016 and *much* bigger in 2020.

But the Deep Axis set the trap years in advance; the Russiagate, Shampeachment, BLAntifa riots, and COVID hoax were opening shots; the stolen election was the final step in the largest gaslighting operation in history. Now, we must fulfill the duties of our higher office, as Mr. Trump suggested in his January 2017 inaugural:

"Today's ceremony…has very special meaning; because today we are not merely transferring power from one administration to another or from one party to another, but we are transferring power from Washington, D.C. and giving it back to you, the American People."

Of course Trump never did that; he was our servant, but his millions of fans wanted a savior instead. Many of his cabinet picks were terrible, and toward the end he embraced the COVID hoax and drove it to a whole new level with Pence, Fauci, Birx, and Big Pharma.

Constitutionally, no president can perform our abdicated duty for us. On their own, presidents have very little power against the Deep State and its lapdogs in Congress. As President Kennedy described the Deep State in April 1961 in the speech that many believe got him killed:

(W)e are opposed around the world by a monolithic, ruth-less conspiracy that relies on covert means…on infiltration instead of invasion…subversion instead of elections, on intimidation instead of free choice, on guerrillas by night instead of armies by day. It…has conscripted vast human and material resources into…a tightly knit, highly efficient machine that combines military, diplomatic, intelligence, economic, scientific and political operations. Its preparations are concealed, not published; its mistakes are buried, not headlined; its dissenters are silenced, not praised. No expenditure is questioned, no rumor is printed, no secret is revealed.

Except for 'Silent Cal' Coolidge, every president left government larger and more corrupt than before. We repeatedly contacted Trump, but he never responded. It was always about himself, a common trait of politicians. Only We The People, if we are repentant and diligent, can end the hijacking of America at last.

Our Historic Opportunity

Almost 80% of sub-Saharan Africa has cell service. An African herdsman can look up weather, learn English, and diagnose maladies that killed his fellow villagers just a decade ago. Technology puts in your hand more information than the Library of Congress. Given all the smartphone applications, it was only a matter of time before we created one to arrest D.C. organized crime. Now we can stop allowing Congress to be run by 19th century procedures in secret, as directed by corrupt industry.

That is textbook fascism, and we can end it. In Lesson 7, you will learn about our proposed mobile app that will allow us to monitor our congressional servants as easily as checking weather, and stop criminals cold.

On social issues, for 50 years a godless urban culture forced our civilization off the rails, always in our face. They claimed this Sodom was America's future, and pantywaist pastors and authors folded, proclaiming 'post-Christian America'. It was all a lie; the only thing 'post-Christian' in America is that the vast majority of pulpits are timid and feckless.

Moral and ethical life continues in America's 31,000 small towns and rural areas. In the 2016 election we defeated and shocked Progressives; we did it again in 2020, but the Deep Axis overthrew the government anyway.

We The People *will not* allow criminals to hijack our republic like this. And we *will not* look to Trump to fix the mess resulting from *our* abdication of duty.

After two generations running from a ruthless, small minority that fights dirty and plays only offense, we in the Remnant *now go on offense, from now on.*

Forget Failed 'Solutions'

Now let's assess the top nine proposed solutions of the past: an Article V convention, nullification, secession, the TEA Party, armed revolution, anarchy, PACs and think tanks, a shadow government, and a D.C. coup.

1. A Constitutional Convention

A heated argument took place among patriotic Americans for several years. In one corner was Dr. Tom Woods and his allies at The Tenth Amendment Center arguing for nullification. In the other corner were celebrities Mark Levin, Glenn Beck, George Soros and a long line of conservatives, libertarians, anarchists, TEA Party folk, Progressives and sexual perverts, all beating the drum for an Article V convention to amend the Constitution.

A latter-day 'ConCon' movement using the moniker 'Convention of States' suggests that by using that label, a constitutional convention becomes a new thing that will not become a runaway convention, like the first and only ConCon, back in 1787. This nonsensical position is debunked by this article by veteran Article V scholar Dan Fotheringham and these articles by former JAG attorney and constitutional scholar Joanna Martin (aka 'Publius Huldah').

Watch this presentation by Robert Brown, exposing the lies being pushed by the COS movement. Then notice these hundreds of liberal organizations pushing for a convention of states to tear our Constitution apart!

The ConCon idea is silly. First: over 11,000 potential amendments have been proposed since 1789. Secondly: our servants violate the Constitution not because it needs amendment but because it needs *enforcement*. Think about it: if the criminals in government have not obeyed the Constitution we have now, why on earth do you think they will obey a new one with all the features that George Soros and the globalists and perverts want to add to it?

2. Nullification

Nullification was first proposed by Thomas Jefferson: when a state's residents disagree with a federal law, the state passes a nullification resolution to block it in that state.

Until our full-spectrum solution is in operation, we support enforcing the 10th Amendment via nullification. But long-term, it's a bad idea for three reasons.

First, it's terribly inefficient for states to spend citizens' time and money in a new rear-guard action every time Congress violates the law. Secondly, it's ineffective: a security fence around one home in a high crime neighborhood does nothing to protect the other homes in the area. Thirdly, nullification would create a constitutional hodgepodge across the republic.

3. **Secession**

As the Confederacy learned from the War to Enslave the States, secession is tactical folly. Small minorities in California, Texas, Colorado and other states have sought to secede or to create new states, but it will never happen.

The families who relocated to New Hampshire in the 'Free State Project' gained nothing. They still face federal and state laws, regulations, and predation by bureaucrats.

4. **The TEA Party**

Like a Rolling Stones 50th Anniversary concert, it was sad to see TEA Party rallies and posters and costumes for ten years while the GOP kept double-crossing its base. Mob actions and electoral politics failed to substitute for law enforcement. The TEA Party was run over by the Trump Train after it created millions of cynical, whipped political activists. For 30 years, the Fear Porn industry had the same destructive effect.

5. **Armed revolution**

Some say it's time to take arms in the streets. Oh? Who will they shoot and what will they do afterwards? You cannot enforce the Constitution by *violating* it.

Jefferson's eloquent Declaration of Independence asserted that our forefathers first exhausted all other options. We now have a Constitution, over which We The People retain every imaginable power over our lives except 17 services that we delegate to the servants. In Article I, Section 8, Clause 15 we stipulate that the Militia must "suppress Insurrections" so the duty of the Militia would be to *stop* armed revolutionaries.

6. **Anarchy**

Of all principles of political economy, anarchy is the most foolish. It refuses to acknowledge human nature and the lessons of history. There is not one example of a successful anarchist culture or economy anywhere on earth.

7. **Conservative Think Tanks and Nonprofits**

The 501c3 industry – PACs, think tanks, the NRA, Americans for Prosperity, Heritage Foundation, CATO Institute, Hillsdale College and countless others that fill your in-box asking for donations – have never reversed a single federal usurpation.

8. **Shadow Government**

Several shadow-government proposals have arisen over the past decade. Tim Turner's bizarre 'Restore America Plan' with its 'Guardian Elders' was updated and re-named The Republic of the United States. There are others, equally strange. Again: you can't enforce the Constitution by *violating* it.

9. Coup d'état

In 2013, Adam Kokesh planned an armed march on D.C. but it never materialized. In 2014, Christian patriots planned Operation American Spring, a 'peaceful coup' in D.C., named after Arab mob uprisings. It also fizzled. We see the passion of our brethren who planned the event, but again: you can't enforce the Constitution by violating it.

Words Matter

Gay makes perversion sound fun; *anti-abortion* makes pro-life people appear evil. Bureaucrats and schools (including private schools) use nonsensical vocabulary to transform our servants into our masters. It's time to detox our civics terms!

Two preliminaries. First, always capitalize *State;* never capitalize *federal* or offices of our servants (mayor, governor, president, congressman, senator, judge), and write *supreme Court* as the founders did. Second, popular sovereignty is *collective,* not individual. We're not each a monarch as 'sovereign citizen' cultists claim. Popular constitutionalism is the *antithesis* of anarchy. Now, ten words to detox…

Nation: America is a constitutional republic; see the Constitution, Article IV, Section 4. A 'nation' is a population under a central government; the tyrannical system hatched by Dishonest Abe and forced on us by D.C. ever since. These united States are a *republic*, not a nation.

Democracy: Calling America a democracy is as inaccurate as calling it monarchy. James Madison wrote: "Democracies have ever been spectacles of turbulence and contention; have ever been found incompatible with personal security or the rights of property; and have in general been as short in their lives as they have been violent in their death." Adams wrote: *"Democracy never lasts long. It soon wastes, exhausts, and murders itself. There never was a democracy yet that did not commit suicide."*

Government: Most people who say, *"I'm against the government!"* in truth are against organized crime. We The People are the highest level of government. So federal government is *only those who perform duties enumerated* in Article I, Section 8. Those who instead skim payroll accounts, counterfeit money, open our borders and spy on us are not government; they are *organized crime.*

Revolution: means overturning government. In our Constitution We The People create, define and severely limit government. The last thing we want to do is overturn it.

Grassroots: We The People are the highest level of government in our republic; why use the brainwashed term *grassroots* as though we are earthworms underfoot?

Voter: We constantly breathe and walk. Why don't we refer to ourselves as 'breathers' or 'walkers'? Don't say *voter;* it's not a noun. Voting is only a small part of our citizen power and duty. Many Americans no longer vote because organized crime turned our elections into a sham. Banana republic *voters* choose puppets.

Elected leaders: Have you ever been *led* by a politician? Statesmen *represent* sovereigns, they do not *lead* us.

Elected officials: If an office is nowhere authorized by us in the Constitution, a person cannot be an *official*. 'Public servant' is a fitting term if they are honest, or 'criminal' if they are not.

Constituent: This one is worse than *voter*, tiny citizens making up one politician. We don't *constitute* servants; we *oversee* them.

Tyranny: is a term used for a corrupt sovereign who becomes ruthless. Today, our servants are financial criminals, extortionists, defrauders, embezzlers, and shameless bureaucrats. This is not tyranny; it's longstanding *crime*.

Like ideas, words have consequences. Let's use accurate vocabulary as we embark on our new way of life. Galileo said, *"All truths are easy to understand once they are discovered; the point is to discover them."* This new life includes responsible *action*, not more words; duty that our fathers shirked. Just one action at a time, we will recover our lives, property, liberty, civilization, and Christian witness.

Death of a Monster

In one generation, Lincoln, Darwin and Marx hijacked America; then, five generations of Christians did nothing as government became a false god walking on earth.

Today, many people believe that the militant Left had gone berserk with 'Trump Derangement Syndrome'. But if we repent, we're actually witnessing the kicking, biting *death* of American communism that has grown like cancer for 150 years.

Think I overstate the case? Go online and Read Karl Marx's 1848 Communist Manifesto. See his ten points that define communism? By the time Woodrow Wilson was in the White House, eight of those points were federal policy; by FDR's reign, all 10 of Marx's points of communism were D.C. policy.

American communism is a century old; like communism all over the world, it is dying; but it never dies quietly, so we are in for quite a ride.

It's All About Jesus

When God lifts His judgment, where *else* can restoration possibly begin? God will not allow anyone but Christians to restore America. All the worthless pastors have cowered in fear long enough. We The People *must* do this.

TACTICAL CIVICS™ is a new way of life for an American remnant as humanity finally learns to use the Internet for self-government. No other people can do this. As silly as we Americans are sometimes, our Christian bedrock and our inspired, powerful Constitution make us unique on earth. Just as one generation hijacked us, now by God's grace, our generation can end the long hijacking.

After you turn 18, perhaps all you can bring to the mission is paying monthly dues, learning the civics, and spreading the word among your contacts. But that makes a powerful difference. Your family and friends will see the change; one day your children and grandchildren will have a full-spectrum plan of action!

With TACTICAL CIVICS™, we hope to forge a network of homes, churches, small businesses, shops, farms, ranches, VFW halls, constitutional Militia units, educated Grand Jury members, and others; Christians who will not run for the hills but will instead join us in repairing the ruins of our civilization.

We had Mr. Trump's back, but either because he did not know the civics or only cared for his own family brand, he never supported We The People, his sovereigns, as we seek to end the Deep Axis's game of thrones. If he was sincere in his inaugural speech, he would have responded to one of our many appeals.

But we should have taken our own advice: We The People, not our servants, are the only level of government who can *enforce* the Constitution.

Lesson 2 Questions for Parents

1. What attitudes and priorities that you have, or had, have contributed to the steady decline of our Republic and how have we individually and collectively enabled and encouraged the vast criminality in Washington DC?

2. We've learned that words matter, and reviewed ten widely accepted words that color our attitudes and actions to benefit those who want us to use those words. Which of those words have you commonly used?

3. Which of the failed 'solutions' have you subscribed to or participated in? Are you ready to move forward to explore Tactical Civics™ as a way of life?

Lesson 3
Applying Romans 13 in America

Many quotations are attributed to Thomas Jefferson but are not actually his. One of these was by John Barnhill in 1914, *"Where the people fear the government you have tyranny; where the government fears the people, you have liberty."*

Thomas Jefferson didn't say it, but the saying is true; and it applies to other human relationships, such as parents who spoil their children until they eventually fear them.

Faced with corrupt and tyrannical government, too many Christians let criminals off the hook by using Romans 13, *"Let every soul be in subjection to the higher authorities, for there is no authority except from God, and those who exist are ordained by God…For the authority is not a terror to those who do good, but to those who do evil. Do you want to have no fear of the authority? Do that which is good, and you will have praise from the same…But if you do that which is evil, be afraid, for he does not bear the sword in vain. He is a minister of God, an avenger for wrath to him who does evil."*

How Christians Pervert This Scripture

Consider this in the context of our Republic as you learned in Lesson 1; we are not ancient Rome under Caesars. So who are 'the higher authorities' in our system? See the first three words of our Constitution: *We the People* collectively are the highest authority. We are *over* the Constitution.

The first Chief Justice of the U.S. supreme Court, John Jay, wrote, *The People are Sovereign… (A)t the Revolution, the sovereignty devolved on the People and they are truly the sovereigns of the country… the Citizens of America are equal as fellow Citizens and as joint Tenants in the sovereignty.*

It is our power and duty to see that the law is enforced when servants do that which is evil. Instead, our arrogant servants have trained *us* to fear *them*.

We the People, the parents who gave birth to our government, must instill proper fear in criminal hearts. In Lesson 7, you will learn how America's sovereigns will have our State Criminal Court 'bear the sword' against any member of Congress or our state legislature who violates our highest law.

Good Guys Have Nothing to Fear

"Do you want to have no fear of the authority? Do that which is good, and you will have praise from the same."

Lesson 6 will explain how the Tactical Civics™ Good Guys campaign will support those who run for Congress standing for our 19 reform laws and against D.C. lawlessness.

For freshmen who decide to follow their bent elders in powerful committee chairs, we don't need to do this the easy way. We can make them *fear the authority* instead. The Indictment Engine™ is unprecedented, but the process will become easier with each felon that we indict, try, convict, and incarcerate via State Criminal Court, with the perpetrator's family assets seized.

Let us review the civics from Lesson 1, because schools have not taught this for generations:

We the People, in the U.S. Constitution, create, define, and severely limit our federal servant in three branches for 17 enumerated services, and for *absolutely no others*. And the *only* duties that We the People stipulate in the Constitution that we are to perform ourselves, are Grand Jury and Militia.

Because we have been ignorant of our Constitution and never taken the law seriously, our servants violate it as impudently as Mexican narcoterrorists violate Mexico's laws. Imagine, brilliant patriots wonder when the Department of Justice and FBI will start rounding up…*their criminal bosses* in Congress!

State-Sponsored Terrorism

With generations of Christians providing render-unto-Caesar cover, D.C. organized crime employs *fear* to defraud its sovereigns. *Terrorism* is defined as violent acts or threat of violent acts, intended to create or instill fear in victims.

Sociopath is an apt label for many in Congress, but beyond Congress' own violations of law is its *criminogenic* nature, teaching state, county, and city agencies in its bent path.

No organization is so feared by so many as Congress' IRS. Millions of Americans work their whole lives but never manage to get ahead. Congress' IRS operation skims every payroll account, allowing criminals in D.C. to live as royalty at your expense while productive Americans do without. In the TACTICAL CIVICS™ Training Center, in the Books & Resources area, we offer a free PDF edition of A Tax Honesty Primer to demonstrate why I and tens of millions of other Americans no longer fear the Wizard of Oz.

Your servants control your life, property, and future. Making illegal 'laws' for us, Congress exempts itself. They have been counterfeiting our money for 150 years. They invite millions of illegals over our border and force taxpayers to pay welfare, healthcare, incarceration, and 'free' government schooling costs so they can gain these illegals' votes and their industry puppeteers can gain the cheap labor.

Meanwhile for their sovereigns, they track, record, and store our conversations, emails, travel and purchase records; fine us for using our own land; regulate everything from lightbulbs to toilet flushes, and legitimize perversion as 'marriage' while muzzling our pulpits. Our abdication created the Caesar that threatens history's most blessed Christian civilization. Repentance demands that we *never again* apply Romans 13 to our Republic as if we are ancient Rome. Repentance is an *action* word!

Pastors and Church Leaders

As their sovereigns, our servants' staggering expenditures, frauds, and abuse of office should fill us with righteous anger, to assure that the higher authorities arrest their crimes as we will outline in Lesson 7. Criminals had a powerful public relations and propaganda machine for five generations. Now the worm turns. *"If you do that which is evil, be afraid"*. Now it's *our* turn, Congress.

Paul's Romans 13 directive to 'the higher authority' – We the People and the U.S. Constitution that we ordained – applies to every American pastor, elder, deacon, teacher and evangelist. Their calling is not only to preach the Word but to call the People to *repentance* and to good works demonstrating to the world that our repentance is *genuine*.

This is not China. Here, church leaders have the same God-given liberty to speak out on issues as does every American. But as leaders in local churches, they also have a *duty* to speak out on moral, ethical, and constitutional issues. Even if they touch on a political party, campaign, or candidate.

Of course, they should not campaign for any candidate; but free speech is the God-given and constitutional right of *every* American.

The Cell That They Built (for Themselves)

The American church that has incorporated itself under IRS Section 501 classification to attract donations, is conditioning its members to seek financial gain (tax write-offs) in Pharaoh's fiefdom rather than doing good works for God's Kingdom. By submitting to the secular authority of corrupt servants of our corrupt servant Congress, they turn civics on its head.

I recommend Peter Kershaw's HushMoney.org; it teaches church leaders to reorganize as a Free Church, leaving 501c3 imprisonment. But even if they do not, nothing in IRS rules prohibits any church from engaging in Tactical Civics™, the People's duty and power of popular constitutionalism.

Even 501c3 churches are encouraged by their state's election division to conduct 'voter' registration efforts as long as they don't do so on behalf of any candidate or party. Here are the current IRS guidelines:

501c3 Churches May:

- Conduct nonpartisan 'voter' registration drives
- Distribute nonpartisan election education materials
- Host candidate/issue forums (including all viable candidates)
- Allow candidates/elected servants to speak at services
- Educate members about pending legislation
- Lobby for legislation (spending only a small amount of their budget on lobbying)

501c3 Churches May Not:

- Endorse candidates from the pulpit on behalf of the church
- Contribute funds, services, mailing lists, or equipment to candidates or PACs
- Distribute materials that favor one candidate or party
- Pay fees for partisan political events from church funds
- Allow candidates to solicit funds while speaking in church
- Set up a PAC that would contribute funds to candidates

501c3 Pastors May:

- Endorse candidates in their capacity as private citizens
- Lobby for legislation in their private capacity
- Participate fully in political committees independent of the church

So, 501c3 pastors may *not* endorse candidates from the pulpit on behalf of the church, but they *may* do so on their own behalf.

Resources for 501c3 Churches

A pamphlet summarizing the legal aspects of pastor and church involvement in the culture war is *Pastors, Pulpits, and Politics* published by Western Center for Law and Policy. Pastors can read it and order the booklet from them here.

There is similar material at the Liberty Council, the American Center for Law and Justice, James Madison Center for Free Speech, and others.

Nothing keeps a church from joining the repentant remnant for Christ and the Constitution. Our book, *Tactical Civics™ for Pastors* teaches pastors how to teach citizens to finally perform our duties in the highest office in American government: enforcing the Constitution and glorifying Jesus Christ, as was once our way before a watching world.

Lesson 3 Questions for Parents

1. Most Americans are ignorant of civics. Were you surprised to learn that *We The People* are the highest authority, even over the Constitution, with the duty to see that it is enforced when our servants do that which is evil?

2. What part does your Christian faith play in your new knowledge?

3. We have learned that God's judgment begins at the Church. Do the leaders in our Church speak out on moral, ethical and constitutional issues? If not, can you see them learning about and accepting this duty demanded by Scripture and our Constitution?

Lesson 4
Dishonest Abe, American Idol

Brace yourself. This lesson will shock you and may make you angry. But as Christ taught, truth will set us free. Hard truths of our history must be faced and hooted off the stage in our homes, churches, schools and colleges if we are to avoid the godless collapse in communist countries and across Europe.

Like so many Russians or Chinese, Americans have been lied to in schools. Even private, Christian, and *most homeschools.* One of the most destructive frauds in our culture is that Lincoln was a great president and a good man. In truth, *he was the most ruthless, destructive president in our history.*

Americans are ignorant of the affinity that Abraham Lincoln had for Karl Marx and his Communist system. Even as liberals have banished the Confederate flag, those who think Lincoln was a hero are as ignorant of our history as the average Russian citizen is of his.

If you think I exaggerate, the first resource I recommend is available at no cost. <u>Reading Karl Marx with Abraham Lincoln: Utopian Socialists, German Communists, and Other Republicans</u> is a 2011 article in *The International Socialist Review,* the communist news source of record, describing the mutual admiration between Marx and Lincoln.

The first book is *Forced Into Glory: Abraham Lincoln's White Dream* by Black scholar and author Lerone Bennett Jr. Impeccably documented with many original source quotes, Bennett paints Lincoln as the consummate White Supremacist and mendacious snake-in-the-grass.

The second book is *Lincoln's Marxists* by Al Benson and Walter Kennedy. It delves into the ties between Marxism, Lincoln's unconstitutional new national army, and the neo-nascent GOP that rose from the ashes of the Whig party. It is a second shocking exposé of our most execrable president and his U.S. Army generals, all proud followers of Karl Marx.

The third book to show you Lincoln's true character and the lasting destruction he wrought is *Lincoln Unmasked: What You're Not Supposed to Know About Dishonest Abe*, by Professor Thomas DiLorenzo. After igniting a fierce debate about Lincoln's legacy with his book *The Real Lincoln,* DiLorenzo now presents stunning new evidence to explode the popular myths about Lincoln. A shocking portrait of a political tyrant, manipulator and opportunist; the antithesis of the idol in American schools.

The fourth book to banish idolatry of America's hijacker is *America's Caesar* by Greg Durand, in two volumes. With a huge number of original source documents, Durand paints a picture of a nineteenth-century agnostic attorney representing riverboat operators and railroad barons; whose only use for Jesus Christ was to lure the masses. This portrait of the most destructive man in American history makes Bill Clinton look like a saint in comparison.

The fifth book is *The Unpopular Mr. Lincoln,* by Larry Tagg, a compilation and analysis of public statements and articles during Lincoln's rule. According to his closest associates, Lincoln was the most despised president in our history.

The sixth book is *A Century of War* by John Denson. It provides copious original source documentation of Lincoln's Northern mercantilist handlers making him defy his cabinet, to sucker the South into firing the first shots at Fort Sumter, where no one was killed or even wounded.

You need not take my word that our former idol was a monster; read any of those resources. You will 'take the red pill' and know that *we have work to do.*

Modern Conservatism is Destructive Denial

If you are not ready to dethrone the god of American government school legend, consider your condition. Our present descent into tyranny while the People do nothing suggests that Americans may have mass insanity. The simple precursor is *cognitive dissonance.* When truth is presented it flies in the face of everything the victim thinks he knows, so he rejects it.

The programming of once-godly, productive, tough-minded folk began in the generation of Lincoln, Marx, and Darwin. Since that generation, we increasingly turned from God to accept every imaginable sin and a few unimaginable ones.

The wages of rebellion is God's judgment. We wander in the desert, oblivious to where we have been and what happened there. Like dumbfounded hijack victims, we simply stare out the windows. Our only path back to sanity is *repentance.*

A second aspect of our national insanity is actual insanity as defined. In the psychological phenomenon called *Stockholm syndrome,* or *capture–bonding,* hostages begin to bond with their captors and eventually even to love and defend them. The victim begins to consider any brief cessation of abuse to be an act of kindness by his captor.

Another defense mechanism known as *Normalcy Bias* may come into play, as we saw in the two oldest generations of former Soviet subjects after collapse of the USSR. In the victim's mind, nothing can alter the conditions to which the victim had become accustomed.

This insanity affects Hillary's and Bernie Sanders' socialist snowflakes of the Millennial Generation (born 1980-95) but also millions in Generation X (1965-79), the Baby Boom Generation (1946-64) and the Silent Generation (1925-45).

Fallen Stalin

A European blogger describes a display of communist statues that had been removed from public squares in Lithuania:

"Families with young children roam the park and it is no exception to see young children posing with Lenin or Stalin while their dad is taking a picture. It is also a strange experience to visit…souvenir shops where you can buy mugs or small glasses with a portrait of Stalin on it. Why would anyone buy a mug with the portrait on it of he who ordered the death of millions? … Bizarre but true."

A park filled with former tyrants' statues is less bizarre than the Lincoln Memorial's shocking idolatry; testament to the power of American school propaganda in place of history. Our schools, like those in China and Russia, were teaching propaganda – and the worst part is, *they still do.*

As you trace history, you discover that our new Washington D.C. master began destroying America's two vital law enforcement institutions, Grand Jury and Militia, during the War to Enslave the States and in 12 years of 'Reconstruction' that followed that debacle. A powerful new mega-bureaucracy hijacked our Constitution, transforming formerly sovereign People and States into serfs, and itself into our master.

American Communism did not begin with Obama. Read any of the books linked in this chapter; you will see that it began with Lincoln. If you perform due diligence but still prefer to honor Abe Lincoln, then don't just hate the Confederate flag; hate the U.S. Constitution too, as he did.

And don't blame me for bringing you hard truth; blame your teachers, whose comfortable traditions – whose *lies* – you prefer to liberty.

Lesson 4 Questions for Parents

1. What is your reaction to learning that we've been lied to for more than a century; that American Communism and the hijacking of our Constitution are not new phenomena, but began during Lincoln's administration?

2. Led by the decision of one man influencing Congress on behalf of the 'Union' nowhere demanded in the Constitution as a one-way forced association, the War to Enslave the States was declared by Lincoln. In 1861-65, half of all property in America was destroyed. As for death toll, adjusted for population growth it would be as though 7.4 million Americans killed one another in four years. Try to imagine that happening now. Compare it to the overthrow, election steal, and cold war gaslighting we're facing now. Which do you think is worse, and why?

3. Do you believe that God will not allow anyone but Christians to lead the restoration of America and that the only way back to restoration of our Republic must begin with repentance?

Why or why not, and what do you think comprises true repentance?

Lesson 5
Split Them Up

We will cover this material again in greater detail in Lesson 13, for this is the most powerful thing We The People can do, to stop D.C. organized crime.

To take Congress out of Washington D.C., we first need a tactical preliminary to change the makeup of Congress. By God's grace, the framers of the Constitution left us just the weapon we need: their first Article in the original Bill of Rights. The only one that has not been fully ratified, it has been gathering dust for over two centuries. So our first action project, called Our First Right, is designed to get our State legislatures to finish ratifying it. As you'll soon see, this has been done before, by *just one man*.

The original First Amendment was designed to preclude exactly the corruption we have today: multimillion dollar campaigns with congressmen reigning over 750,000 citizens that they cannot know, much less represent.

Two years before the Bill of Rights was finalized, on the last day of the 1787 Constitutional Convention, Nathaniel Gorham made a motion to change one word in Article I, Section 2, Clause 4 of the new Constitution: "the number of Representatives shall not exceed one for every forty thousand" would now read, "…for every *thirty* thousand". Others seconded the motion, then George Washington rose to speak for the first and only time in the four month long convention, as James Madison describes on page 644 in *Records of the Federal Convention*:

When the President rose…he said that although his situation had hitherto restrained him from offering his sentiments…he could not forbear expressing his wish that the alteration proposed might take place… The smallness of the proportion of Representatives had been considered by many members of the Convention an insufficient security for the rights and interests of the People.

He acknowledged that it had always appeared to himself among the exceptionable parts of the plan…as late as the present moment was for admitting amendments, he thought this of so much consequence that it would give much satisfaction to see it adopted.

The delegates passed the change unanimously.

For the next two years the State legislatures deliberated about ratifying the new Constitution. On June 8, 1789 Madison's team introduced 39 amendments. On September 25, Congress did pass the Bill of Rights, but only twelve of the 39 articles of amendment, and sent them to the States for ratification. We were taught that the Bill of Rights had ten amendments; in truth, it had twelve. But the first two were not ratified by the necessary three-quarters of the States so they remained open in the States, gathering dust...*for two centuries.*

Then in 1983, University of Texas student Greg Watson ran a campaign to get 29 more State legislatures to ratify the original Second Amendment. It stipulated that if Congress gives itself a pay raise, it does not take effect until an election intervenes. After Watson had toiled away for almost ten years, in May 1992 the U.S. Archivist certified that three-fourths of the States had ratified and that 'Article the Second' of the Bill of Rights was now the 27th Amendment.

Every article in our Bill of Rights is ratified except the first and most important one. It has 11 ratification votes; it needs 38. So when we get 27 more State legislatures to ratify it, the original 'Article the First' will become the 28th Amendment. If a college student could get this done, so can we.

Since Congress already passed the Amendment, Washington D.C. can't stop us and no constitutional convention is needed. Our State legislatures have a duty to ratify our full Bill of Rights so that we can finally restore the People's House.

What This Will Accomplish

Congress today spends $5.85 billion annually on operations, opulent lifestyles, imperial palace, and massive staffs. No sane employer allows employees to set their own pay, staff, benefits, and office arrangements.

Making districts small will reduce House members' power but our big payoff is that Capitol Hill will not accommodate 6500+ House members and staffs, so we can bring Congress home where we, not lobbyists, control them.

The Bring Congress Home Act will stipulate that the (approximately 6,600+) congressmen and 100 senators will now work full-time back home in one modest office each and be limited to two terms, either house. We do not need a term-limits amendment; it they were able to limit the House to 435 seats without an amendment, they can limit their terms, too.

Capitol Action Teams

Nothing can be done at any 'state palace' until we have a sufficient number of active TACTICAL CIVICS™ chapters and members in that state.

Once we do, we will deploy Capitol Action Teams consisting of one very adept public speaker to do the press and social media events in each capital city, and a team of canvassers comprised of TACTICAL CIVICS™ chapter volunteers to go to each state legislator's office and make our demand to hold the vote on Our First Right, at last.

Twelve state legislatures – CT, KY, MD, NH, NJ, NY, NC, PA, RI, SC, VT and VA – already voted to ratify it, but CT failed to turn in its paperwork. So we need 27 more states out of the 38 who have not acted on it, to just vote 'yes'.

Remember basic civics; mob action isn't for sovereigns so we specifically do *not* want large mobs at these events. We only need small teams to do the canvassing and our national OFR spokesman to do press events in the capital city. Our two-person Capitol Action Teams go to every state legislator and get them on video, answering one question:

"We sent you a 28th Amendment Fact Sheet and model Joint Resolution. This is a simple issue with no political downside. Will you bring to the floor the ratification vote of the original First Amendment, the First Right in our Bill of Rights?"

They make the legislators answer yes or no; no excuses or bloviating. They get it on video. They will be firm but cordial. They will be upbeat, offering the politician a gift! Equal representation for all, at last! The teams will send materials to every state legislator once they get their email address; Appendix B is the 28th Amendment Fact Sheet with history of the original First Amendment and Appendix C is the model Joint Resolution.

Logistics and Schedule

Most State legislatures open their session in January and end by May or June but calendars vary. If you live in AR, MT, ND, NV or TX, the legislature only meets in odd-number years (not in 2022, 2024, etc) unless a special session is called.

Deadlines for submitting bills and floor or committee actions don't matter; we are telling the legislature to hold a *ratification vote*, period. It can happen anytime in the session, and in the first few dozen states it has no political downside.

The teams must remember: politicians are *never* to be trusted, even self-proclaimed Christian ones. Once they win a place under the granite dome, your servants are *never* on your side, no matter *what* they say. Your state capitol is no better than Capitol Hill. Recall civics from Lesson 1.

A citizen does not have to yell at servants, but politicians and their staffs have a habit of foot-dragging. They always try to appear very busy, unless a wealthy donor drops by; for *them* they will drop *everything*.

This is not typical political action nonsense. It is the crucial first step in the most powerful popular sovereignty transformation in history.

Our next lesson introduces Tactical Civics™ Good Guys, to help thousands of citizen-statesmen stand up to become the most historic Congress in history – and explains how we Bring Congress Home, forever.

Lesson 5 Questions for Parents

1. [Not for citizens of KY, MD, NH, NJ, NY, NC, PA, RI, SC, VT and VA, which already voted to ratify.] What is the likelihood that our state could be one of the 27 needed to ratify the original First Right in our Bill of Rights? What actions must the citizens of our state take to achieve this?

2. Discuss the practical advantages of significantly reducing size of congressional districts as the founders intended. Are there any disadvantages?

3. Do you think the Capitol Action Team strategy is sound, to push the ratification vote as the first step in the most powerful people's reform in history? Do you think it can succeed in our state? Why or why not?

Lesson 6
Bring Them Home

"If we lose freedom here, there is no place to escape to. This is the last stand on Earth. And this idea that government is beholden to the people, that it has no other source of power except to sovereign people, is still the newest and most unique idea in all the long history of man's relation to man... Whether we believe in our capacity for self-government or whether we abandon the American Revolution and confess that a little intellectual elite in a far-distant capital can plan our lives for us better than we can plan them ourselves". (Ronald Reagan, Oct. 1964)

Washington D.C. is earth's most corrupt and powerful city-state, working for the 534 billionaires and every industry in America. Idealistic statesmen win office, move to D.C., receive orientation, then are surrounded by veteran staffers, other unelected D.C. bureaucrats, D.C. law firms, and single-issue lobbyists.

By turning the tables, We the People demonstrate to the world that Americans truly are self-governing; that we still have a Constitution that we enforce, even if it means incarcerating incumbents in Congress. But that shouldn't be necessary; step one is 'Our First Right', to transform congressional elections forever.

After the States ratify the 28th Amendment, the next congressional election will be for approximately 6,600+ representatives in compact, local congressional districts rather than 435 huge, gerrymandered fiefdoms for industry.

I predict that as soon as we ratify the 28th Amendment, most incumbents will suddenly need to *"devote time to my family so I will not be running for re-election".*

Good riddance!

Losing Our Royalty Fetish

Because we have been ignorant of civics for generations, we have had a childish attitude toward presidents, a caricature of I Samuel 8, when Israel's judges (short-term, rather than lifetime lords and masters) had become corrupt:

"And it came to pass when Samuel was old, that he made his sons judges over Israel. Now the name of his firstborn was Joel; and the name of his second, Abiah. They were judges in Beersheba. His sons walked not in his ways, but turned aside after money, and took bribes, and perverted judgment."

That describes the average federal judge or politician.

The people told Samuel that they wanted a king to rule over them. Samuel warned them that kings would take 10% of their substance and make their lives difficult:

"But the people refused to hearken unto the voice of Samuel; they said, 'No, but we will have a king over us, that we may be like all the other nations'".

Like the British, too many Americans are unwilling to govern themselves and instead seek monarchs like Barack and Michelle or like Donald and Melania with their Arab sheikh-style opulent lifestyle, to rule over them. We liked the Trumps; our point is that a gold-plated first couple made Americans gawk like Brits, and far too many Americans already had a fascination with celebrity.

If we accept or even demand celebrity of our public servants, we have no right to oversee them, or even to vote, because celebrities will prey on productive citizens due to *moral hazard,* the economic principle of spreading theft around so that you only steal a small amount from each of a vast pool of victims. Productive Americans are losing ground against bloated bureaucracy, supported by wealthy predators at the top and hordes of parasites at the bottom.

Tactical Civics Good Guys: Popular Constitutionalism

It is time to wake up, repent, and take our lives back. The world awaits such hope; a model of what can be done. It must begin with repentance, then duty.

Every two years, one out of 50,000 of us can take responsibility to represent the others, obeying and supporting the U.S. Constitution as the oath of office demands, and co-sponsoring our reform laws. Surely there are a few hundred thousand intelligent, patriotic Americans who will accept our Good Guys challenge after we ratify the 28th Amendment.

If you're honest and of average intelligence, you're far superior to the average member of Congress today. It will hardly be a sacrifice: half of a congressman's salary is $90,000 per year and you won't have to move to D.C. or keep a second home. The new U.S. House of Representatives can fulfill the Founding Fathers' dream of the People's House: serve for two or four years, then return to regular life. No careers in politics. No rich, famous narcissists and showmen. Just citizen-statesmen representing self-governing citizens.

The one in 50,000 citizens will have simpler duties than the mayor of a city; any competent adult can read the Constitution and obey it better than today's D.C. incumbents do. Self-government is just applying morality and common sense to the issues we face as a republic. Largely, it requires plain fiscal discipline, to shut down unconstitutional agencies, bureaus and programs; impossible for a politician seeking a lifelong career, but a no-brainer for any productive American.

No one expects perfection in a congressman; only honesty and common sense. But after you turn 18, even if you do not feel called to the Good Guys challenge to serve in Congress from your community, surely you will know at least one person of character and integrity in your town that you will be able to nominate and support to take the challenge.

Time for a Mass Extinction Event

Why do we despise politicians? Because whether local, state or federal, they speak lies, cut deals, and daily huddle with one another in a world of make-believe, spending our hard-earned money like drunken sailors at a magic ATM machine. Congress runs earth's most powerful city-state as organized crime, for the benefit of a bewildering list of powerful industries and groups.

We the People believe we can't win because we can't get to the billionaires. But we only need to get their puppets; the control mechanism of our Constitution. When we take Congress out of that corrupt city-state to work from their communities, *D.C. organized crime loses its grip on productive America's payroll accounts.*

One statesman out of every 200 politicians – statesmen like Ron Paul or Josh Hawley – are painted by lapdog media as curmudgeons because they remind us that Congress is violating the Constitution. Because they appeal to honesty in a city of liars. Trump did the same thing, but he tried to do it all alone and take the credit. As we explain in the next lesson, ending D.C. organized crime is the job of We The People!

Our first reform law is the *Bring Congress Home Act* or 'BCHA'. Something like the 2013 resolution called HR287 to bring Congress home to work from their district offices via *telepresence*, which is common tech today, with thousands of participants able to meet by desktop, laptop, tablet or even smart phone.

The BCHA stipulates that all members of Congress will work full-time back home in one modest office each, with staff of two for a congressman or six for a senator; limited to two terms, congressmen making half their present salary since districts will be 1/14 as large, and they receive no benefits or pensions. *Congress should be short-term public service, not a career.*

What About Cost?

Even with 6600+ congressmen, with their small new staff and only one small office each, the BCHA will decrease Congress' $5.85 billion annual operations budget, as we will illustrate in Lesson 13. But more importantly, we will save *trillions* in pork and illicit agencies and projects.

As the next lesson explains, the Indictment Engine™ will let you see your servants' proposed legislation on your mobile device *before* it is passed rather than having to lobby to nullify or overturn it *after* it has wrecked your life.

The Transition

Our first 'big Congress' will do what all past ones have done: set up their office and staff in their district, but then instead of moving to D.C., they will simply meet at a large D.C. venue on January 3 (of 2025 or 2027, for instance) for one item only, to enact the BCHA. The president signs it and makes history, then they go home to their lease office and telepresence system.

Organized Crime on the Potomac

Because there are more than 100,000 lobbyists in D.C. and thousands of concession and support businesses there, that city-state's network of businesses and contractors will resist reform with all their might. So our duty is simple: We The People must break the battle down into 3,141 county-level skirmishes, where we outnumber the criminals by hundreds-to-one.

We now have a full-spectrum, long-term plan of action that is lawful, peaceful, practical, and designed to last as long as the Constitution does. Our duty is to build county chapters and get the word out that We The People are now in charge of our servants, and need to bring them home. Then it all becomes a matter of public relations, perseverance, and faith in the LORD.

When journalists speak of the huge army of D.C. lobbyists, they do not even include most of the parasites in that city-state of self-serving industries, law firms, think tanks, nonprofit foundations, event managers, hotels, caterers, restaurants, special-interest and single-issue organizations who will fight to the death to keep their great gigs. But if it's Washington D.C. vs. America, *my money is on America.*

Some Days the World Just Changes

Despite their great wealth and power, Pharaohs did not have flush toilets, cars, or air conditioning.

By the grace of God and over 66,000 hours of due diligence and R&D by 44 volunteers, in the fullness of time, mankind's inventions will again change the world. Tactical Civics™ with Our First Right and the Bring Congress Home Act will be the most powerful acts of popular constitutionalism since shopkeepers, farmers and planters changed the world in 1776.

It's time to *bring Congress home.*

Lesson 6 Questions for Parents

1. Now that we're aware of the depth and breadth of corruption in D.C., and its hijacking of America, we can no longer turn a blind eye or we become complicit. Duty demands action; besides Tactical Civics™ chores, what changes can you think of making in your family and community life that help teach others about our authority and duty as the collective sovereign?

Are you obeying illegal mask or jab mandates, or mandates for church and home gatherings?

Especially if you're self-employed, will you consider no longer financing illegal and immoral acts through paying taxes to Congress, by learning Tax Honesty? (Get the free *Tax Honesty Primer* in our Books & Resources area or buy it at Amazon for under $5.) What else can we do as individuals and families?

2. What effect do you think Bring Congress Home Act will have on elections?

3. As we begin to remove career politicians, do you believe that enough patriotic Americans will step up and serve as U.S. senators and representatives? Would you? Why or why not?

Lesson 7
True Law Enforcement

Our operating principle for TACTICAL CIVICS™ is that we will only take on one project at a time, focusing all effort on that project until we achieve it. Our ancestors did nothing for 150 years; we will not repair the ruins overnight. We will crawl before we walk, and walk before we run.

We have everything we need, but detoxing generations of propaganda still takes time. In this lesson, we will peek at our long-term goal: like the invention of the telephone or car, but with today's amazing tech. And hopefully with a maverick president on our side.

The Tenth Amendment stipulates that the sovereign States and People retain all powers except the 17 that we delegate to Washington, DC. *It has no sovereignty in any other area of life, or jurisdiction in any other area of the world.*

Read that last paragraph again. Slowly. *Twice.*

By now you're aware that our servants have been perpetrating massive crimes for generations. Organized Crime: The Unvarnished Truth About Government is Tom DiLorenzo's book exposing a century of D.C. crimes. AmericaAgain! – The Movie presents Congress' top seven crimes: Counterfeiting, Fraud, Grand Theft,

International and Domestic Racketeering, Extortion, and Criminal Invasion of Privacy.

Yes, Organized Crime

Of the many hundreds of whistleblower books exposing D.C. organized crime operations, I recommend *War is a Racket,* the 1935 classic by General Smedley Butler, and *Theft of The Nation*, the detailed 1969 survey by criminologist Donald Cressey, describing how local, state, and federal governments 50 years ago were already operating organized crime. Cressey named mafia families in American big cities, in statehouses, and in Washington D.C.; and things have gotten much worse since that time. On their counterfeiting, see Appendix H; it's multi-*trillion*-dollar crime! We're not being melodramatic; our governments are operating exactly as those in Russia, Venezuela, or North Korea.

The Mask is Off Now

The Russia hoax, Shampeachment, Plandemic, theft of an election (thus our entire government) and the massive gaslighting covering it all up in true Soviet style, is illustrating to the world that D.C. organized crime and its minions in countless corrupt American cities will not just disappear if we elect 'better politicians'. *Elections will never arrest criminals.*

Investigative journalist Peter Dale Scott, over 50 years, has published 40 books including *American War Machine*, and *Drugs, Oil, and War* and his latest book, *The American Deep State*. We produced a 6-part podcast series in 2019-20 entitled *Who Killed America's Militia?* that is available in the Militia topic of the Discovery section of the TACTICAL CIVICS™ Training Center. In those nine hours of podcasts, we explain in detail the who, what, when, where, and why of the FBI, CIA, DOJ and other useless D.C. agencies who run interference for mafia, to make you believe, decade after decade, that things will all be better if you just "trust the Plan".

AmericaAgain! is a perpetual charitable trust whose action mission, TACTICAL CIVICS™ recruits, educates, supplies, and tactically organizes Americans to enforce the U.S. Constitution by restoring Grand Jury and Militia in every county and eventually by using the Indictment Engine™, a mobile app whose algorithms assign felony indictment target value to every bent member of Congress.

Our long-term staffing plan includes legal personnel to recruit field attorneys and support Grand Jury and Militia to superintend their state prosecutor, judge, and county sheriff as these servants learn to perform their duty at last, and support us as we learn to perform ours in Grand Jury and Militia.

State Judges Trump federal

The Constitution has been violated for generations by our servants because We the People have never *enforced* it. From now on via State criminal courts, we will.

Remember: the Supremacy Clause, which is Article VI, Section 2, stipulates that *the Constitution,* not federal government, is supreme. It says that State judges are bound by it, but that means bound to *enforce* it as well as obey it.

Even adults with backgrounds in government or law will be befuddled reading American civics for the first time. As you complete this tutorial, if you bring this powerful truth up in a room full of law professors, you will see a few seconds of head-scratching, followed by strident defense of existing arrangements.

John Marshall, the first chief justice of the U.S. supreme Court, was an ambitious, articulate jurist. Few people outside the legal profession can appreciate how a single unelected man over two centuries ago could build an entire federal law industry and guild as if he was an emperor. But in a side-remark called a *dictum* that was not even an official part of his ruling in the 1803 case of *Marbury v. Madison,* the first chief justice built a towering artifice of jurisdiction for federal courts that we never granted them; then, the arrogant, multibillion-dollar federal law guild have extended this lawless artifice for over two centuries.

Our founders rejected titles of nobility for public servants, to erase all vestiges of aristocracy. The original program for attorneys was that they had no special schools; they simply read law until they could stand before the bar and be found competent to practice. The original principle for judges was that they not be lawyers like the mechanics practicing before them; just men who demonstrated wisdom and integrity.

Flying in the face of these original norms and ideals, for 212 years Americans have bowed and scraped before an arrogant priesthood of professors and judges, the most arrogant being federal judges – the servants of our servants! (In Article III of the Constitution, We the People create a U.S. supreme Court, then allow Congress, which we created in Article I, to create its inferior federal courts.)

Should We the People defer? Think logically: no State Court was created by the U.S. Constitution; the States were pre-existing, sovereign parties to it. All inferior federal courts are created by, and serve at the pleasure of, Congress. That means that federal courts must recuse themselves in any case involving a member of Congress. Since the U.S. supreme Court is complicit in Congress' largest, longest-running financial crimes and crimes of foreign occupation ('insular cases'), *it has to refuse jurisdiction.* And finally, federal courts have no jurisdiction in State crime cases anyway.

So you see that our legal authority is clear. As former Stanford Law School dean Larry Kramer suggests in *The People Themselves,* when federal government violates the Constitution, the People are superior to the U.S. supreme Court.

All we needed was a mechanism to help us exercise our lawful power. Now we have one, but these things will not happen on their own.

We have chores!

How the App Will Operate

The Indictment Engine™ is actually a planned combination of a software app, AmericaAgain! Legal Section staff work, and peaceful, perpetual citizen action to superintend servants via *tactical force-massing*.

That means a Grand Jury and Militia work to bring a criminal legislator under felony indictment in State criminal court on felony charges under the politician's *State* laws that coincide with the omission, commission, support for, or acquiescence in Congress' violating our highest law. The legal principle *qui tacit consentit* regards any accessory to a crime; 'silence implies consent'.

Our Legal Section prepares the felony presentments beginning with financial crimes against residents of your State by a fellow resident of your State who happens to be a member of Congress or your State legislature.

Each time we get a State Grand Jury to hand down a criminal indictment against a legislator for a State Penal Code offense, our plea bargain deal will be like the one offered by the Saxons to King Ethelred in 1014 A.D., or by the English barons to King John in the *Magna Carta* in 1215 A.D., or by Congress' IRS thugs to every 'Taxpayer'... *"Agree to our terms or go to prison with your assets seized."*

Those members of Congress not yet targeted will receive the same offer, but as an immunity deal (cooperate, and you are immune from prosecution).

Before all of that, our TACTICAL CIVICS™ Good Guys campaign will offer every candidate and incumbent an opportunity to step away from D.C. organized crime before being targeted.

They stop engaging in Congress' felonies and they sponsor our reform laws restoring what D.C. organized crime has stolen from the American people. It's not rocket science.

Debunking Common Objections

Those who say that Congress enjoys sovereign immunity from prosecution are wrong. The U.S. supreme Court ruling in *Langford v. United States* is a strident reiteration of a basic premise of 1,000 years of western law – no one is above the law, especially legislators.

Those who say that the perp will file for Removal Jurisdiction in federal court when indicted by the State court, are also wrong. Title 28 U.S. Code, Section 1441 ('Removal Jurisdiction') is only available to defendants in *civil* cases; only arising under the U.S. Constitution or other federal laws; and only when there is 'diversity of citizenship' (plaintiffs and/or defendants are from different states).

Neither the U.S. supreme Court nor the U.S. district courts have jurisdiction over a criminal defendant who is a resident of a state that indicts him for violating its own State Penal Code, when all plaintiffs are also residents of that state.

Those who say that state prosecutors lack courage or honesty to indict members of Congress should be aware that in 2010, the State of Texas convicted Tom DeLay for financial crimes committed while he was the second highest ranking member of the U.S. House of Representatives. Moreover, every county Grand Jury can pursue corrupt or dishonest prosecutors and judges and work for *their* indictment if necessary.

Those who say that DeLay's was an insignificant case should review the State of Oklahoma's 15-count, $11 billion fraud indictment of WorldCom CEO Bernard Ebbers, who had his assets seized and is serving out the rest of his life in prison. The Oklahoma Attorney General allowed the federal court to take jurisdiction but was prepared to re-indict if the federal court failed to satisfy Oklahoma.

Looking Ahead

Let me reiterate: TACTICAL CIVICS™ will only pursue one major project at a time, concentrating our chapters on one achievable goal rather than allowing proponents of each of our 19 reforms to pull in a different direction, diluting our offense as patriots have done for 50 years. But let us look ahead just a bit, to the restored popular sovereignty that we hope for in the longer term.

The Grand Jury

This subject is covered in much more detail in our Field Handbook #2, *Grand Jury Awake*. But basically, when We The People finally enforce the U.S. Constitution, we cause public servants to "be in subjection to the higher authorities" and we also keep the Leviathan state from growing back like a cancer.

The Indictment Engine™ will produce presentments for Grand Juries, citing specific felony counts that the targeted legislator is planning to perpetrate with passage of the legislation (s)he is sponsoring. Unfortunately, our presentments cannot also name as indicted co-conspirators the attorneys and individuals in the corporations that drafted the proposed bill, for that would make it a federal case.

Called to Duty

Most states have similar Grand Jury process. Ideally, your county clerk (elected position) randomly picks names of potential jurors from the county driver license or voter registration records, and calls you to jury duty. When you arrive, they tell you whether you're being asked to serve on a Grand or petit (trial) jury.

When you agree to serve jury duty, in Common Law countries, you become the highest authority in the legal system. No judge can countervene the jury; it has ultimate disposition of the case. The Grand Jury has more power and discretion than a judge, as the late U.S. supreme Court justice Antonin Scalia wrote in U.S. v Williams (1992):

"Rooted in long centuries of Anglo American history…the Grand Jury is mentioned in the Bill of Rights but not in the body of the Constitution…(i)t is a constitutional fixture in its own right…it belongs to no branch of the institutional government…Although the Grand Jury

normally operates…in the courthouse and under judicial auspices, its institutional relationship with the judicial branch has traditionally been…arm's length. Judges' direct involvement in the functioning of the Grand Jury has generally been confined to…calling the grand jurors together and administering their oaths of office…The Grand Jury requires no authorization from its constituting court to initiate an investigation…the Grand Jury generally operates without the interference of a presiding judge…(i)t swears in its own witnesses…the Fifth Amendment's constitutional guarantee presupposes [that the Grand Jury is] *independent of either prosecuting attorney or judge…the Sixth Amendment right to counsel does not* [apply for] *an individual… summoned to appear before a Grand Jury, even if he is the subject of the investigation…the whole history of the Grand Jury institution, in which laymen conduct their inquiries unfettered by technical rules."*

Behold the power of the People!

The Grand Jury can serve for months, but is not a full-time thing; sometimes only one day per week or less. It considers only capital cases and other 'infamous crimes' (like stealing an election). The Grand Jury can make its own presentments based on any information its members discover themselves, or that is brought to them. The Grand Jury does not rule on the law at issue, nor does it determine guilt or innocence; that's for the 12-person petit jury.

The Grand Jury only decides whether to issue a bill of indictment for prosecutors to take the target to trial.

TACTICAL CIVICS™

Since the beginning of its existence over a thousand years ago, the Grand Jury has been a *secret* function, to assure the safety of Grand Jurors and so they are not unduly influenced.

The Indictment Engine™ process discovers the presentment material in any proposed bill filed by the legislator; our Legal Section will 'load the hopper'; the target is then brought before an informed Grand Jury. Each time we acquire a new target, we will publish it in the county and state. Members of the Grand Jury are unknown to the public, but they can see and act on our targeting package as they would do with any presentment they come up with on their own.

The Indictment Engine™ will prepare a comprehensive presentment including the text of the filed bill, names and association(s) of the individuals or corporations that drafted the bill for the politician to sponsor, and the relevant State Penal Code sections that it violates, besides violating the Constitution.

Next, the Grand Jury hands down the bill of indictment. To assure the case is not hijacked by a corrupt or timid prosecutor, our members in that county's TACTICAL CIVICS™ chapter will put public pressure on the prosecutor's office. If they are corrupt, *they* will be the next Grand Jury target.

As you read the history of Grand Juries in America, you see We The People stopping organized crime in government, and that's how the People have done it since 997 AD!

American Militia 2.0™

At this point, another aspect of our TACTICAL CIVICS™ trifecta is vital: well-regulated Militia. See our book, *Time to Start Over, America* for much more on constitutional Militia; but our mission is not Militia! We only brief and educate militia groups, and get them to pass our County Militia Ordinance.

On the local level, we will offer TACTICAL CIVICS™ Affiliate membership to retail stores, professionals like doctors and lawyers, and others who want to support and further our mission. American Militia 2.0™ is our project to make Militia fun, cool, and popular again; as patriotic here as it is in Switzerland and valued as highly as your local Volunteer Fire Department. We The People have a constitutional duty! We already have the world's largest and most active firearms and shooting culture; now, we just add American Militia 2.0™.

Although Trump claimed to be a 'law and order' president amidst unprecedented lawlessness and violence across America, he didn't understand that law enforcement is a local and state function, *not* the job of presidents or their bureaucracies. And he obviously also did not know that the 'Department of Justice' is an illegal agency that began a century ago when a part-time job for one man was created without constitutional authority. The agency shouldn't exist!

'Gun Rights' Dinosaurs

I was a member for decades, but I dropped my membership after noticing that the 150-year-old NRA has never even *attempted* to restore constitutional Militia. Like most 501c3 organizations, it's a money-mill. If it ever allowed a real solution to the crisis it pretends to want to solve, you stop donating every month for the latest 'attack on your gun rights'. Like all Fear Porn, it's a simple business model: milk five million members for donations while playing Whack-a-Mole with an endless covey of threats rising out of the brambles from your pals in Congress.

Think: what is the primary law enforcement and defense force in the U.S. Constitution? *The Citizen Militia.* And what is the first duty of the Militia? *"To execute the Laws of the Union"*. So constitutional Militia restored to every community will be the most powerful law-enforcement, border-and-riot-control and national defense force on earth. See the problem for NRA's revenue stream? When we split Congress into 6,500+ tiny units scattered far from lobbyist-land and NRA's imperial headquarters, it will sink into the tar-pit like the cruel dinosaur it is.

People's Power and Pantywaist Pastors

Your county TACTICAL CIVICS™ chapter first pushes our Constitutional Militia Ordinance through your county so your servants will appoint officers and provide training in every town with a willing Militia. Every State has the legal duty to provide for a true Citizen Militia, per Article I, Section 8, Clause 16 of the U.S. Constitution; but the state palaces now try to disarm us instead, so now we go to our counties to cure the violation.

Incidentally, to any pastor who is afraid of the responsibilities of citizenship, I suggest they run, and keep running until no Bible-honoring American can reach them. They should either find courage or find another line of work. Remember, *judgment begins at the Church*. Read our book, *Tactical Civics™ for Church Leaders*.

In most efforts of Tactical Civics™, an 81-year-old woman can do as good a job as an 18-year-old man. Yes, it's more threatening to America than a world war, but wisdom trumps testosterone in arresting domestic enemies. We the People serving in Grand Jury are the most powerful actors in American government. Together, the People have always had ultimate authority over government.

President Trump suggested this in his inaugural address, but then he operated like a benevolent dictator, constantly saying "I". He doesn't know civics, bless his heart; neither do his most ardent fans because all of us have been ignorant of popular sovereignty and American rule of law. No other people on earth have this, even theoretically – and until the advent of the Internet and social media, We the People could never make it real. *Now we are fools if we do not.*

This is the most exciting time to be alive in America. But if you're not an AmericaAgain! member, you're still part of the problem. If you're 18 or over, you can make history in your county; join your chapter of TACTICAL CIVICS™. Then get your closest friends to join; we'll support you as we make history.

Some Days, the World Just Changes

After the Potsdam Conference ending World War II, the city of West Berlin became an oasis of liberty surrounded by communist East Germany. Germany itself was divided into communist east and democratic west, but Berlin fell fully within the communist side so it was cut in half, the western half of town being free, the eastern half communist.

Life on the two sides was as different as night and day, but the one bright spot in the bleak life of communist East Germany was West Berlin. If you ever visited as an East German, you got a taste of real food, real tea and coffee, real cigarettes, clothing, appliances, everything. A black market developed for all of those things – and for airline tickets out of West Berlin to destinations in the free world. For years, every communist dreamed of taking that flight from West Berlin to freedom. But even that one hope was extinguished, literally overnight.

If you woke up in Berlin on August 13, 1961 you discovered that overnight, Soviet forces had constructed a high fence between East and West Berlin. Topped by sharp concertina wire, it closed off all escape to West Berlin. If you had a family, job, or fiancé in West Berlin, that morning put an end to the relationship. Telephone lines into West Berlin were cut, so you could not even inform your family on the other side.

For 28 years, the Berlin Wall changed the world of all East Germans. But like communism itself, their ruthless artifice could only remain standing by force or fraud. *Then Ronald Reagan spoke six words.*

His challenge, *"Mr. Gorbachev, tear down this wall!"* sparked the imagination of Mikhail Gorbachev and kindled East German hearts. The world changed back again. Tasting liberty at last, the German people destroyed and carried away every chunk of the Berlin Wall almost as quickly as the Soviet crew had erected it.

God turned a page of history for the Germans when Ronald Reagan spoke those six words. God is also turning a page of history for us, as a brash casino owner and real estate developer was made president by millions of conservatives, then cheated out of re-election that he fairly won.

For the LORD will not cast off his people, neither will He forsake his inheritance. But judgment shall return unto righteousness: and all the upright in heart shall follow it. Who will rise up for me against the evildoers? or who will stand up for me against the workers of iniquity? Shall the throne of iniquity have fellowship with thee, which frames mischief by a law? They gather themselves together against the soul of the righteous, and condemn innocent blood. But the LORD is my defense and my God, the rock of my refuge. He shall bring upon them their own iniquity, and shall cut them off in their own wickedness; yea, the LORD our God shall cut them off.

Psalm 94 has always been a major inspiration for the staff at AmericaAgain!. We believe that God is raising a repentant Remnant to cut off those who 'frame mischief by a law'. We the People *can* enforce our U.S. Constitution from now on. The corrupt city-state and federal law guild greedily held their place at the head of the table in American law, as powerful guilds held Medieval Europe in serfdom…

Until they didn't.

Lesson 7 Question for Parents

1. The model ordinances will restore Grand Jury and Militia to work hand in hand to investigate potential crimes in public offices in our county by bureaucrats, politicians, and law enforcement.

How likely do you think the people of our county will be, to support returning to the People's two ancient institutions of law enforcement? What actions can you think of, that might increase the odds of successfully restoring them?

Lesson 8

Nineteen Steps to America Again

We the People intend to draft, refine, and push through the following 19 reform laws. This lesson is only an overview; a complete summary text of the proposed laws appears in the AmericaAgain! Declaration (see Appendix F).

As a plea-bargaining package offered to any member of Congress criminally indicted using the AmericaAgain! Indictment Engine™ or as an immunity package for those who have not yet been targeted, we will allow them to agree in writing to co-sponsor these reforms and vote for them without amendment.

1) Shut down D.C. organized crime by passing the **Bring Congress Home Act** that relocates all members of Congress to offices in their home district, via telepresence technology.

2) End the imperial, immoral rule of federal courts by passing the **Constitutional Courts Act**, which will disallow any case involving abortion, euthanasia, marriage, sexual practices, healthcare, education, religious laws (e.g. sharia), or state voter ID laws, out of federal court jurisdiction, including the U.S. supreme and lower courts.

Subject matter jurisdiction is a prerogative of Congress stipulated in Article III, Section 2, Clause 2 of the U.S. Constitution. This reform law also outlaws 'administrative law', assuring that no administrative law 'judge' can bind any citizen, and outlawing the use of terms such as 'court', 'order', 'subpoena', 'due process', 'the record' and other judicial terms by administrative bureaucrats including so-called 'tax courts'.

3) Drastically Shrink Federal Government by enacting the **Non-Enumerated Powers Sunset Act**, providing for creation of a House Standing Committee to Defund Non-Enumerated Powers, to fund and support a nationwide Citizens' Volunteer Research Service, which shall have the authority to review and de-fund any federal regulation, agency, bureau or program and its associated officers and staffing if not within a power *specifically* enumerated by We The People in the U.S. Constitution as a power of federal government.

By this legislation, any creative interpretations applied in the past by Congress and presidents using 'elastic clauses' (interstate commerce, general welfare, necessary and proper) and tax revenues sent as foreign aid outside the borders of the fifty States, will be de-funded and outlawed. This act will end virtually every alphabet-soup agency including DHS and all federal meddling in education, farming, and the environment (for the most part) as well as all foreign aid, which should only be a *voluntary* function for Americans and private organizations.

4) Outlaw back-door pork and tyranny by enacting the ***Clean Bill Act***, outlawing any omnibus bill or the addition of riders, unrelated-issue amendments, and earmarks to legislation. This act will also require that all filed bills list the names and contact information of every private-sector individual and/or entity who initiated, proposed, or suggested or drafted elements of the bill.

5) Secure our Border and civilization by enacting the ***Secure Borders Act***, acknowledging each state's duty to field a Militia for border defense, calling for construction or completion of the border wall, and immediately de-funding and outlawing all agencies, bureaus, policies and programs that encourage, facilitate or support illegal immigration. This legislation shall also bar from entry into the U.S. any adherent to sharia law, whether or not the person attempting to enter the U.S. is a resident of an officially Islamic state.

6) **End the 'Anchor Baby' tactic** by enacting Senate Joint Resolution 6 of the 111th Congress, stipulating that a person born in the United States shall not be a citizen unless one parent is a citizen, an alien lawfully admitted for permanent residence, an alien performing active service in the Armed Forces of the United States, or the person is naturalized per the laws of these United States.

7) The ***Congressional Anti-Corruption Act*** provides first, SEC insider trading rules will apply to members of Congress. It will be a federal crime for a member of Congress, directly or through proxies, trusts, or other entities, to purchase or sell stock in any company materially affected by legislation of which the member of Congress may be reasonably expected to have knowledge. Secondly, no member of Congress can be a lobbyist for five years after leaving office and *for life*, no former member of Congress or staffer for a member of Congress can lobby for a foreign government. Thirdly, it will be a federal felony to require a member of Congress to raise money as prerequisite to leadership or committee assignment.

8) Restore Privacy by enacting the ***Citizens' Privacy Act***, reiterating 4th Amendment privacy of the People's persons, houses, papers, data communications, vehicles, and effects from any government surveillance, seizure, detainment, or file storage by any method including drones, mini-drones, hidden cameras, etc. The law makes any such activity a federal offense unless preceded by issuance of a specific, bona fide judicial warrant issued upon probable cause. Repeals any parts of the FISA, RFPA, USA Patriot Act, NDAA, Intelligence Authorization Act of 2004 or any similar legislation present or future that violates the constitutional rights of any American.

9) The ***Religious Treason Act*** will first, outlaw religious laws or subversive activities meant to incite violence in the name of a religion or any foreign interest operating in the U.S.; secondly, stipulates a 'three strikes' policy eventually outlawing Islam in this republic if its adherents perpetrate three terrorist attacks; and thirdly, makes it a felony for any elected or appointed U.S. public servant to travel to a foreign country with the travel funded by a foreign government or a

foreign or domestic private foundation or lobby group on behalf of any foreign country, people or religion.

10) We will secure the Internet for citizen use by enacting the ***Internet Liberty Act***, making it a felony to disable Internet service within the USA, or selectively ban or hamper any individual's free access to a public Internet service on the basis of that individual's political or religious position unless espousing or calling for violence.

11) The ***Constitutional Supremacy Act*** based on the 1953 Bricker Amendment, will stipulate first, that no treaty will be valid if it violates the U.S. Constitution; secondly, that all Senate votes for a treaty must be recorded; thirdly, that no Continuity of Government (COG) order can contravene, violate or suspend the Constitution; fourthly, that federal courts will have no jurisdiction in any matter arising under this legislation; fifthly, making it a felony for any individual or group to engage in or materially support actions that threaten the legal or financial sovereignty of any of the sovereign states without the consent of the legislature(s) of every affected State.

12) The ***American Sovereignty Restoration Act*** of 2009 (HR 1146) of the first session of the 111th Congress, will terminate authorization of funds for the U.N. and withdraw diplomatic immunity for U.N. employees or delegates.

13) The ***Lawful Wars Act***, ends wars of plunder, disallowing funding for foreign hostilities without a Declaration of War and proof to Congress that such mobilization is necessary to defend against demonstrable threat to these 50 States.

14) We end federal grants to cities, counties, and States by enacting the ***Federal Pork Sunset Act***, making all federal grants/aid be remitted to the States as block grants for three years, after which all federal aid or grants end, and any further federal payment to States, counties or cities will be a federal crime.

15) We help restore the Citizen Militias of the States via the ***Minuteman Act***, to help Americans in their own counties to "execute the Laws of the Union, suppress Insurrections, and repel Invasions". This law will repeal every federal statute, regulation, executive order or other directive including the National Firearms Act of 1934 and later variations and preempts every such measure present and future of any State, county or city that infringes on or burdens the right to purchase, keep, carry, transport, or sell firearms, ammo, and accoutrements suitable for Militia service or that interferes with lawful design, manufacture, repair, or sale/distribution of arms, ammunition, etc.

16) We enact the ***Non-Conscription Act***, declaring that Congress, presidents, and federal courts have no authority to conscript Americans of any age into involuntary servitude for any purpose.

17) We restore sovereign State lands and foreign countries by enacting the ***Return of Sovereign Lands Act***, stipulating that other than land for military installations, federal government has no constitutional power to claim or control any private land, water, timber, oil, gas or other natural resources in, on, or under

any sovereign State, for any reason, under any conditions, without the *"Consent of the Legislature of the State in which the Same shall be"*.

Much more comprehensive than Utah HB142 passed in 2013, all federally held or controlled lands and natural resources within each sovereign State *and any foreign country* will revert within 36 months to full ownership and control of that sovereign State or country. Repeals all federal land-use regulations, national forest and park acts, and like federal controls, subject only to laws of the States.

18) We finally end the long rule of banksters, government-sponsored FED counterfeiting, the 'fractional reserve' loan fraud, and the gargantuan derivatives industry built on those frauds, with the **Lawful United States Money and Banking Act** which will have aspects of, but be more comprehensive than HR 459, 833, 1094, 1095, 1098, 1496, 2768 and SB 202, restoring lawful gold and silver U.S. money, and outlawing the FED cartel and any privately-owned entity ever having control over production of, or determining the value of, U.S. money. For much more on Congress' financial crimes, see Appendix H.)

19) We end secret intelligence agencies and projects that are nowhere authorized by the Constitution, enacting the **Intelligent Republic Act**, based loosely on the *Smart Nation Act* sponsored by Congressman Rob Simmons (R-CT), transitioning to Open Source Intelligence and outlawing any government program kept secret from Congress, which is clearly illegal.

Lesson 8 Questions for Parents

1. The 19 reform laws, once enacted, will bring us full circle to the Founders' intentions for America. Which three are most compelling to you, that you believe will have the greatest impact?

2. Has your optimism about America grown as your child learns this material that you had never seen before, understanding that their generation will be more likely than your generation, to begin restoring our rule of law? If not, why not?

Lesson 9

Granite Dome Syndrome

This lesson is the transcript of the most popular 'TED Talk' I have delivered so far on our Sunday night national conference calls. It's the best way I know to prepare you for this new way of life; by showing you how the hired help has twisted American civics, and our lives, all backwards and upside-down.

I'll discuss Granite Dome Syndrome, Moral Hazard, and our abdication of our sovereign prerogative that has resulted in full-blown Washington D.C. Communism and Fascism. I mean *literal* communism and fascism as Marx and Mussolini defined them).

Let me first define sovereign prerogative. *Sovereign* just means one who exercises the supreme, permanent authority. That's established in the opening three words of the supreme Law of our Land.

In its first important decision in 1793, *Chisolm v. Georgia,* the U.S. Supreme Court held that the *People* are the collective sovereigns in our form of government. *Prerogative* means the exclusive right and power to command, decide, rule, or judge. So this will be a key Tactical Civics lecture because it will give you civics knowledge that you won't hear anywhere else but that's vital for overcoming the psychological conditioning that you've suffered all your life.

So. First, *this* idea.

The power to *think* – to initiate and conduct those electrobiological processes called human thought – is the most profound gift that God gave mankind alone, among all species of His creatures on earth.

Because rational thought is our most valuable possession from God, it's especially discouraging and dangerous to see how few Americans spend much time actually *thinking* about *important* things. With each passing year, our days and weeks and years seem to be more packed full of noise. Of *busy*-ness and amusements that you only realize at the *end* of life were a total waste. Worthless; yet we spend the vast majority of our lives on these frivolous things.

Tonight, I want to challenge you to start doing things differently. And further, I want to challenge you to winsomely and in a friendly and helpful tone, also start influencing those around you to do the same: to just start *thinking* about things that matter in life, and to start immediately tuning out worthless nonsense when you see or hear it.

In the whirl and din of our Internet-and social media-mediated lives today, it's harder than you think, to just tune out every message that's just distraction on Facebook and YouTube and such. The average American 15 and 20-year-old, as much as 60- and 70-year-old, is like a child at an arcade, wasting hours every day that they will never recover; that they *could* spend thinking about and doing things that might change their family's entire history.

So that's the challenge; my first point tonight. If you want your life to count when you leave this earth, stop wasting precious hours on *nonsense*. You can't get those hours back.

Now tonight's main subject. I want to break down criminogenic American government into several psychological artifacts of mass-conditioning so you start to perceive how the system creates and maintains its oxen: 'taxpayer', 'consumer', 'voter'. Not sovereigns; on the contrary, just *oxen*.

I've spoken before on these calls about public architecture – what I call *Granite Dome Syndrome*. I've explained to you what happens right in the first week after a legislator or even their staffers get an office space under a granite dome. You've seen the incredible scale and opulence of the state capitols and of Capitol Hill. Not only the sheer massiveness and celestial beauty of the frescoed rotundas and massive colonnades, but the dining rooms with gold-trimmed china and silverware. The overstuffed leather chairs. The tapestries and portraits and Persian rugs.

I've explained how this does for those public servants exactly what it would do to *you* if you suddenly were given a palatial mansion. You'd wake up every day and see all around you the fact that you're now *very* special in society. This deference to elected servants is trained into American schoolchildren from a very early age.

Okay, so we know what Granite Dome Syndrome does for the servants, but what does it do to the sovereigns…to us? Well, it does the same thing as if you lived in a 70-year-old blighted tenement house, and you walk into a marble-floored 20,000-square-foot, 14-bedroom mansion. You definitely are *not* going to be able to conceive of yourself as the boss of the person in that mansion, right? So Granite Dome Syndrome is a no-brainer, and we need to do something about it.

Until we do take them out of those palaces – by the way, I propose that you start calling your state house the *capitol palace* from now on. So at least when the snot-nosed legislative aide looks down his or her nose at you, you'll keep in mind that the young fool is the servant of your *servant*, and you're the *boss* of their boss!

Okay, now a *second* element: Moral Hazard.

In economic theory, the principle called *Moral Hazard* holds that the larger a taxpayer population grows, the less each taxpayers will care about a given expense because it impacts each one so little. Notice how central governments tend to be more corrupt and opulent as a function of population. The larger the victim pool, the less each victim feels the hit. That's Moral Hazard.

The label *Moral Hazard* derives from the phenomenon that when times are good and taxpayers aren't hurting much, the corrupt activities, agencies, bureaus and debt load that would normally make you furious, don't bother you. Because the hit is spread over a lot of people, each one doesn't feel like it's worth the trouble to confront it. Even if they're presented with a practical arrest mechanism for the crimes, they just won't bother. That's what makes it so dangerous and why it's called Moral Hazard.

Now, a *third* element of criminogenic tactics: *distance.*

Federal government puts legislators far away from their communities. Their sovereigns can't see who they're meeting with for breakfast, brunch, lunch, cocktails, or dinner. This distance makes it very unlikely that you'll take the time or spend the money to check up on them. If you don't see their day-to-day shenanigans with attorneys and consultants for corporations and single-interest groups, it's like it's not even happening. Do you see how the factors add up?

A *fourth* element is *unaccountability*. What difference will it make when we pass the Bring Congress Home Act and not only bring them home and cut their salaries and limit their terms, but also demand annual audits of our servants' expenditures, posted on a public website? Isn't it *ridiculous* that we've never demanded this before? And why on earth do we not get to determine their salaries rather than *them* doing so themselves?

Now the *fifth* element, 'mass civics deception'. Fraudulent labeling of the lawless form of government we've allowed to grow right inside the shell of our supposedly constitutionally-limited one.

Washington D.C. Communism is never called by its accurate name, yet the D.C. government today meets all ten of Karl Marx's stated goals in *A Communist Manifesto*.

The same goes for Washington D.C. Fascism. Mussolini defined *fascism* as the alliance of central government with the corporations, to control the people in the service of the State. Ending D.C. Fascism is simple; after we strip them of their Granite Dome palace, we begin filling those legislators' seats ourselves, and we stipulate in law that legislation *must actually be written by legislators* and specifically *not* by industry.

When we break down the House districts into small, local ones and take Congress out of Washington D.C., then we can enforce Article I, Section 8, Clause 17 – that's where We The People grant Congress exclusive legislative jurisdiction over the District of Columbia. See how nice that will be when Congress isn't there anymore but all the D.C. *tentacles* remain there? The responsible remnant can end D.C. Communism and Fascism *without firing a shot.*

You see how the American mind is conditioned, and why young people seek careers in politics? Political careerists *never* lose their granite dome, perks, and pay (better pay than private-sector jobs). And what about us? Well, if we oxen fail to pay property tax on our *paid-for* farm, home, or shop – we lose everything to the arrogant hired help when *the sheriff* sells it on the courthouse steps.

So the *sixth* element of corrupt government is closer to home. The *ad valorem* property tax scam in America stokes the fires that make us fear our servants. You fail to pay for whatever your legislature wants this week, and you'll face your county tax collection lawyers and your friendly, neighborhood sheriff!

That's the *predator* aspect of the crime spree; what about the *parasite* army? Well, that's the *seventh* element of criminogenic American government. *Criminogenic* means it teaches criminality by example...and that's precisely what government in D.C. and your state palace has done. It has taught your county, city, and school district bureaucrats and boards to be as criminal in their presumptions as Congress is, with its $22 trillion debt burden palmed off on *our* backs.

So. The parasite army is a huge catalyst, a multi-generational welfare horde including 30 million illegal aliens, riding the coattails of our corrupt servants and 20 million public employees in agencies, bureaus and departments. That's 50 million people extorting and bleeding productive America!

Our First Right and the Bring Congress Home Act are our last serious line of defense against rogue states that declare themselves *sanctuaries*. From under those granite domes, the state governments of California, Colorado, Illinois, Massachusetts, New Mexico, Oregon and Vermont have declared their states *outlaw territories*, against law and against the interests of productive citizens. Close behind are many cities and counties in Iowa, Pennsylvania and Washington State.

With state governments proclaiming rule of law dead, do you see how Obama's administration including 'Resident' Biden, Hillary's open corruption, Bernie Sanders' candidacy and George Soros' astroturf hordes forged a coordinated attack by American Communism against rule of law?

This public, shameless rebellion against Productive America is straight out of Saul Alinski's book. It's the Cloward-Piven Strategy in full metastasizing cancer mode. We will explain how these tactics took notes from the long history of success in the infanticide and sexual perversion communities.

TACTICAL CIVICS™ is the answer – but sincere repentance is Step One. As we've explained, Americans have been taught to self-label as *taxpayer* and *voter* like farmers use the terms *ox* and *mule*.

The war, banking, and oil industries piled on because no conditioning tool works as well on mules and oxen as the shock of war: Lincoln's war, Wilson's, FDR's, LBJ's, and the open-ended Bush-Clinton-Bush-Obama-Trump war are a one-way ratchet; a growing burden on productive America.

But things are finally changing, and TACTICAL CIVICS™ is the point of the spear, even though we're only a mustard seed today. You see, the ox is beginning to despise the growing blue whale on its back, but there are still millions of complaining, fearful, angry, cynical Americans on social media every day who (even the angriest among them) suffer from Granite Dome Syndrome without even knowing it.

So. Now you know more about your mental and emotional condition and its origins, than you did a few minutes ago. This course is designed to prepare you to break free, and help forge a far better life for your grandchildren than your grandparents handed down to your parents.

Let's review TACTICAL CIVICS™ again, and how it will work. We all know the problems: every day, Americans are more fearful, angry, frustrated and cynical about America's direction. Abortion, perversion and transgenderism even in grade schools, Congress opening our border to hundreds of thousands more illegal aliens to add to the tens of millions already here. Cheap labor for industrialists and free votes for evil politicians. Muslims are winning elections to city, county, state governments and to the U.S. Congress.

Antifa rioters and random shooters pop up as regularly as clockwork. These planned distractions keep us from noticing D.C. mega-crimes. They give state and federal tyrants more reasons to disarm the law-abiding citizenry, and frighten and destabilize Americans, at least the more limp-wristed ones, to reject the idea of constitutional Militia more than ever.

Some governors are so wicked now that they're *openly* destroying our civilization. Some state legislatures are actually pushing the murder of not only pre-born infants, but those who have already been born. As Christians warned a decade ago, the homosexual army expanded the gaping hole in our morals to now allow pedophiles and transgendered perverts to follow. Marxists are pushing so-called Critical Race Theory to further tear our civilization apart. Where will this end, and what can *you* do to help?

To reiterate, AmericaAgain! Trust is a charitable trust and member organization whose mission is to recruit, train, support and organize the American remnant in a new way of life called TACTICAL CIVICS™, the result of over 66,000 hours of research and development by 44 volunteers. It is unprecedented; the only full-spectrum action solution in our republic. TACTICAL CIVICS™ has discrete milestones, detailed processes and personnel plans for execution, and metrics for reaching each milestone before proceeding to the next one.

The unique, powerful facts of American civics are that We The People, as the *creators* of all three servant branches in Washington D.C., are the *only* human authority *above* the US Constitution. Collectively, we occupy the highest office in our government. No other population in history has had that lawful authority.

TACTICAL CIVICS™ includes five unprecedented objectives...

First: We restore our original law enforcement institutions: the State Grand Jury and the constitutional State Militia. Most importantly, now we *jointly deploy* them. Eventually, every State Grand Jury can have the lawful firepower of its corresponding constitutional Militia to serve and arrest potential criminals in public office at the school district, city, county and state levels, as well as members of Congress now living and working full-time in their own communities.

TACTICAL CIVICS™, with our Operation Restoration, seeks to clean up the images of America's Grand Jury and Militia, to expose impostor groups. I am referring to so-called grand juries who seat themselves, and private militant groups who are unaccountable to their State government as stipulated in the Constitution, and who instead operate as private vigilante groups. Operation Restoration will bring together all those who are ready to serve *constitutional* Militia duty in their community and State, as the Founding Fathers intended.

Our local Militias should be much like all of our local Volunteer Fire Departments. TACTICAL CIVICS™ is committed to restoring clean, law-abiding, all-American, locally-controlled constitutional Militia for a new sense of community, liberty and security that is of, by, and for The People Themselves.

Second: We finish ratifying the first right in our Bill of Rights, breaking the U.S. House into small districts. You are learning about this amazing gift left to us by the Founding Fathers. All we have to do is finish that chore; 'Our First Right' in the original Bill of Rights is already ratified by 11 states; it only needs 27 more.

It was the first one of twelve articles in the original Bill of Rights; keeping congressional districts small, to reduce corruption. It was the only subject on which George Washington stood before the Philadelphia convention to speak about in 1787. When we finish ratifying Our First Right, a U.S. House campaign will cost a few *thousand* dollars, not millions. This will make a U.S. House seat appealing to *millions* of regular, honest, hard-working Americans.

Third: Once we've broken Congress down into about 6,600+ small districts represented by citizen-statesmen, we *Bring Congress Home*, to be the world's first distributed legislature, now under *our* watchful eye. In this 21st century, while over 40% of American businesses are using telecommuting and online meetings, why do we allow our arrogant, corrupt servants in D.C. to remain there, in the most ruthless, corrupt city on earth, while we pay all their bills? It's *insane*.

The Bring Congress Home Act stipulates that they get just one modest office per member of Congress and it must be in their district. We limit them to two terms, House or Senate and *no* benefits; they can pay their own way like most of *us* have to. We cut Congressmen's salaries to half of what they pay themselves now, and we annually audit their office operations, as any good employer should.

Fourth: We deploy our Indictment Engine™ mobile app, to track and arrest legislation violating the U.S. Constitution. Its language artificial intelligence algorithms search the proposed legislation to match it against the applicable sections of the sponsor or co-sponsor's State Penal Code sections, and the Indictment Engine™ outputs a felony presentment for each attempted crime. Those presentments can be used by the State Grand Jury to pass down a criminal indictment count against the politician proposing the lawless legislation, for each such violation of his State Penal Code.

Fifth: Through our 19 Reform Laws, TACTICAL CIVICS™ will help citizen-statesmen in our new, distributed Congress, over time, to scrape back all that We The People lost to D.C. organized crime over the past 160 years.

TACTICAL CIVICS™ county chapter founders and leaders are holding meetings from coast to coast in hundreds of counties. They are learning the same civics that you are learning in this tutorial, and spreading the same good news that we hope you will spread as you become an amazing American, mingling in society.

With county chapters from Alaska to Florida and new Chapter Founders joining every day, TACTICAL CIVICS™ is not politics, needing majorities. It's *popular constitutionalism;* the People enforcing the Constitution for the first time, and from now on. Since it is law enforcement rather than electoral politics, we only need half of 1% to meet our objectives and rebuild America's walls.

We do not deny that we are witnessing the noisy, messy, cursing, spitting collapse of American Communism after a century; and of the massive Deep State and media empires who have enjoyed fat careers on the backs of a population that have never enforced our highest law. There are hundreds of thousands of complainers and Fear Porn hawkers, who daily spew 'passion' on social media. They point out evils both real and imagined. But they never deliver solutions or actually get to work.

What good does it do, to continually complain about the gathering darkness? Even if America is collapsing – at some point we'll have to clean up and restore normal life, right? So TACTICAL CIVICS™ has already *begun*.

We The People, just a remnant, are now doing our best every day, to take America back. We have the only full-spectrum action plan in this republic. No one else – no private sector startup, no one in academia, no nonprofit – has anything even *approaching* this mission. Yes; of *course* it will be difficult! Of *course* it will take years! Restoring rule of law in the largest free republic in history, when the criminals have had generations to perfect their game – what would you *expect*?

Sincere Americans must wake up, *now*. Perform your own research to corroborate our shocking assertions in this tutorial course. The hard truth is that Americans were lied to in school and defrauded in college for over a century. We've been propagandized by the servants whose salaries and benefits we pay.

Now the good news: this is the *best* time to be alive in America, and God is blessing us yet again, if the responsible remnant will only do our duty.

Lesson 9 Questions for Parents

1. Honestly, were you aware of the elements of Granite Dome Syndrome before you saw this lesson, or have you always felt a certain inferiority whenever you entered our capitol palace?

2. After We The People finally bring Congress home to serve us from regular lease offices in their communities, do you think we should bring our state legislators home too, instead of letting them team up against us under the granite dome? If not, why do you think it's better to leave them operating there?

Lesson 10
What's Under the Hood?

Many times I have been asked, "What are the subjects of our 19 reform laws?"

You can read the draft reform laws in our *AmericaAgain! Declaration,* Appendix F. For a simpler draft of the 19 reform laws, see the final lesson in the book, *Mission to America: A Seven-Week Crash Course in Tactical Civics™*. Some of it is hard reading, but our blessed civilization has been transmogrified into a godless nightmare and crime spree over 160 years by powerful cartels; so We The People need to grow up, repent our dereliction of duty, and start doing our chores.

Below is our proposed Reform Law #2, as an example of the extent of the research and planning that our team invested over a decade, to bring this mission to Americans so that the remnant can introduce it and live it out in their own counties. We already did the hardest work so that others wouldn't have to.

Reform Law #2, The Constitutional Courts Act

Section 1. A consensus exists among the American public that the federal courts have been corrupted and are manipulated by powerful individuals and by lobbyists for industry and special interests, rendering moot the stipulated limitations placed by the People through the U.S. Constitution on its creature, federal government.

a. James Madison, Father of the Constitution, in his Virginia Resolution of 1798, and Thomas Jefferson, in his concurring Kentucky Resolution, wrote that the States, as the creator parties to the U.S. Constitution, have the right and duty to judge when the U.S. Constitution has been violated by federal government; that the federal government cannot judge of its own infractions

b. In Article III, Section 1 of the U.S. Constitution, the People grant to Congress the authority to create the inferior federal courts, thus the subject matter jurisdiction of the inferior federal courts is entirely within Congress' discretion.

c. In Article III, Section 2 of the U.S. Constitution, the People grant to Congress the authority to withhold subject matter jurisdiction even from the U.S. supreme Court, using "such Exceptions, and…such Regulations as the Congress shall make".

d. In Article VI, Section 2 of the U.S. Constitution, the People stipulate, *This Constitution…shall be the supreme Law of the Land; and the Judges in every State shall be bound thereby…,* which binding includes *enforcement* as well as obedience.

e. Every federal legislator is now performing his federal duties full-time within his or her own district, which is the jurisdiction of his State Grand Jury and State Court.

[N.B.: This bill will not be attempted until after we have enacted Reform Law #1, The Bring Congress Home Act.]

f. Therefore, pursuant to the power granted by the People to Congress in U.S. Constitution Article III, Section 2, Clause 2, after the effective date hereof, no federal court shall have jurisdiction in any case in which a member of Congress is charged by his or her own State Grand Jury with violating, or conspiring to violate, the U.S. Constitution.

g. In no such case shall removal from state jurisdiction be available to the accused, whether pursuant to 28 USC 1441, or any subsequent federal law.

Section 2. The American People stipulated in Article I, Section 8 of the U.S. Constitution, that *The Congress shall have power…to constitute tribunals inferior to the supreme Court…,* and in Article III, Section 1, that the federal courts are, *such inferior courts as the Congress may from time to time ordain and establish,* and in Article III, Section 2, Clause 2, that the U.S. supreme Court, *shall have appellate jurisdiction…with such Exceptions, and under such Regulations as the Congress shall make.*

In *Turner v. Bank of North America* (1799), Justice Chase wrote, *The notion has frequently been entertained, that the federal courts derive their judicial power immediately from the Constitution; but the political truth is, that the disposal of the judicial power…belongs to Congress. If Congress has given the power to this Court, we possess it, not otherwise: and if Congress has not given the power to us or to any other Court, it still remains at the legislative disposal.*

In *Ex parte Bollman* (1807), Chief Justice John Marshall wrote, *Courts which are created by written law, and whose jurisdiction is defined by written law, cannot transcend that jurisdiction.*

The power of Congress to create inferior federal courts, necessarily implies, as written in *U.S. v. Hudson & Goodwin* (1812), the *power to limit jurisdiction of those Courts to particular objects.*

The U.S. supreme Court held unanimously in *Sheldon v. Sill* (1850) that because the People in the Constitution did not create inferior federal courts but authorized Congress to create them, that Congress by necessity had power to define and limit their jurisdiction and to withhold jurisdiction of any of the enumerated cases and controversies.

The high court even acknowledged Congress' power to re-examine particular classes of questions previously ruled on by the U.S. supreme Court, as stated in *The Francis Wright* (1882): *(A)ctual jurisdiction under the* [judicial] *power is confined within such limits as Congress sees fit to prescribe…What those powers shall be, and to what extent they shall be exercised, are, and always have been, proper subjects of legislative control…Not only may whole classes of cases be kept out of the jurisdiction altogether, but particular classes of questions may be subjected to re-examination and review…*

In *Lauf v. E.G. Shinner & Co* (1938), the U.S. supreme Court declared, *There can be no question of the power of Congress thus to define and limit the jurisdiction of the inferior courts of the United States.*

In *Lockerty v. Phillips* (1943), the U.S. supreme Court held that Congress has the power of, *withholding jurisdiction from them* [federal courts] *in the exact degrees and character which to Congress may seem proper for the public good.*

Section 3. Therefore, Congress hereby excludes from federal court jurisdiction any and all cases involving:

a. Taking of human life, from point of conception;

b. Sexual practices or the institution of marriage;

c. Healthcare;

d. Education;

e. Official recognition or application of any foreign law or code within these united States or any of them; and

f. Claims of United States control, possession, or jurisdiction over any land outside of that granted by We the People and the States, as stipulated in Article I, Section 8, Clause 17 of the U.S. Constitution.

Section 4. What constitutes due process in all courts within the United States or any of them shall be defined and determined exclusively from within the Bill of Rights and the American common law, in that order of precedence.

Section 5. In Article III, Section 1 of the U.S. Constitution, the People stipulate, *the judicial Power of the United States shall be vested in one supreme Court, and in such inferior Courts as the Congress may from time to time ordain and establish;* therefore within 12 months of the passage of this Act:

a. No 'administrative law' tribunal in these United States shall bind any citizen;

b. No administrative adjudicator shall be referred to as 'judge';

c. No administrative tribunal shall be referred to, or refer to itself, as 'court';

d. No administrative process or tribunal shall describe its processes in terms such as 'order', 'subpoena', 'warrant', or 'the record', which are reserved for constitutional judiciary.

Section 6. Pursuant to provisions of Section 3(f) above and the proposed Return of Sovereign Lands Act, 24 months after enactment of this legislation and thereafter, it shall be a federal felony for any agency, agent, bureau, department, officer, contractor or other representative of the government of these United States of America to claim, own, maintain or operate a purported U.S. court or detention facility that is not located within the land or property stipulated in Article I, Section 8, Clause 17 of the U.S. Constitution.

Section 7. Because Federal Rules of Criminal Procedure Numbers 6 and 7 appear to create an unconstitutional barrier to the established prerogative power of the People when serving in their State Grand Jury, no federal judicial rules shall have any bearing or authority over any State Grand Jury.

As U.S. Supreme Court Justice Antonin Scalia wrote in *U.S. v. Williams* (1992):

"(T)he Grand Jury is an institution separate from the courts, over whose functioning the courts do not preside...Rooted in long centuries of Anglo American history, the Grand Jury is mentioned in the Bill of Rights, but not in the body of the Constitution. It has not been textually assigned, therefore, to any of the branches described in the first three Articles. It is a constitutional fixture in its own right...

"In fact, the whole theory of its function is that it belongs to no branch of the institutional government, serving as a kind of buffer or referee between the government and the People...The Grand Jury requires no authorization from its constituting court to initiate an investigation, nor does the prosecutor require leave of court to seek a Grand Jury indictment...[T]he Grand Jury generally operates without the interference of a presiding judge. It swears in its own witnesses, and deliberates in total secrecy."

Section 8. As stipulated in Article I, Section 8, Clause 15 of the U.S. Constitution, the several States retain the power to enforce this legislation by appropriate State legislation and duly authorized Citizen Militia enforcement action within their respective jurisdictions.

[End of draft bill.]

Not Like All The 'Restore America' Plans

So. We aren't being hyperbolic or self-aggrandizing, merely factual, when we make the claim that, *AmericaAgain! Trust has created and defined, and is leading a new market and a new way of life called Tactical Civics™, the only full-spectrum, lawful, peaceful solution to the destruction of our republic by organized crime and its bureaucratic hordes and media and academic allies under the guise of government.*

Our team took 12 years just to bring this mission to Americans because as you now see, digging deep into the crimes of our servants and their masters, the billionaires and global corporations, required us to perform *years* of investigative research, legal drafting, 'war gaming' under strictures of Common Law and constitutional precedent, and fine-tuning language to make it as comprehensible as possible to American adults of average intelligence.

With each of our proposed reform laws, we didn't just make it up as we went along. We sought out the best minds in America who had already been working the problem and publishing their solution to that problem (crime) before we began constructing that reform law.

In the case of this particular reform, our inspiration and information originated at the desk of Professor Philip Hamburger of Columbia University, who has been preaching this truth for decades.

Becoming one of 'We The People'

If you decide to live this new way of life, after your 18th birthday please re-read the *AmericaAgain! Declaration* once a year or so, as you become a 'Constitution tutor' in your county.

Thinking about reading pre-law type materials and introducing this kind of thing to adults might intimidate you today. I remember that feeling, years ago! You will overcome it by doing your chores: reading, meditating on what you just read, discussing it with others in the Tactical Civics Training Center and in your county chapter group. You will quite often need to read things several times.

This is called *due diligence*. It is the price of being an American in full. It's how you become one of *We The People,* when almost everyone around you is too slothful or fearful to lift a finger.

God made mankind for work, and truly *meaningful* work is rare on the earth today.

Isn't it about time we did some?

Lesson 10 Question for Parents

1. Until the late 19th century, to stand for the bar exam only required that the candidate read and study enough law and cases to pass the bar; it did not require a college degree.

The *Void for Vagueness* doctrine in American law holds that a law is void if a person of average intelligence can't understand it.

How do these facts change your view of our duty to learn enough about laws and legal process to oversee our servants in government, thus maintain our constitutional rule of law…even to draft and propose reform laws ourselves?

Lesson 11
The People Themselves

TACTICAL CIVICS™ is a new way of life following the thesis first proposed in 2004 by then-Stanford Law School dean Larry Kramer and in his book **The People Themselves: Popular Constitutionalism and Judicial Review**, as quoted in earlier lessons.

Dean Kramer asserted a truth that is obvious to any third grader reading the first three words of our Constitution: *We The People hold the highest public office.* We are the boss of government that we created in that supreme Law of the Land. *We are constitutionally (legally) superior to the U.S. supreme Court. Thus, we are obviously* far *superior to the inferior federal courts.*

TACTICAL CIVICS™ is the responsible remnant of Americans, for the first time and from now on, actually *enforcing* our highest law. Here is how the enforcement aspect against federal and state legislators will operate:

When any legislator files a bill that we believe violates the U.S. Constitution, if we find a harmonizing State Penal Code section on which to indict the sponsors and co-sponsors of that bill – even before it becomes law, the sponsors have committed *felony conspiracy*. The plan is for this analysis and targeting to eventually take place in our Indictment Engine™ mobile app; a major feat of Language Artificial Intelligence.

The Indictment Engine™ outputs a felony presentment to each County Grand Jury of each co-conspirator; that is, each co-sponsor of the bill. Next, those Grand Juries instruct their associated Militia in each district of each co-conspirator to serve that target with a felony indictment.

Why the Militia? Because *the Constitution is our highest law and Militia is the only authorized force to enforce it (see Art I, Sec 8 Clause 15)*. At least in the early years of this new way of life, paid 'law enforcement' will not confront powerful politicians. We The People need to make an intimidating show of armed force, as IRS, FBI, BATF, and police or sheriff SWAT teams do, to prove to criminal legislators that We The People mean business. They either obey the law or we have the court seize their assets and send them to their State Penitentiary to do hard time.

Contrary to what KrisAnne Hall and former sheriff Richard Mack (Constitutional Sheriffs and Peace Officers Association) teach: *sheriffs are not America's highest constitutional law enforcement officers.* Yes, in any county, the sheriff is higher legal authority than any federal actor; but in ancient Britain, the duty of the *shire reeve* – the origin of our word *sheriff* – was to be the crown's chief enforcer of the crown's rules and collector of taxes from the people, using force when necessary. And *that is what sheriffs still do.*

No Private Property in America

For instance, it is a demonstrable fact that private property no longer exists in America. After you pay off the bank or mortgage company, you still only *rent* your land, business, farm, or home from all the taxing entities: school district, city, and county. Their unelected bureaucrats build palatial buildings for themselves, buy fleets of new vehicles, get the latest computer tech and other goodies…all paid for by hard-working people, many of whom cannot afford a new home, new vehicle, or new computers.

The People pay all the bills but have *zero* control over the bureaucrats' decisions to build and buy fancy stuff. *How dumb can we be?* An American might spend half a lifetime paying off his home, but if he can't make a property tax payment that the taxspenders demand, the sheriff will hold a foreclosure sale on the courthouse steps! *If this is not Communism, in what way would Communism be worse?*

So no, Mr. Mack; the sheriff is no friend to the U.S. Constitution as long as his two top allegiances are to bureaucrat taxspenders, and to getting re-elected.

Sheriff is Not Found in the Constitution

In our highest law, We The People do not mention police, sheriffs, or constables. The only law enforcement we authorize is found in Article I, Section 8, Clause 15: …*Militia to execute the Laws of the Union, suppress Insurrections, and repel Invasions.*

Two things you may conclude from this. First, we need to bring all members of Congress into *State* Criminal Court jurisdiction. They and our other servants defy and violate the Constitution and our liberty…governors, mayors, sheriffs, judges, constables, policemen and others take liberties and are deeply corrupt; yet being ignorant of our authority and duty when serving on Grand Jury and Militia, Americans think we have no recourse other than trying to fight tyrannical mandates and tax hikes! How *foolish* of us.

Secondly, we need to restore the Grand Jury and Militia in every county, and make sure they coordinate operations so that We The People maintain control.

I am not suggesting that all sheriffs are corrupt; but almost none of them know this true, unfortunate history of their institution. And no politician in your county is more aware than sheriffs are, of those cameras in re-election campaigns. In any state with property tax, the sheriff is the enforcer, which makes him one of the oppressors, not the defender of the Constitution that many claim to be.

Repentance: Not Words But Action

Anyone over 18 years old may join the remnant, launch a TACTICAL CIVICS™ county chapter, learn the civics and tactics, and spread the good news to inspire friends to be the founders of their county chapters, too.

The enemies of our civilization are many. But a faithful remnant can win this war against D.C. organized crime and its minions in state, county, city, and school district bureaucracies. Not only can we win it more quickly than you might imagine, but We The People of this unique constitutional Republic are the only population on earth, at any time in history, who grant to ourselves the highest office in all government.

The opposite of rebellious or unlawful talk, this is American civics; the norms and principles laid down by our founders.

Gaslighting is a Communist Tool

Gaslighting is a criminal tactic in which the perpetrator continually presents lies as truth, and tries to convince the victims that they are going insane.

Since the 9/11 operation, and especially with the Plandemic and Election Steal 2020 operations, there remains no question which side the major media, Big Tech, and Hollywood are on. But it is a simple matter to test our servants who are legislators, judges, and paid law enforcement, to discover which side of this existential war they are fighting for. Do not believe it when they attempt to make you think that basic civics and the Constitution are too difficult for you to grasp. Never believe such liars. *This is not China; at least not yet.*

If we give honest statesmen our support, they will increasingly show themselves and grow in number and influence. But repentance in our civilization must not be limited to our servants. For We The People too, now is the time to take up our duties, and allow the watching world to learn from our faithful example.

Lesson 11 Questions for Parents

1. What do you think of the assertion of former Stanford Law School Dean Larry Kramer, that We the People are constitutionally (legally) superior to the U.S. supreme Court in deciding what the Constitution says?

2. In Article III, Section 2, Clause 2 of the Constitution, We The People authorize our servants in Congress to create their own federal courts and limit their subject-matter jurisdiction and even that of the U.S. supreme Court. Does this change your view of the importance and power of SCOTUS judges?

3. Had you ever realized that the sheriff is still the tax enforcer for the 'crown'?

4. In the Constitution we stipulate that our Militias *alone* can 'execute the Laws of the Union', yet most Americans fear and loathe the very word *Militia*. Consider who stands to lose; who do you think propagandizes and gaslights the American People, causing them to run from their authority and duty?

Lesson 12
Republic, Republic, Republic!

Over a decade ago, 30-year veteran New York City school teacher John Taylor Gatto published a trenchant indictment of government schools entitled **Dumbing Us Down: The Hidden Curriculum of Compulsory Schooling**. But that scholar omitted one crucial point of government programming that I will bring to your attention.

Americans are ignorant of civics. We don't know how our system of government works or even what form of government we have.

I'm not referring to those ditzy high school and college kids that Mark Dice interviews, who don't know third grade material. I'm talking about most of our presidents, members of Congress, university professors, journalists and others who should know better. Like most adults trained in government schools, they believe that Abe Lincoln was our greatest president, a preposterous 'fact' of propaganda on which Washington D.C. has relied for 150 years. In Essay 34, we link to six books and a website that debunk that destructive lie.

But they also cannot comprehend the stipulations set out by We The People in our U.S. Constitution; the most basic fact of civics, that these united States of America are a *republic*, a form of government guaranteed by We The People to each of the States in Article IV, Section 4 of the U.S. Constitution.

You see, *country* can mean many things; if I say I live in the country, I don't live in the city. Using the word 'country' doesn't settle the matter.

In anthropology, *nation* refers to a common cultural group (see Colin Woodard's book, *American Nations*). In political economy, *nation* refers to a population living under a unitary government. On the other hand, *republic* refers to a confederation of sovereign states each with its own government but unified for only limited and specified purposes. Read the Constitution; that's us. It isn't rocket science. In fact, the average fourth grade homeschooler has no problem grasping and remembering it. But senators and presidents apparently do.

These united States of America have been a republic for 227 years. America has never been a *nation,* even if many past presidents have used the word because it was handy. If you think this American *republic* is no big deal, you have no idea. Watch Europe over the next few years and you will begin to appreciate the value of our Christian civilization, our constitutional rule of law, and the republic that We The People guarantee to every sovereign State in Article IV, Section 4:

The United States shall guarantee to every State in this Union a Republican Form of Government...

James Madison, Father of the Constitution and the unimpeachable authority on such questions, explained this clause of the new constitution in **Federalist #39**: *Each State, in ratifying the Constitution, is considered as a sovereign body, independent of all others, and only to be bound by its own voluntary act. In this relation, then, the new Constitution will, if established, be a federal, and not a national constitution."*

But our ignorance of civics is not limited to the fact that most Americans do not know what form of government we have by law. They also do not know that We The People are the highest level of government, standing over our U.S. Constitution as its creators, interpreters, and enforcers.

For generations, government schools and even private, Christian, and so-called classical schools have trained Americans to demote ourselves with words like *voter* and *grassroots*. You will not have that handicap; we cleared that up in Lesson 2. Having never read our own Constitution, written at sixth grade comprehension level, most Americans are clueless. Once you recognize our duty and power as America's collective sovereign, you will never again use the word *nation* to refer to our *republic*. You also will stop using propaganda phrases such as 'elected leaders' and 'elected officials' to refer to arrogant criminals. These people are elected to represent and serve us, and to scrupulously obey the Constitution. Instead, they serve themselves and the elite, and violate America's highest law every day, many times per day. And listen to them; they are proud of it!

If a clueless employer referred to his employees or servants as "my elected leaders" (since he does have to hire them from a pool of candidates), how long would it take for the hired help to take the employer captive? Those 'elected leaders' set their own working conditions, staffing, salary, benefits, luxury travel – and send their IRS thugs after the taxpayers to fund it all.

Mr. Gatto and many others have pointed out the seminal part played by the government schools in destroying our republic. We have swallowed and regurgitated a great deal of destructive foolishness, and the ruins are generations deep. There is work to be done. By the grace of God, over 50 years, America's growing army of homeschoolers have been training a remnant to take up our duties and powers that our ancestors abdicated, and this tutorial is now the consummate example.

As Europe flies apart under this same curse of criminality, America is pushed to the gates of Hell, with the Millennial generation pushing for Communism, smiling all the way, courtesy of government schools. It's time to reform our vocabulary and repent our way of life.

Unlike complaining 'save America' groups and websites that do nothing but quote Founding Fathers and ask for donations, TACTICAL CIVICS™ chapters have formed in hundreds of counties from Alaska to Florida. It is now easier than ever for We The People to begin rebuilding the fallen walls of our *REPUBLIC!*

Lesson 12 Question for Parents

1. Article IV, Section 4 of the Constitution opens with this warranty language:

The United States shall guarantee to every State in this Union a Republican Form of Government…

In Federalist 39, James Madison offered additional warranty language:

Each State, in ratifying the Constitution, is considered as a sovereign body, independent of all others, and only to be bound by its own voluntary act. In this relation, then, the new Constitution will, if established, be a federal, and not a national constitution.

Can you give one example of Washington D.C. violating the warranty found in Article IV, Section 4, explain who is supposed to enforce that warranty, and how they are supposed to do it?

Lesson 13

Our First Right

This is the story of a crime. Of how a tiny mistake 140 years earlier set us up for it, how We the People have always had the power to reverse it, and how we can take Congress out of Washington DC, making that corrupt city irrelevant again.

America was hijacked by Washington DC – the most ruthless, powerful, criminal city-state in the history of the world – when Congress stole our First Right in the original Bill of Rights. This virtually hidden mega-crime stole all representation in the U.S. House and Electoral College from residents of 31,000 American small towns; about 90% of America's land mass.

The millionaire lapdogs of billionaires and industry distract us with week-to-week nonsense as they fund pork, multibillion-dollar wars and multimillion dollar campaigns for huge districts with as many as 900,000 citizens – all because of a small error of just *one word*.

The Founding Fathers' Plan

It began on the last day of the five month long Constitutional Convention in 1787. Delegate Nathaniel Gorham made a motion to change one word in Article I of the proposed Constitution – "*the number of Representatives shall not exceed one for every forty thousand...*" to read, "*for every thirty thousand*".

George Washington rose to speak for the first and only time to address the convention. On page 644 of *Records of the Federal Convention*, James Madison describes the scene:

"When the President rose…he said that although his situation had hitherto restrained him from offering his sentiments…he could not forbear expressing his wish that the alteration proposed might take place… The smallness of the proportion of Representatives had been considered by many members of the Convention an insufficient security for the rights and interests of the People. He acknowledged that it had always appeared to himself among the [disagreeable] parts of the plan…as late as the present moment was for admitting amendments, he thought this of so much consequence that it would give much satisfaction to see it adopted."

The change was adopted unanimously. State legislatures deliberated ratifying the Constitution. Madison's committee proposed 39 amendments; on September 25, 1789 Congress passed the 12-article Bill of Rights, sending it to the States to ratify. Article 1 guaranteed small districts…

Article the First. – After the First Enumeration required by the First Article of the Constitution, there shall be One Representative for **every Thirty Thousand***, until the Number shall amount to One Hundred; after which the Proportion shall be so regulated by Congress that there shall not be less than One Hundred Representatives, nor less than One*

*Representative for **every Forty Thousand** Persons, until the number of Representatives shall amount to Two Hundred, after which the Proportion shall be so regulated by Congress that there shall not be less than Two Hundred Representatives, nor more than One Representative for **every Fifty Thousand** Persons.*

Some people contend that *'not more than'* in the last sentence means they sought to *restrict* the number of representatives. But that word *'more'* in the last sentence was a transcribing error, as you see from Washington's speech, the convention vote, and the bold clauses above.

A Slip of Mister Otis' Pen

On the day before Congress officially passed the Bill of Rights, they agreed to correct a transcribing error to change the word *less* in *"the last line less one"* and to insert the word *more*. So the last sentence should end, "nor less than…":

Though confusing, the final phrase fits with the prior sentences. But the scribes making copies for the States received bad instructions from Samuel Otis, who reported that they should replace the word 'less' in the last **place** in the article, rather than in *'the last line less one'*. So the copies sent to the states contained an error that made the last passage read exactly *opposite* of what the Founding Fathers intended.

The handwritten copies were sent to all 13 states so their state legislatures could ratify as stipulated in Article V. By 1790, twelve states had ratified: CT, KY, MD, NH, NJ, NY, NC, PA, RI, SC, VA and VT.

Our First Right, Hidden in the Basement

In 2011, a disbarred New Jersey attorney named Eugene LaVergne discovered that Connecticut's vote sat unrecorded, so only eleven votes were counted…all because of Mr. Otis' pen.

LaVergne discovered that the Connecticut House voted for the original First Amendment in October, 1789 and its senate voted for ratification in May, 1790. That made Connecticut the ninth state to vote for ratification out of 12 states at the time; exactly three-fourths of the states, the number required to ratify an amendment per Article V of the Constitution (now needs 38).

When its senate voted to ratify, the Connecticut House wanted to retract its earlier vote until Otis' error could be corrected. The transcription error was trivial; everyone knew the intention of that article was small districts. Since a ratification vote can't be retracted, Connecticut buried its ratification vote record in its state archives in the basement, and it was never recorded.

Although LaVergne sued in 2012, the court threw out the suit. You can see why, if you read Article V of the Constitution. We The People do not give the courts any jurisdiction in the matter. The only way forward is for the State legislatures to finish the ratification process, as we stipulate in Article V.

Congress already passed it, so we don't need a constitutional convention; just 27 more ratification votes. DC can't keep 27 more State legislatures from restoring our First Right at last. But you may wonder, why did we wait so long?

Congress's Crime of '29

The founders designed the People's House to keep politicians from amassing power. The number of districts of the House of Representatives was supposed to increase after every census to keep districts small. But the shock-and-awe of Lincoln's War and 'Reconstruction' were a devastating 16-year distraction. Elite puppeteers bought politicians, increasing their power and riches as their districts grew. Then, their only job was to distract America with an unending series of political scandals…

Congress reapportioned districts in 1872 with a random formula creating **292** districts, yet our First Right required **765** districts at that point. In 1890, the House changed its calculation to ensure that no state lost a seat due to shifts in population, yet our First Right required **1,844** districts as of the 1910 census, when Congress fixed the U.S. House at a random **435** districts.

Our First Right required **2,120** districts as of the 1920 census, but using convoluted math, Congress passed its Reapportionment Act of 1929, that did not even *mention* districts. When they used the excuse that the House chamber could not accommodate more than 435, congressman Ralph Lozier said:

I am unalterably opposed to limiting the membership of the House to the arbitrary number of 435… There is absolutely no reason, philosophy, or common sense in arbitrarily fixing the membership of the House at 435…

Openly violating the Constitution, Congress arbitrarily fixed the size of the House, knowing that the original First Amendment was still before the States, open for ratification. Career politicians wanted power, and their billionaire handlers wanted it even more. Now we know *precisely* how it was done.

It's Our Responsibility

Isn't it amazing? This hijacking began with a one-word clerical error, followed by a shock-and-awe war and counterfeiting operation by Lincoln, a president that most American schools teach was one of our greatest. For copious evidence that Lincoln and the 37th Congress hijacked our lawful (silver) U.S. Dollar and defrauded us into a civil war, read any of three books on the subject by Thomas

DiLorenzo, or see the six books that I link to in Essay 34 of my book, *A Republic to Save*.

Several of those books also explain that Lincoln and Karl Marx were mutual admirers, and most of Lincoln's Union generals were fans of Marx. By the time Tom 'Woodrow' Wilson was in the White House, eight of Marx's 10 points in his Communist Manifesto were already federal policy. Yes, *our federal servant has been Communist for generations.*

At this writing, a usurper 'resident' acting as president and his thousands of colluding minions in Washington DC are carrying Lincoln's hijacking to an entirely new level. Either We The People arrest DC and end American Communism on our watch, or our historic window of opportunity may be gone. The Internet is shaking humanity as the printing press shook the medieval world. Reclaiming our First Right and restoring the People's House is up to We The People, the top level of government.

First Things First

Before we can push this unfinished business through 39 state legislatures to get at least 27 of them to vote 'yes', TACTICAL CIVICS™ is building our county chapters and membership, so that we can pack our state palaces when we are ready to call for the vote in each legislature.

If We The People do not first build massive numbers and get organized, today's Deep Axis will kill our rule of law. We will be toast unless we get serious ***now.***

There is Precedent

Did you know that the original *Second* Amendment, after 203 years sitting idle in the states, was finally fully ratified because of the efforts of one man?

In 1983, a University of Texas student named Greg Watson began working to get 29 more State legislatures to ratify the amendment, which stipulates that if Congress gives itself a pay raise it does not take effect until an election intervenes. After ten years nagging the state legislatures, in 1992 that one man got it ratified, and it is now the 27th Amendment. If one diligent citizen can do it, then surely we can get 27 more state legislatures to ratify our First Right and make it the 28th Amendment.

State Legislators

Remember, this is merely a state legislature ratification *vote,* not legislation. Yes, we must still deal with the long, drawn out calendar and rules and other nonsense in state legislatures; but the vote can be taken in a single day. No legislation, reconciliation bill, or governor's signature is required.

See Appendices B and C, Fact Sheet for legislators and a draft Joint Resolution that they can use to call for the vote. If you live in KY, MD, NH, NJ, NY, NC, PA, RI, SC, VA or VT, your legislature already ratified the original First Right.

Granite Dome Syndrome

We The People must *never trust a legislator*. In Lesson 9, we explained the power of architecture on the human psyche. Ancient Rome employed it to make conquered chieftains and princes cower in awe when they visited Rome, the seat of their new master's power. Granite Dome Syndrome hits within a week of taking office.

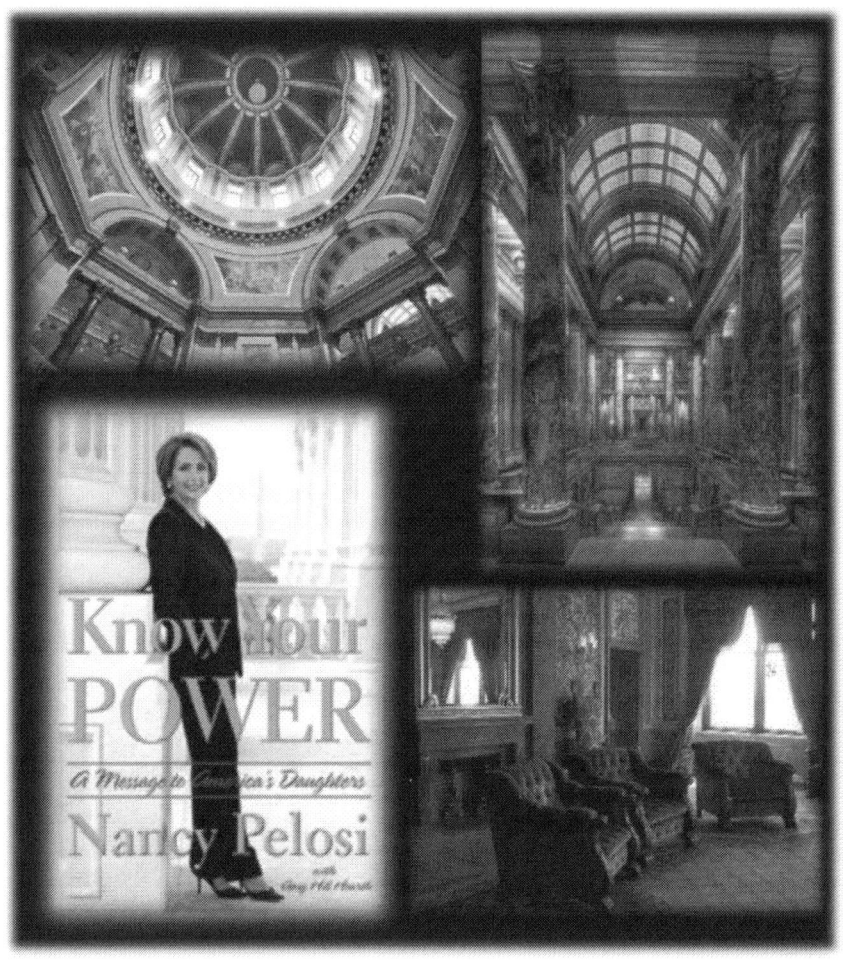

The People pay for it, so look carefully and imagine that this instant opulence became *your* playground for the rest of your life. It's like a middle-class person being given a free mansion with staff and amenities. The architecture alone makes the person consider himself very special. Their staff reinforces this self-assessment, and they learn to think: *"The people pay all my bills…the fools even come hat-in-hand to my door every day! They pose for pictures with me! They send their children by the busload to get a glimpse of me! They call me 'Honorable'! This is better than being a drug lord; I'm a rock star and my constituents are idiots!"*

As their sovereigns, we must put our foot down as our ancestors failed to do. We must stop expecting criminals to reform themselves. Why is the Internet not being used for self-government, as citizens become daily more aware of the systemic corruption in government, industry and professions? Responsible role-reversal demands that we *must* finish ratifying Our First Right.

City Mouse: The Most Common Objection

Those who object to *small* congressional districts claim that it will only increase the number of House seats for big cities, and they don't want a bigger Congress and even *more* power for the big cities! But they aren't thinking.

Every U.S. map of election results has shown a very *conservative* America, with only big cities being liberal. Yet for a century, big cities have had *all* power in House and Senate while America's 31,000 small towns have had *zero* voice in Congress – or in the Electoral College, since states get one elector for each member of Congress.

To explain the mechanics of *The Crime of '29* we'll use City Mouse and Country Mouse and call each House seat a cheese.

Congress in 1929 illegally capped the number of U.S. House districts at 435, ballooning each cheese until it only goes to every 750,000 people. *Country Mouse gets no cheese, ever.*

America is a sea of red and Country Mouse is everywhere, but each cheese is huge so Country Mouse has no political machine or media (for instance, to steal elections and lie about it after). *City Mouse gets all the cheese, always.*

Now, let's change the game and make a cheese be just 50,000 people. Suddenly *there is cheese everywhere across the red areas.* Sure, it's true that City Mouse gets more cheeses, *but they're smaller* and City Mouse no longer gets *all* the cheeses. Even in the cities, the patches of 50,000 Country Mice who were trapped in conservative ghettos for generations, now get cheese, too!

America will suddenly appear to become more conservative, but *actually we will have simply ended a century-old crime.*

The Bring Congress Home Act

Since 6,600+ members will definitely not fit in the House chamber, it's time to bring them home, via our Bring Congress Home Act (BCHA), stipulating that:

- No member of Congress can have an office in D.C.

- Every member gets one modest lease office, *in their town*

- Congressmen get 50% of their present salary

- Congressmen get a staff of two (senators, six)

- All members are limited to two terms

- End all benefits immediately

- They work via telepresence, off-the-shelf tech today

In each congressman's office space there will be one extra telepresence workstation for citizen use when we testify before a congressional committee or subcommittee. Why should we have to take time off, fly to them in DC, and pay for travel just to have them look down their noses at us, their sovereigns?

A New Chapter in American History

Once we set the precedent by bringing Congress home to modest lease spaces and small staffs, Americans in every state capital will get other great ideas. Already, former gubernatorial candidate and businessman John Cox of California has launched a state-level project to break up the *state* legislature and have them serve full-time from their hometowns. https://neighborhoodlegislature.com/

It will take time to reclaim life in America, but Our First Right can stop the Deep Axis wars, corrupting our money and plundering the world in our name.

What About The Expense?

Imagine an employer allowing employees to set their own salaries, benefits, fancy offices, working conditions, staffing levels, and opulent perks; a recipe for business failure! Americans complain about government excess, but don't see how they can reduce Congress' countless unconstitutional expenditures.

Americans still send their children on D.C. bus tours to gawk at 535 politicians who *each* spend an average *$11 million annually* on their operations; who *each* have as many as *eight* offices and staffs; whose Capitol Hill palace is more opulent than those of kings, popes, and emperors: white-glove exclusive dining rooms, gold-plated china, limousines, spas, private jets and more. All paid for by us, their sovereigns; $5.85 billion annually for Congress' operations.

We The People abdicated our sovereign role, allowed our corrupt servants to control every aspect of life and steal us blind for generations. We allowed them to rack up $22 trillion in debt and $190 trillion in unfunded liabilities.

Congress' Operating Cost

See the two following pages; smaller districts will *not* cost us more. A distributed local Congress made of normal Americans *will cut tens to hundreds of billions* in federal expenditures besides saving us $800+ million annually in Congress' operations. As Melancton Smith said in the 1788 New York ratification debate:

The man who would seriously object to this expense to secure his liberties, does not deserve to enjoy them. By increasing the number of representatives, we open a door for…the substantial yeomanry of our country, who, [having] habits of economy, will be cautious of…expenditures…a greater saving will be made of public money than [needed] to support them.

Every 1/10 of 1% that we cut spending *offsets the entire cost of operations for 6,600+ congressmen and 100 senators,* so we will not have to pay more to maintain the same 100 senators plus a 6,600+-member U.S. House when we Bring Congress Home.

Our Reform Law 3, the **Non-Enumerated Powers Sunset Act**, will acknowledge the People's own Citizens' Volunteer Research Service (CVRS) to review and de-fund any federal regulation, agency, bureau or program and its associated officers and staffing if not within a power *specifically* enumerated by We The People in the Constitution. *Remember Amendment X; we retain all such powers.*

So forget the chickenfeed on these spreadsheets, and imagine the savings that We The People can produce when 6,600+ citizen teams begin to review and cut!

Congressional Operating Budget

Each year, 535 members spend $5.85 billion; per member that equals:	$10,934,579
If 6,400 House & 100 Senate members split same $5.85B, each gets:	$900,000

House Operations Budget Item Description	Annual
Legislator $98,000 salary plus 40% burden	$137,200
Senior staffer (ofc manager) $65,000 salary plus 40% burden	$91,000
Junior staffer, research & clerical $45,000 salary plus 40% burden	$63,000
Office rent ($3000/mo)	$36,000
Utilities ($800/mo)	$9,600
Phone & Internet service ($1500/mo)	$18,000
Publications (no mailing; website only, plus PDF) allow $3,000/mo	$36,000
Research expenses and publications ($5,000/mo)	$60,000
Copying services (for legislative and other publications; $5,000/mo)	$60,000
Legislative drafting services ($5,000/mo)	$60,000
Computer systems support ($500/mo)	$6,000
Website maintenance ($400/mo)	$4,800
Insurance (fire/theft/casualty; $500/mo)	$6,000
Very limited travel	$25,000
Office supplies, furniture rental ($3,000/mo)	$36,000
(4) computer systems (one for the People testifying before committees)	$14,000
Alarm & security services ($500/mo)	$6,000
Gasoline allowance (to attend events only in the district; $500/mo)	$6,000
Auditor selected by the People of the district ($1500/mo)	$18,000
Total Budget (less contingencies)	$692,600
Contingencies (10%) audited and posted quarterly on website	$69,260
Total Budget Required per U.S. House member	$761,860

Senate Operations Budget Item Description	
Legislator $198,000 salary plus 40% burden	$277,200
(2) Senior staffers $75,000 salary plus 40% burden	$210,000
(4) Junior staffers, research & clerical $50,000 salary plus 40% burden	$280,000
Office rent ($5000/mo)	$60,000
Utilities ($900/mo)	$10,800
Phone & Internet service ($2500/mo)	$30,000
Publications (no mailing; website only, plus PDF) allow $7,500/mo	$90,000
Research expenses and publications ($8,000/mo)	$96,000
Copying services (for legislative and other publications; $10,000/mo)	$120,000
Legislative drafting services ($5,000/mo)	$60,000
Computer systems support ($1,000/mo)	$12,000
Website maintenance ($400/mo)	$4,800
Insurance (fire/theft/casualty; $500/mo)	$6,000
Travel	$75,000
Office supplies, furniture rental ($5,000/mo)	$60,000
(8) computer systems (one for the People testifying before committees)	$28,000
Alarm & security services ($750/mo)	$9,000
Gasoline allowance	$9,600
Auditor selected by the People of the district ($1500/mo)	$18,000
Total Budget (less contingencies)	$1,456,400
Contingencies (10%) audited and posted quarterly on website	$145,640
Total Budget Required per member	**$1,602,040**
Total expense for 6400 congressmen at $761,860 each:	$4,875,904,000
Total expense for 100 senators at $1,602,040 each:	$160,204,000
Total Congress Operating Expenses after we Bring Congress Home	**$5,036,108,000**
Current Operating Expenses (535 members total)	**$5,850,000,000**
The Bring Congress Home Act can save us $814 million!	

Lesson 13 Question for Parents

1. On page 83, we explained how globalists who own and run Congress like game pieces, got them to (supposedly forever) limit the number of House seats, thus massively increasing the power that a billionaire obtains with each game piece.

We also showed, as with all other aspects of the hijacking (our lawful U.S. Dollar, our constitutional Militias, our sovereign States having total liberty except in the 17 enumerated powers), they did it while Americans were still under the shock-and-awe of the deadliest war in our history, Lincoln's D.C. against America.

Can you now see how billionaires and industries control D.C.? If so, do you think that breaking 'cheese' back down to small districts as our Founding Fathers intended will, at this advanced stage, begin restoring power from corrupt big city machines, back to the American Heartland?

If not, what elements do you see keeping organized crime in control?

Lesson 14
The Last D.C. Congress

Imagine Washington DC *with Congress no longer there.*

Envision the American people setting the standard for government reform on earth, by forcing our Congress to become the first distributed legislature of the twenty-first century. Imagine your members of Congress working from a modest office just a few miles from your home, full-time.

If we should face a financial collapse and Great Depression II, imagine We The People forcing our state legislatures to finally ratify the original First Amendment (making districts 1/15 as large as they are today) and keeping our new, more representative Congress home, full-time. Whatever the people face, the elected servants face!

This is a vital aspect of the TACTICAL CIVICS™ way of life; a self-governing people finally having real-time oversight of what our servants are doing in government. Citizens should not have to wait weeks just to see the congressman who is their servant.

Imagine, you will walk into your U.S. congressman's office and see only a staff of two, who treat you as their employer – as indeed you are. This is what our mission can help Americans do: provide the world with the first example of *true* popular sovereignty. Of course it will take a few years; yet of all populations on earth, this is something that only the American people can do.

Incidentally, no president can do anything like this. We The People never invested the office of the president with so much power. Presidents have often done great damage to our republic, but seldom great good. As one of our memes says, *Presidents are only hood ornaments on the freight train of America's moods.*

Last lesson you learned about Our First Right; our plan to push for the final ratification of the original First Amendment. When 27 more state legislatures ratify, it will become the 28th Amendment and will change everything, limiting congressional districts to 50,000 people as the Founding Fathers planned. It will result in 6,600 members of the U.S. House of Representatives.

If you think this is too many, we have 7,383 members in our state legislatures, representing the same 334 million Americans. Which legislature impacts us more, federal or state?

The major goal of ratifying the amendment is to pass the *Bring Congress Home Act* (BCHA), which will remove Congress from Washington D.C. and make all U.S. congressmen and senators work full-time from their home district, using today's off-the-shelf telepresence technology.

Behind the Washington, D.C. Tourist Facade

First, you need to know why elections can never change things. The Potemkin Village erected for D.C. tour buses is all a lie to keep the masses working and paying taxes. Actually, Washington D.C. is the most powerful, corrupt, ruthless city-state in history, operating in its own moral, ethical, and economic universe. Treachery, fraud, theft and perversion are the norm.

Of course this was true in ancient Byzantium, Athens and Rome and is true in London, Paris, Moscow, Beijing, Brussels, Mexico City, and many others. But the big difference with D.C. is the sheer *scale* of evil power concentrated there.

Today, new freshmen arriving in Washington D.C. are handled by career staffers who run them through orientation. The freshman is first put in awe of the massive scale of D.C. architecture, the countless monuments, and opulent furnishings; *"We're not in Kansas anymore, Toto!"* Next, he witnesses the ancient, Byzantine, often clandestine traditions of standing committees – each a fiefdom in itself; especially the Rules and Calendar committees.

By the end of orientation week, even the most idealistic freshman is overwhelmed; then he begins to face the human side of D.C. organized crime. Not only are the huge staffs impressive, but the sheer range of services available to a legislator with just a call can make a believer out of the new solon.

They also learn a little-known fact: many D.C. career staffers earn more than members of Congress do. Also, they were there years before the freshman member arrived and they will be there years after the member loses re-election to another freshman with big ideas.

Career staffers are more powerful than many members of Congress and they make larger salaries. The tens of thousands of unelected bureaucrats in the D.C. Deep State watch presidents come and go. Including the 'Senior Executive Service' of 9,000 industry moles, they are unknown and untouchable by their sovereigns, the American People. Does all this seem lawless and ruthless? Welcome to Washington D.C., freshman legislator.

Next, the new freshman discovers who actually writes the laws: As we said before: lobbyist law firms with hundreds or thousands of staff. These firms fill entire buildings on K Street and inside the Beltway. Their largest clients span the globe, having no allegiance to one country. These industry players and multi-billionaires enjoy first-name access to federal judges, presidents, cabinet members, and top committee chairs in Congress. (When it absolutely, positively has to be done overnight with total deniability, they use CIA and other 'black bag' assets.)

Do you begin to see the problem in trying to 'reform America' when so many aspects of our lives are determined by the Deep State? Once installed in the most powerful and corrupt city-state on earth, a new member of Congress is not even a blip on the radar. He's just a cipher. *A nothing.*

D.C. 'Woodshedding'

Early in conditioning, the freshman is invited to a meeting with career staffers, a lobbyist, and a Big Dog (committee chairman, deep-captured by D.C. organized crime). At that meeting, the idealist dream from back home becomes a rerun of *Mr. Smith Goes to Washington*. Reforming visions melt in the presence of all that *power*. The message is, *"Little congressman or senator, you are nothing until we give you a committee assignment; and that's only if you play the game. And if you don't play the game, the FBI and NSA have complete dossiers on you. We can make your life a living hell."*

This has always been the system used by organized crime; and 'woodshedding' is also received by every president and federal judge, in different forms. *This is real life in D.C., the most ruthless, powerful city-state in history.*

But let's return to the good news that we can all help make a reality, as we come together in TACTICAL CIVICS™ chapters in countless small towns, then move in state phalanxes on our state legislatures to take Congress out of D.C. forever.

I'd like to see Trump back in the White House in 2024 because if the Last D.C. Congress enacts the Bring Congress Home Act, Trump may be the *only* president brazen enough to sign that most powerful reform legislation in two centuries.

The Last D.C. Congress

Here is how it would go down.

Once the original First Amendment is ratified by 27 more states, the first truly representative congressional election in over a century will be held. The huge new Congress will meet only for a short time, perhaps a week, in a large D.C. venue for only two purposes: first, to have the thousands of new freshmen receive their video orientation of how America's new distributed Congress will work. Second, to pass the BCHA, holding the floor debate and House and Senate votes, then getting the BCHA signed into law.

That will be the last gathered Washington D.C. action of the U.S. Congress ever required. From then on, we join the 21st century; Congress can do its work under our supervision from back home.

Because their districts will be one-fifteenth as large as they are today, congressmen will have only one office, a staff of two, and will be paid half their present salary. Senators will still make the same salary, but will also only have one office and staff. The BCHA also stipulates that both houses of Congress will be limited to two terms, and members will receive no benefits. We need to make lifetime careerists extinct and encourage citizen-statesmen; men and women who will serve for a few years then return to real life.

After passage of the BCHA, every member of Congress stays in their hometown rather than destroying their families by having a second home – and often a secret second life – in the secretive city-state.

America's public servants became our masters because We The People abdicated our rightful powers. We The People, in creating history's first distributed legislature, will demonstrate to the world how to finally apply 21st century technology to self-government, the last frontier of mobile apps.

Over generations, our servants have treated themselves to offices with 20-foot ceilings and marble floors, under massive granite domes. In D.C. and every state capitol, the architecture is a subliminal, overpowering aspect of psychological warfare, turning sovereigns into servants. Now We The People, by allowing them only modest workplaces, assert that public servants will respect the constitutional hierarchy of American government. *We The People are the boss!*

The first distributed Congress will work out the kinks in the telepresence system over a few months, but the efficiency will be clear. For instance, citizens who wish or need to testify before a committee of Congress can now simply show up at their nearest congressman's office, and when called on by the committee, log on to the citizens' telepresence workstation. No more wasting our time, money, and travel fatigue to go to D.C. to appear before *our servants*.

Once we the American People make history in self-governance, no corrupt government on earth will be safe. And this is even before we deploy our Indictment Engine™ or pass the 18 other reform laws described in Lesson 8!

Some Days The World Just Changes

Despite their great wealth and power, the Pharaohs did not have air conditioning. Despite their incredible intellect and wisdom, the Founding Fathers didn't conceive of jet air travel. *Some days, the world just changes.*

Not many years ago, smart phones, FedEx, Amazon, eBay, search engines, and a hundred other innovations were unthinkable; now, Americans consider them indispensable. TACTICAL CIVICS™ can be, too; a totally logical new way of life for the Information Age. The end of pointless politics, and the beginning of popular constitutionalism.

Lesson 14 Questions for Parents

1. Can you actually see us bringing Congress home?
2. Name a few major benefits of taking them out of Washington D.C. forever.

Lesson 15
Our Job, Not Trump's

Two mega-trends are causing great upheaval around the world in our generation. First, the Internet is threatening corrupt, bureaucratic governments worldwide; no government will come out of this the same size as it entered the Internet Age.

The second mega-trend is the exposure and collapse of Karl Marx's system in America. Over a century, our federal government has adopted all ten points in the *Communist Manifesto* as official policy. Now, hordes of Latin Americans pour across our southern border, supported by big business, the massive D.C. welfare state, and the Clinton-Obama-Biden machine with its lawless minions almost everywhere employing Saul Alinski's *Rules for Radicals*.

It's time for productive America to get *serious*. We cannot continue to live and think as we were programmed, while our republic burns. Americans must stop complaining on social media and *take responsibility*.

Melania Trump was the finest First Lady in history, and Donald Trump proved to be the best president in over a century. But he was *far* from perfect. Anyone who thinks he could be America's savior is deeply mistaken; presidents cannot restore our land. *Only God can,* and He demands our repentance and responsibility! Our forefathers slept and so have we, as predators and parasites took over our culture and government, replacing them with European-style counterfeits. The norms and nobility that animated our founders are fallen and must be rebuilt.

A communist-dominated U.S. House of Representatives began its cancerous work in January 2019, and had a plan backed by George Soros' money, Barack Hussein Obama's 250 field offices of 'Organize For America', tens of thousands of Obama-plant holdovers in the Deep State, and D.C. staffers who play equally well for either party as long as they get their cut.

What are *we* going to do about this, fellow American?

The Chinese philosopher-general Sun Tzu wrote, *"If you know the enemy and know yourself, you need not fear the result of a hundred battles. If you know yourself but not the enemy, for every victory gained you will also suffer a defeat. If you know neither the enemy nor yourself, you will succumb in every battle."*

Because they didn't know basic American civics, our parents and grandparents didn't know our authority and duty over the Constitution and over our servants that we create by that law. Very few Americans know anything about Grand Jury and constitutional Militia. So Americans don't know their responsibility for this mess, or even basic facts such as, American Communism began when Dishonest Abe and Karl Marx were pen pals and mutual admirers. Or the fact that most of

Lincoln's illegal, full-time U.S. Army generals were also followers of Marx, the creator of Communism.

Because Americans don't know that American Communism began generations ago, they also don't know that the donkey party is not the whole problem. *Both* parties are distraction theater, designed to keep us waving pom-poms while the Deep State robs us blind and enslaves us forever. Americans are clueless of the fact that *politics can never be law enforcement.*

We The People don't face a simple enemy, but massive organized crime working in league with a foreign enemy (Chinese Communist Party) and public education from kindergarten through graduate school. Too many Americans think that war is only kinetic conflict: troops, ships, and planes attacking one another. But when two Chinese bureaucrats (Qiao Liang and Wang Xiangsui) wrote *Unrestricted Warfare* in 1999, they explained with shocking honesty how China was *already* exploiting America's weaknesses and how to attack us using nontraditional means, especially in our schools and universities and in the culture, using propaganda, high technology, and as much sex, perversion, and drugs as they can manage, to break the bonds of American family and society. The COVID scam and Election Steal 2020 were the most effective stages of that warfare to date. But the solution is not civil war; it is law enforcement.

TACTICAL CIVICS™ was developed by 44 volunteers after more than 66,000 hours in research and development of the only full-spectrum solution in our republic. It is *not* politics, but a responsible new way of life. Restoring our republic is *our* job, not the job of our presidents; it's above their pay grade. We must stop being cheerleaders for presidents and perform *our* responsibilities, since We The People occupy the highest office in government.

If we do our job, then what we are witnessing is the ugly *death* of American Communism, *not its birth.* To restore our Republic before it is destroyed, we have to stop cheering for presidents and start doing *our* job, in our *higher* office of government. We must stop writing letters to politicians! As things stand now, incumbent politicians can do *nothing* to stop the Deep State. Instead, let's take responsibility as our Founding Fathers demanded. First, as Sun Tzu suggested, we need to know ourselves and our enemy. And then we need to *stand.*

Lesson 15 Question for Parents

1. Did you ever consider the fact that collectively, We the People really occupy the highest office in American *government,* or have you always seen government as us vs. them?

Lesson 16

Cabbages, Kings, and Tactical Civics™

Over time, stupidity kills civilizations. It sometimes strikes me that we Americans may be the stupidest people in history. Or at least up there among the top few.

There is a difference between *ignorance* and *stupidity*. The former can be remedied by study; the latter cannot. Stupidity is a conscious *choice*. It's where we get the words *blockhead* and *recalcitrant*. And you can think of others.

The Bible clearly directs us to avoid certain things and to do other things. For about the first eight generations after landing here, Americans followed those directives. But for the past five generations we have increasingly rebelled against all that God-stuff. So we are paying the price. That's one level of stupidity; eternal things; but there is also the temporal level of stupidity.

For instance, consider the first three words of our Constitution: *"We The People"* and then, *"do ordain and establish…"*. In other words, when it comes to government in our Republic, the most basic principle is that *We The People are Boss.*

In that highest *law* for all public servants, We The People stipulate clear, concise orders. We *create* the federal servant branches, then we *define* and severely *limit* them. That includes legislators, presidents and judges; *they* work for *us*. And they *have* to obey the Constitution.

The accurate definition of American civics: *Who is Boss?*

The accurate definition of patriotism: *We The People, making our servants obey the Constitution.*

An American is one of 'We The People' if (s)he takes responsibility. Collectively, we are the *boss* of legislators and the *boss* of presidents, and the *boss* of all federal judges. All of them love to be called, *"The Honorable…"*, or *"Mr. President"*, or *"Your honor"* but *don't you dare do that!*

I never used titles of nobility or distinction with Carter, Reagan, Bush I, Clinton, Bush II or Obama. And although I liked him better than those others because he was not a politician, I never used the title with Trump, either. He may be a billionaire, but he worked for us and had to obey the Constitution. To the extent he did, we could thank him for his service. But always remember: *it's their job.*

It matters not what style manuals or English teachers taught us; when you, an American, address your public servant federal judge, president, state legislator, or dog-catcher, use only their last name as any employer does with an employee. Sure, if you are a public employee, you will use terms such as, "Mr. President!" or "Yes sir, Senator, sir!" – because that is expected of underlings. But *all* those public office holders are *our* underlings, by law.

One bedrock principle of Tactical Civics™ is that We The People have perverted *our office,* the highest office in the land. Because we wanted monarchs, we have them – right down to imperious, corrupt city councils and school boards!

Most of us never learned rudimentary American civics as you are doing; we were ignorant. That is easily remedied by studying our books, articles, podcasts, and videos in our Training Center at TacticalCivics.com.

You are in a tiny cohort of Americans learning the hard truth about the mess we made by abdicating our oversight duties, leading to organized crime taking over our federal government and most state, county, and city governments and school district bureaucracies.

Now you are learning *honest* civics. Once you complete this tutorial and fully understand what this mission is designed to accomplish, please reach out and tell others. We have many restoration projects to complete, and only the People can do them. Look at Europe: once a people loses its civilization, *it's gone.*

Tens of millions of Americans still love Donald Trump, but it was foolish to act like lovesick puppies following Donald as though he was an emperor. The many transformative powers to be exercised in coming years must be exercised by the Big Boss – *We The People.*

Please, never again address your servants in the statehouse or on Capitol Hill as *"the Honorable".* Americans are in this huge mess of our own making because we were ignorant. Now let's dispel our ignorance. Repairing these ruins begins with remembering civics: *we are the boss* (collectively, not individually) and our lifelong duty as Americans is to *assure that our servants obey the Constitution,* at all levels of government from school board members to our federal servants in black frocks.

We stipulate in the opening words of our highest law, the most powerful and basic American civics: *We The People…do ordain.*

Now it's time that we start doing some ordaining.

Lesson 16 Question for Parents

1. Do you agree that the best definition of patriotism in our Republic is, *We The People, making our servants obey the Constitution?* If not, what is your definition?

Lesson 17

The Fear Porn Industry

Like the horror film genre, the Fear Porn industry is a perverse kind of entertainment that excites the limbic system of the brain, inciting daily cycles of anxiety, fear, and anger. Like all pornography, it is false, cruel, and destructive; but it produces great revenues because Americans are predictable consumers.

Over the past generation, many young Americans came to love horror films. In the same way, millions have become addicted to conservative talk and pointless 501c3 groups, making Fear Porn potentially worse for America's future than open communism. Some of these stars admit that they are entertainers; most of them do not, and most listeners cannot discern that conservative talk is just that: *talk*.

During my lifetime, Americans transmogrified from an industrious people with time only for factual news – into self-obsessed consumers, seeking entertainment in place of news. Today, a factual news report won't garner market share; too many limbic systems have been conditioned to want fear, anxiety, and rage, which have become like a drug for millions of conservatives.

Does this describe you? Be honest; do you visit social media to argue, knowing you won't improve a thing? Do you daily listen to talk show hosts, knowing that nothing they say *ever* improves anything?

How the Industry Operates

Consider the passionate hero that you listen to or read every day. Having invented the market, Rush Limbaugh removed his mask years ago; he readily admitted to being a GOP shill and an entertainer. But don't you ever wonder who will give himself a heart attack first, Mark Levin or Alex Jones, from all his screaming?

Conservative radio, TV and Internet 'news' shares an entertainment market with ABC, MSNBC, CNN, FOX, et al. And the political parties. And the non-profits. Here's the drill: keep the folks hopping mad. Fear and loathing brings audience, who buy your brand-name tea, or your precious metals merchant's stuff, or your colloidal silver, water filters, and emergency food – or they will run their credit card for your latest 'money bomb' campaign or Holy Land cruise.

Joe and Liz Farah milked their huge audience for $274 million in gross revenues from Farah's 2009 *Send Congress a Pink Slip* campaign that did nothing to stop Obamacare. In fact, those *billions* of tiny pink slips only went to the Capitol Hill dumpsters. Farah knew it was impossible to physically deliver them. But the campaign was a huge success for Farah's Fear Porn empire, and today he still begs for donations! How long can you milk a sheep? Decades, apparently, as Farah, Limbaugh, Beck, Hannity, Levin, Jones, and countless other Fear Porn vendors have demonstrated.

Now, don't shoot the messenger, angry patriot. If you are sincerely upset and want to restore America, the stars of Fear Porn won't help you.

Joe, Rush, Sean, Glenn, Mark, Mike, Alex, Dennis, Laura, Michael – as well as NRA, GOA, Cato Institute, Heritage Foundation, Hillsdale College, and many other 501c3s comprising 'conservatism' today are only *conservative* in the sense of *conserving their golden goose*. It's just business. Media moguls, talk stars and 501c3 donation mills are businessmen in a Fear Porn market that mines a rich, growing demographic vein: productive, disgruntled patriots.

The GOP needs the Democrat party and vise-versa, to remain profitable because politics junkies pay to see a fight. Similarly, the world of Fear Porn (conservative talk, media, non-profits) always need a crisis and a bad guy: mass murder, potential war, economic woes, organized crime in government, BLAntifa riots, natural disasters, rise of the police state – the Fear Porn industry gives you what your limbic system demands every day.

Try to grasp the Farah/Beck/Jones/Levin business model: they must mentally condition you to inaction and cynicism, so you *never take action* on solutions. They can only grow their empire as long as you keep tuning in, so their book sales, advertising revenues, and brand presence grow.

American Christians Have Been Here Before

You would think that gullible Americans learned their lesson after decades of public exposure of charlatans Kenneth Copeland, Benny Hinn, Creflo Dollar, Kenneth Hagin, Marilyn Hickey, Joyce Meyer, Joel Osteen, Oral Roberts, Pat Robertson, and others. But when P.T. Barnum said *"there's a sucker born every minute"*, he was too conservative.

Don't get me wrong. It's a free country and you can do as you like with your money; it's none of my business. My point is that no amount of listening or donating to Fear Porn will ever restore America. Real solutions would put the entertainer out of business, and no entertainer or think tank can restore our Republic. Popular constitutionalism is real restoration by *citizens,* not celebrities.

The Gun Lobby and Non-Profit Industry

Fear Porn is not limited to radio, TV, and the Internet. For instance, the NRA and GOA will never restore the citizen militia of the several States, as demanded by law. Your dues to them is wasted on political fireworks, nothing more.

Besides repeating what you have already heard, when have you ever seen any nonprofit (Heritage Foundation, Cato Institute, et al) actually sponsor action for reform? Like government agencies, conservative think-tanks reform *nothing.* They produce monographs and studies, and sponsor expensive conferences that at the very most are reactive, but will never restore what we already lost.

They scare you, to stir the same political pot that attracts the stars of 'conservative talk'; the goal of Fear Porn is to keep you angry, afraid, and buying or paying to fight 'crises'. In time, all this pointless donating without any restoration will make you cynical; but by then, the 501c3 has already hooked your kids or grandkids after making a pile from *your* purchases and donations.

First Step in Recovery: Stop Your Denial

If you listen to the talkers or read WorldNetDaily or Infowars every day, you will never become part of a solution, as a result. You can go to the WND or Infowars site and learn how to buy gold and ammo, hide in the boondocks, feed yourself, and kill the hungry neighbors pounding at your door when the time comes. You can sign up for any of the NewsMax pop-up ads, and receive a *"super-special, eye-opening, life-changing report, FREE!"* – along with a gazillion pieces of junk mail for the rest of your life. Fear Porn stars will never lead a critical mass of citizens to become a unified force to enforce and restore our Constitution. Have you ever seen a celebrity even *attempt* it?

The same applies to your social media addiction. Face it, no amount of posting patriotic quotations or pictures will change anything. Think! Has your favorite conservative website, radio or TV show or social media site *ever* promoted a real solution, or does it just stir up your fear, loathing, and blood pressure every day?

How about your conservative talk-star's action plan? Did Glenn Beck's or Mark Levin's first five 'final solution' plans work out for you, or did you finally get the picture that building ratings and ad revenue is what the stars were really after? Levin is not actually as blood-spittingly angry as he sounds; that's his radio show persona. *An act.* Mark is actually quite *happy* with his millions in ad revenue.

Do you wonder how they can drum up a new cauldron of righteous indignation again tomorrow, and the next day, and the next? Well, that's entertainment; it's the celebrity's talent. After Limbaugh made his first $50 million, he was able to start having fun as his former 'anger' mysteriously cooled. The others learned the trick, and their estates are growing apace by keeping you on the hook.

Over 1,500 local American radio stations now play nothing but wall-to-wall conservative talkers with their wall-to-wall advertisements. God rest his soul, Rush Limbaugh gave birth to an incredible cash cow.

Passive listening – even if you *scream* at your radio! – changes nothing. It's not the kind of life lived by sovereigns. We became passive couch-potatoes when the Fear Porn industry moved in to feed on a demographic pig-in-a-python. *And you know you're shirking your chores.*

A Destructive Feedback Loop

Each of these actors built and refined his own shtick and on-air persona. These performers should be *ashamed* of themselves for doing this; but when you listen to them and pay them, *you* are half of the feedback loop that makes Glenn cry, makes Mark scream as though he's about to have a heart attack, and makes the veins in Alex's neck and forehead pop out as he almost turns clinical. In his divorce lawsuit, when his ex-wife accused him of being full of anger, Jones admitted that his on-screen anger was all an act.

You have told the Fear Porn celebrity what you like. As is true of horror movie fans, you've told them that you *want* the ranting, the tears, the never-ending fear and loathing. Understand the sin here, fellow Christian: as with adultery, alcohol or drug abuse, or pornography and masturbation, you give yourself over to gradual self-destruction. Of *course* the drug dealers, liquor stores, and porn industry *love* you! But you *can* stop this, fellow American. You *can* grow up and take responsibility.

Please don't suggest that I'm barking up the wrong tree. The conservative talk and non-profit industries are *not* about solutions. To start regaining what we have lost, we must tune out the Fear Porn, repent, and get to work.

Some Exceptions

Mike Church, on his eponymous radio show for years taught history, civics, and the Constitution to his audience even though it meant smaller market share. He was a unique 'Re-Founding Father' in the conservative talk industry.

The same goes for Tim Brown, former editor of Freedom Outpost, now with Sons of Liberty and several other news sites. Other exceptions include Mark Goodwin at Prepper Recon and Jim White at Northwest Liberty News. Best of all was the late Joyce Riley, who on her *Power Hour,* dug deep every day for real solutions and grilled her radio guests for facts, not infomercials.

Some Bridges Need Burning

If you think I'm attacking potential allies of TACTICAL CIVICS™, truth is *never* bad policy. They'll never promote a solution like TACTICAL CIVICS™ because ending the crimes they harp about every day would kill their golden goose. Besides the exceptions mentioned, if my assessment is wrong in the case of a rare conservative talker, he will support TACTICAL CIVICS™. But I won't hold my breath; the conservative talk and 501c3 Fear Porn industry is holding American Christianity back as the Reagan presidency did *and it is more dangerous, because Fear Porn addicts can claim it's a solution, though in 35 years it has not been.*

In a 2017 article, Tobias Stockwell posted the best explanation I've ever seen, of how the Internet is transforming our minds, actions, and society.

Repent Your Addiction

The answer to the Fear Porn industry is: *turn them off.* Show this analysis to your addicted friend who spends hours per day listening to conservative talkers – or who spends just as much time posting futile arguments, quotations, pictures, or cynical jokes on Facebook or on Fear Porn site comment threads.

What's the point? Listening to talkers instead of taking action will never restore our civilization. Cynicism and venting at the radio or on social media only makes you *more* cynical.

Cynicism and paranoia have already taken millions of patriots out of the fight. From Joe Farah to the NRA and Heritage Foundation and Hillsdale College, cynical Americans now expect them to sell products and beg for donations while bringing the latest atrocity or 'crisis', with no improvement, world without end. So the Fear Porn-weary consumer just 'checks out' of his responsibilities.

Conservative talkers are not conserving anything, but We The People now can. So turn off Fear Porn, and start walking the talk.

Lesson 17 Question for Parents

1. If you regularly read, watch, and/or listen to celebrities or organizations that you know perfectly well have never improved anything except their own bottom lines, will you try just one week of detox to see how your emotional and spiritual health improves?

Lesson 18
The Founders, Right Again

Like rambunctious Siamese twins from Satan's womb, the fraudulently labeled 'Convention of States' (COS) outfit and 'National Popular Vote' (NPV) scheme call themselves *conservative,* while burning across state legislatures trying to destroy our Constitution under the guise of 'badly needed reform'.

Whatever their actual motivations, both schemes march in lock-step with today's unmasked American Communism. Both also align with Progressives and urban metrosexuals against the conservative 95% of American landmass comprising America's 31,000 small towns and the country where Americans still know right from wrong.

In Lesson 19, we will expose the treachery and fraud of the COS scheme, but we believe there will never be another constitutional convention. If the States have been unable to finish ratifying a single Article V item on their plate for over 230 years (the original 'Article the First' in the Bill of Rights) there is little chance they can pull off a constitutional convention.

Praise God for that fact; James Madison said, *"Having witnessed the difficulties and dangers experienced by the first Convention...I should tremble for the result of a second."*

As for the second scheme, at TACTICAL CIVICS™, we don't feel it necessary yet to delve into it, as court challenges would tie up any attempted popular vote scheme for years. By that time, we hope to have already broken up the U.S. House into the small districts demanded by the Founding Fathers, and hope to have brought Congress home, which will turn the tables on today's Communist-Progressive-Pervert-Abortionist-Illegal-Islamic hijacking of America.

More importantly, the mendacious minions behind the preposterous National Popular Vote scheme may play ignorant, but they are well aware that the only way to get their way is for states to defraud their people and violate Article II, Section 1 of the Constitution. It simply won't work; the Constitution controls, and it is clear. If these treacherous schemers want the NPV for presidents, they have to amend the U.S. Constitution.

That raises the same challenge facing the other shameless liars running the COS scheme. But tens of millions of Americans in 'flyover country' already have their number.

To put into perspective the attempted hijacking of the already terribly adulterated Electoral College, as a concise primer on the institution, we reprint the following 1992 piece authored by a federal election commission bureaucrat who actually did a decent job with the facts.

Essay in Elections: The Electoral College

William C. Kimberling

In order to appreciate the reasons for the Electoral College, it is essential to understand its historical context and the problem that the Founding Fathers were trying to solve. They faced the difficult question of how to elect a president in a nation that:

- was composed of 13 large and small States jealous of their own rights and powers; suspicious of a central national government

- contained only 4,000,000 people spread up and down a thousand miles of Atlantic seaboard barely connected by transportation or communication (so that national campaigns were impractical even if they had been thought desirable)

- believed, under the influence of such British political thinkers as Henry St. John Bolingbroke, that political parties were mischievous if not downright evil, and

- felt that gentlemen should not campaign for public office (The saying was "The office should seek the man, the man should not seek the office.").

How, then, to choose a president without political parties, without national campaigns, and without upsetting the carefully designed balance between the presidency and the Congress on one hand and between the States and the federal government on the other?

Origins of the Electoral College

The Constitutional Convention considered several possible methods of selecting a president.

One idea was to have the Congress choose the president. This idea was rejected, however, because some felt that making such a choice would be too divisive an issue and leave too many hard feelings in the Congress. Others felt that such a procedure would invite unseemly political bargaining, corruption, and perhaps even interference from foreign powers. Still others felt that such an arrangement would upset the balance of power between the legislative and executive branches of the federal government.

A second idea was to have the State legislatures select the president. This idea, too, was rejected out of fears that a president so beholden to the State legislatures might permit them to erode federal authority and thus undermine the whole idea of a federation.

A third idea was to have the president elected by a direct popular vote. Direct election was rejected not because the Framers of the Constitution doubted public intelligence but rather because they feared that without sufficient information about candidates from outside their State, people would naturally vote for a 'favorite son' from their own State or region. At worst, no president would emerge with a popular majority sufficient to govern the whole country. At best, the choice of president would always be decided by the largest, most populous States with little regard for the smaller ones.

Finally, a so-called Committee of Eleven in the Constitutional Convention proposed an indirect election of the president through a College of Electors.

The function of the College of Electors in choosing the president can be likened to that in the Roman Catholic Church of the College of Cardinals selecting the Pope. The original idea was for the most knowledgeable and informed individuals from each State to select the president based solely on merit and without regard to State of origin or political party.

The structure of the Electoral College can be traced to the Centurial Assembly system of the Roman Republic. Under that system, the adult male citizens of Rome were divided, according to their wealth, into groups of 100 (called Centuries). Each group of 100 was entitled to cast only one vote either in favor or against proposals submitted to them by the Roman Senate. In the Electoral College system, the States serve as the Centurial groups (though they are not, of course, based on wealth), and the number of votes per State is determined by the size of each State's Congressional delegation. Still, the two systems are similar in design and share many of the same advantages and disadvantages.

The similarities between the Electoral College and classical institutions are not accidental. Many of the Founding Fathers were well schooled in ancient history and its lessons.

The First Design

In the first design of the Electoral College (described in Article II, Section 1 of the Constitution):

- Each State was allocated a number of Electors equal to the number of its U.S. Senators (always 2) plus the number of its U.S. Representative (which may change each decade according to the size of each State's population as determined in the decennial census). This arrangement built upon an earlier compromise in the design of the Congress itself and thus satisfied both large and small States.

- The manner of choosing the Electors was left to the individual State legislatures, thereby pacifying States suspicious of a central national government.

- Members of Congress and employees of the federal government were specifically prohibited from serving as an Elector in order to maintain the balance between the legislative and executive branches of the federal government.

- Each State's Electors were required to meet in their respective States rather than all together in one great meeting. This arrangement, it was thought, would prevent bribery, corruption, secret dealing, and foreign influence.

- In order to prevent Electors from voting only for a 'favorite son' of their own State, each Elector was required to cast *two* votes for president, at least one of which had to be for someone outside their home State. The idea, presumably, was that the winner would likely be everyone's second choice.

- The electoral votes were to be sealed and transmitted from each of the States to the President of the Senate who would open them before both houses of Congress and read the result.

- The person with the most electoral votes, provided that it was an absolute majority (at least one over half of the total), became president. Whoever obtained the next greatest number of electoral votes became vice president; an office which they seem to have invented for the occasion since it had not been mentioned previously in the Constitutional Convention.

- In the event that no one obtained an absolute majority in the Electoral College or in the event of a tie, the U.S. House of Representatives, as the chamber closest to the people, would choose the president from among the top five contenders. They would do this (as a further concession to the small States) by allowing each State to cast only one vote, with an absolute majority of the States being required to elect a president. The vice presidency would go to whatever remaining contender had the greatest number of electoral votes. If that too was tied, the U.S. Senate would break the tie by deciding between the two.

In all, this was quite an elaborate design. But it was also a very clever one when you consider that the whole operation was supposed to work *without political parties* and *without national campaigns* while maintaining the balances and satisfying the fears in play at the time.

Indeed, it is probably because the Electoral College was originally designed to operate in an environment so totally different from our own, that many people think it is anachronistic and fail to appreciate the new purposes it now serves. But of that, more later.

The Second Design

The first design of the Electoral College lasted through only four presidential elections. For in the meantime, political parties had emerged in the United States. The very people who had been condemning parties publicly had nevertheless been building them privately. And too, the idea of political parties had gained respectability through the persuasive writings of such political philosophers as Edmund Burke and James Madison.

One of the accidental results of the development of political parties was that in the presidential election of 1800, the Electors of the Democratic-Republican Party gave Thomas Jefferson and Aaron Burr (both of that party) an equal number of electoral votes. The tie was resolved by the House of Representatives in Jefferson's favor - but only after 36 tries and some serious political dealings which were considered unseemly at the time.

Since this sort of bargaining over the presidency was the very thing the Electoral College was supposed to prevent, the Congress and the States hastily adopted the Twelfth Amendment to the Constitution by September of 1804.

To prevent tie votes in the Electoral College which were made probable, if not inevitable, by the rise of political parties (and no doubt to facilitate the election of a president and vice president of the same party), the 12th Amendment requires that each Elector cast *one* vote for president and a *separate* vote for vice president rather than casting two votes for president with the runner-up being made vice president.

The Amendment also stipulates that if no one receives an absolute majority of electoral votes for president, then the U.S. House of Representatives will select the president from among the top three contenders with each State casting only one vote and an absolute majority being required to elect.

By the same token, if no one receives an absolute majority for vice president, then the U.S. Senate will select the vice president from among the top two contenders for that office.

All other features of the Electoral College remained the same including the requirements that, in order to prevent Electors from voting only for 'favorite sons', either the presidential or vice presidential candidate has to be from a State other than that of the Electors.

In short, political party loyalties had, by 1800, begun to cut across State loyalties thereby creating new and different problems in the selection of a president. By making seemingly slight changes, the 12th Amendment fundamentally altered the design of the Electoral College and, in one stroke, accommodated political parties as a fact of life in American presidential elections.

It is noteworthy in passing that the idea of electing the president by direct popular vote was not widely promoted as an alternative to redesigning the Electoral College. This may be because the physical and demographic circumstances of the country had not changed that much in a dozen or so years.

Or it may be because the excesses of the recent French revolution and its fairly rapid degeneration into dictatorship had given the populists some pause to reflect on the wisdom of too direct a democracy.

Lesson 18 Question for Parents

1. Today, 48 states have a winner-take-all scheme, requiring all electors in the state to cast their vote for the candidate with the most *popular* votes in the state.

Do you think this popular vote adulteration at *state* level, negates the *national* purpose of the Electoral College?

Or do you think the Electoral College, by all ballots going to the popular vote winner in *conservative* states, offsets disproportionately large numbers of votes in big cities and liberal states?

Lesson 19
The ConCon Come-On

"Having witnessed the difficulties and dangers experienced by the first Convention... I should tremble *for the result of a second."* — James Madison

"A constitutional convention is a horrible *idea. This is not a good century to write a constitution."* — US Supreme Court Justice Antonin Scalia

The staff at TACTICAL CIVICS™ and AmericaAgain! are often asked why we do not align ourselves with proposed 'solutions' such as an Article V convention, nullification, secession, the TEA Party, armed revolution, anarchy, PACs and think tanks, shadow government efforts, or a DC coup. None of those proposed 'solutions', even if they accomplished what they propose, would restore America's rule of law. As to why we do not support an Article V constitutional convention, or 'ConCon', let me explain.

A latter-day ConCon movement using the moniker Convention of States (COS) claims that by using that label, a constitutional convention transmogrifies into a new creation, impervious to a runaway convention as happened at the first and only ConCon in 1787. This nonsensical position is summarily dismissed by this article by veteran Article V scholar Dan Fotheringham, and it is completely eviscerated by these articles by former JAG attorney and constitutional scholar Joanna Martin, aka 'Publius Huldah'. Finally, this excellent presentation by Robert Brown of John Birch Society ends all debate, in my view.

Scroll down this massive far-left coalition list of Soros-affiliated groups calling for a ConCon. Imagine them amending our Constitution!

Moreover, logic suggests that a ConCon is ludicrous, because more than 11,500 amendments to the Constitution have been proposed since 1789. Washington D.C. violates the Constitution not because it needs *amendment* but because it needs *enforcement*. Criminals will not obey an *amended* Constitution any more than they obey the *existing* one. Tom Glass, a former Texas Attorney General candidate and constitutionalist, makes the case cogently, here.

Finally, our trump card against those who propose Article V action by the States to curb D.C. organized crime. There has been an open Article V amendment awaiting action by the States for over 230 years! As an open Article V action, it does not require a ConCon; it was already passed by Congress in 1789 and as stipulated in Article V; it only awaits ratification by the States, 11 of which have voted to ratify so far.

'Article the First' — the first article in the parchment Bill of Rights and the only subject on which George Washington felt passionately enough about to speak publicly at the first ConCon in 1787 – stipulates small congressional districts, not to exceed 50,000 people.

This would accomplish three powerful reforms in American self-government. First, it will eviscerate the power of industries and lobbyists to buy political races. Today's huge, gerrymandered U.S. Congressional districts allow only the wealthy and well-connected to compete for a House seat.

Secondly, state legislatures finally finishing their Article V duty on this pending amendment will give a vote in the U.S. House and in the U.S. Electoral College to America's 31,000 small towns *for the first time in over a century.*

Third and most importantly, it will logistically require our Bring Congress Home Act, a reform law removing Congress from D.C. and requiring them to work full-time from their hometowns. *This would mean the end of law firms for industry writing most federal laws and running our lives.*

We the People will be in control of our servants in Congress at last! They will have small districts, one modest office each, a staff of two for congressmen, half their present salary, and both houses limited to two terms, no benefits. They can stay in their own town to serve in the U.S. House, so hundreds of thousands of honest, productive citizen-statesmen would run for *the People's House,* as the Founders called it.

Imagine: perhaps in January 2025 or 2027, a president Trump could be cutting the ribbon on the world's most amazing high-end redevelopment project: a new hotel/retail/office rehab of the former U.S. Capitol. Imagine dining, shopping, staying the night, or even having a lease office in the former imperial palace of today's DC mafia, who will never again sit as though they are our masters, under that celestial granite dome.

No ConCon can do that.

Lesson 19 Question for Parents

1. Did you ever support the 'convention of states' scheme, and if so, why?

2. Do you now agree that another constitutional convention would destroy our Constitution? If not, why not?

Lesson 20

Allegiance to What?

I do not recite the Pledge of Allegiance.

This gets me in a trouble with some of my fellow Americans. If you want to be despised by otherwise good, patriotic Americans, just tell them that you don't recite the pledge.

Here's the irony: Americans' childhood programming was like that of any Soviet or Chinese citizen, rendering us ignorant of our history and what the D.C. government has done to us over five generations.

As we explain in the segment from 8:14 to 8:47 in *AmericaAgain!- The Movie*, the Bellamy Pledge was developed by a fascist/socialist to program America's children. If you are interested in the birth of the Bellamy Pledge, you can find more history here.

In his article entitled *What's Conservative About the Pledge of Allegiance?*, Gene Healy of the CATO Institute analyzes Bellamy's pledge and asks why any constitutionalist should chant a pledge to Washington D.C.?

Well, because most Americans are programmed and ignorant of facts of history. For instance, you now know that Dishonest Abe Lincoln and Karl Marx were pen pals and mutual admirers, and that Lincoln was the original hijacker of our Constitution, as explained in Lesson 4 with its links to six books.

See? Americans for six generations have been cheated in school. With the exception of homeschoolers, every generation alive today is a victim of fascist conditioning that began 150 years ago. The Marxist Obama wrought destruction on our society but did not launch American communism; *Abe Lincoln did.*

By Woodrow Wilson's administration a century ago, seven of the ten points of the Communist Manifesto were D.C. policy; today, it's 10 out of 10. As we demonstrated in Lesson 12, by law (Article IV, Section 4, U.S. Constitution) America is a constitutional *republic* of sovereign States, not a unitary *nation;* an important distinction. Centralized power is dangerous! So no, I will not pledge allegiance to the D.C. organized crime operation of career politicians.

TACTICAL CIVICS™ is our mission to rebuild America's walls as in the Book of Nehemiah; a new way of life for self-governing Americans; popular constitutionalism. One major goal: detox our minds of 150 years of communist programming in government schools, colleges, universities, and bureaucratic agencies reinforced daily by mainstream media. The first three words of the U.S. Constitution make clear that the sovereign power and duty of We the People over our servant government is *perpetual.* As Mark Twain said, *"No country can be well governed unless its citizens as a body keep religiously before their minds that they are the guardians of the law and that the law officers are only the machinery for its execution, nothing more."*

It's time to repent our sloth, gullibility, and misplaced allegiance; time to learn basic civics, and to take responsibility. This tutorial is designed to give you true history and civics, to empower you as no generation of American scholars has been empowered in two centuries.

Of course, true liberty is impossible without Christ. As Jesus said of Himself and His gospel, *"You shall know the truth, and the Truth will make you free"*. It's true in civil affairs, too. So I do not recite the Bellamy Pledge.

Instead, I pledge allegiance to Christ and the Constitution. I hope you will, too.

Lesson 20 Question for Parents

1. Have you looked up the Bellamy Pledge, and/or watched AmericaAgain!- The Movie, to learn more about the origin of this mass conditioning tool, or do you think, deep in your heart, *"They can't take Lincoln and the Pledge from me!"* ?

2. Now that you understand how D.C. organized crime operates, are you beginning to appreciate why corrupt cartels and careerists want to keep Americans cheering for 'Uncle Sam' rather than digging up hard facts of history?

3. Which do you consider more revolting: a textbook shattering your lifelong programming, or your servants running organized crime, gaslighting you, and skimming your payroll checks to pay for their lifestyles?

Lesson 21

Culturism is Not Racism

In 1835, after spending many months traveling our republic of sovereign States, the French Statesman Alexis deTocqueville finally published his 700-page, two-volume ode to our civilization, entitled *Democracy in America.*

Tocqueville's *magnum opus* remains the most cogent analysis, criticism and celebration of America ever written by a non-American. Despite his family roots deep in Roman Catholic law and customs and Gallic monarchy, the young Frenchman plumbed the soul of the American people to point out the Anglophile, Christian roots and ground of this radically unique new culture.

America's culture was shockingly different from England's, yet America's culture began with Anglo-Saxon seed stock coming here for the glory of Jesus Christ and His gospel. Ours was never the culture of the Spaniards, French or Dutch who also came to North America to colonize. What caused America to become the leading driver of all the civilizations on earth?

It was *our culture*. And not all cultures are ethically equivalent, however loudly the multiculturalist horde may protest. Ideas are the stuff of cultures. Ideas can kill or give life. Ideas can enslave or liberate. *"America is great because she is good; and when she ceases to be good, she will cease to be great,"* the Frenchman wrote.

Precisely; for it is not culture or intellect alone. Egyptians, Persians, and Europeans had those in spades before America was colonized. While Germany, France, Italy, Spain, Mexico, Argentina, India, Persia (Iran), Egypt and others may be only a fraction as large as America, they all have great natural beauty and some of their ancient civilizations made great discoveries in science, mathematics, astronomy, art, music and more. Yet, Americans are not teeming to Russia, China, Iran, Egypt, India, Mexico or any other Latin American country.

And it cannot be our vast land area and natural resources, for Russia is twice as large, China and Canada are equal in land area to us, and Brazil is almost so.

But those cultures have common origins in monarchy, serfdom, slavery, and castes. Much of Europe, Canada and Latin America also are deeply influenced and controlled by the Vatican. So one can certainly find Mexicans, Canadians, Venezuelans and Brazilians with fair skin, blue eyes, blonde hair, and related European ethnic characteristics, yet certainly not sharing our culture.

The People: Keepers of Norms and Law

I will gladly be labeled a culturist, but never a racist. In his unique way, this is Trump's position, too, which he drummed home regularly. This drove his feral, perverse enemies insane.

Before it became an aristocratic category, *noble* meant simply virtuous. American *nobility* is our collection of behavioral artifacts from English progenitors, including our unique system of law. It began in ancient England but was re-crafted by our fathers in our Constitution.

In our highest law, We The People empower and entrust ourselves to control the evil passions of man, whether in ourselves, our neighbors, or elected servants. But only via the stipulated institutions of the Grand Jury and Militia of each sovereign State. This unique American system fascinated Tocqueville, who mentioned that Mexico had attempted with its 1824 Constitution to closely mimic ours but could not pull it off.

Among many cultural disparities were two glaring cultural facts: first, the conquering Spaniards in Mexico were Vatican minions and their Constitution made Roman Catholicism the official religion. Secondly, large populations of barbarian Mesoamerican Indians remained committed to their former idolatry, cannibalism and tribal rivalries.

Americans began to demonstrate in real life, the theories of classical economics. This followed logically from New Testament Christianity only when stripped of the Vatican's hierarchies, superstitions and taxation of even the very poor. The Vatican held France, much of Europe, and much of Canada under its power when Tocqueville wrote. Thus he marveled at the unfettered Americans, living our lives and making our plans with so little direction from 'above'.

The Frenchman did not gloss over the coming cataclysms with American Indians and African slaves. In fact, as he was writing, our Indian wars were ongoing. Then the whole foundation shifted just a decade or so later, when Washington D.C.'s troops captured almost half of Mexico, and ended African slavery while enslaving *all* Americans under a new D.C. master.

After Lincoln and 'Reconstruction', our unique system of State sovereignty was hijacked. Our republican form, limited central government, copied by Mexico's 1824 and 1857 constitutions, was placed in indefinite confinement.

America's British Roots

As for the seed stock, added to the predominantly British colonial population of several million, a steady stream of British subjects, a total of 2.7 million, moved to America throughout the 19th century. In that same century, five million Germans and almost a million Italians legally immigrated here, followed by millions more Italians plus millions of Russians in the first two decades of the 20th century. Still, the Anglo-American roots of our laws and norms held fast.

Cultural Wrecking Crews

The original residents of this land, American Indians from Alaska to Florida, predominantly remain on reservations where gambling, alcoholism, drug addiction and broken marriages prove the dictum that ideas have consequences.

Despite the silly concept of the 'noble savage', worshiping your Stone Age ancestors, wolves, and trees by seeking to live like them in the 21st century is a recipe for failure.

The fact is, Americans descended from Stone Age peoples from literally all over the world. But by the lights of New Testament Christianity and eventually an ingenious Constitution, we left the ancient barbarism of our fathers and for centuries have led the world in missionary work, charitable giving, inventions, and individual liberty. Quite simply, *multiculturalism is a cruel joke.*

Of America's dozens of immigrant demographic cohorts, five of them have sought to break or destroy American culture rather than assimilate: Africans, Hispanics, Muslims, atheists (including secular Jews who feed Hollywood), and a home-grown alien cohort of virulent sexual deviants.

Now, the 'racism' war re-kindled by the Obamas has been taken up as an electoral Hail Mary Pass by American K-12 schools, colleges, and universities, by berserk congress members, Antifa rioters, Hollywood's continuing attack on morality, and ruthless industrialists and Democrat Party operatives who import illegal aliens to harvest their votes and cheap labor. The bogus 'Critical Race Theory' faction-baiting has nothing to do with race, and everything to do with ruthless pursuit of Communist power.

Our surest defense is to return to America's norms and nobility – New Testament Christianity, the rule of law and limited government codified in our Constitution, the defense of private property, and our fervent support of, and praise for, individual initiative.

American or African; not 'African-American'

Africans were brought here by the millions until the first half of the 19th century, and that cruel method of 'immigration' is indefensible, except that within one generation, Black American couples enjoyed a quality of life here that was unavailable back in Africa.

Despite generations of execrable racism by whites, by the late 19th century, families whose great-grandparents had been slaves captured by *other* Africans and sold to *black* slave traders, enjoyed a standard of living above that of Africa's *kings*. Christianity had made the strong, nuclear family the norm for American blacks. Because grinding poverty is no better than slavery, America's culture (the systems of law, ethics, and economy it built) drew tens of millions of Italians, Germans, Irish, Russians, Swiss, Austrians, Norwegians, Hungarians, Swedes, Chinese, Polish and 4.8 million Canadians to these United States.

America's First Slaveowner Was Black

Millions of Americans of African origins have left African culture and hard stories of slavery, behind. Yet too many blacks do not know that the first legal slaveholder of a lifetime slave in America was a black Angolan who took the name Anthony Johnson. After earning his freedom after seven years, Johnson was granted land by the Virginia colony. He became a successful tobacco farmer in Maryland and attained great wealth, being referred to as the Black Patriarch of "the first community of Negro property owners in America".

The hypocritical Johnson filed a lawsuit against another African who sought to leave Johnson's plantation when his period of indenture had finished. The court granted Johnson's request to make Casor a slave for life. Thus, a black former slave was the instigator of African chattel slavery in America (whites were also enslaved by indenture). Yet, the ruthless, tireless 'African lobby' driven by the Democrat Party continues to turn the knife at every opportunity. A wicked alliance seeks to overthrow productive America; and if you read the 1958 book *Color, Communism, and Common Sense* by Manning Johnson, a black former Communist, you'll understand that Obama's race war is nothing new.

Spain to Mexico to America – And Back Again

Hispanics, especially Mexicans, are another unique case. There were approximately 90,000 Mexican citizens living in what became the states of California, Arizona, Nevada, New Mexico, Colorado, Utah and the former Republic of Texas, when the Treaty of Guadalupe-Hidalgo was signed on the 4th of July 1848.

Beginning in the early 1930s during the Great Depression, mass 'repatriations' of Americans of Mexican descent took place across these states. These were American citizens – and the ironic worst case was the City of Los Angeles, home to the majority of America's population of Mexican descent. The City government cracked down on tens of thousands of Hispanic Americans.

By that time, including illegal aliens, the region was home to over a million Mexicans and Mexican-Americans. Some had deep family roots on the land; most felt that the land had been 'stolen' from Mexico. Whatever the case, they rejected American culture, reveled in Mexican folkways and beliefs, and steadfastly refused to be *agringolados*. They considered, and many of them still consider, themselves to be Mexicans, occupying our American States in imaginary *Reconquista*.

Like far too many Black and White Americans, these Hispanics simply allow the productive *gringos* to pull the load while generations of their family depend on communistic welfare programs that are inimical to the Protestant work ethic of America's founders.

But all is not lost; the zoological assortment of rock-throwing, screeching fascists and communists are destroying the Democrat party at this writing. The pendulum of history swings both ways; the berserkers, with help from media, are making millions of former Democrats shake their heads in amazement at the utter lunatic asylum that their party has become.

But setting aside the failed "Racism!" tactic, since my first book, *This Bloodless Liberty,* I've maintained that we are actually witnessing the messy, screaming *death* of American communism, which began ideologically with Lincoln and in practice with Woodrow Wilson. For a century, this bloodiest system of government has twisted and strained America's roots, but by the grace of God, has not broken us. The Obamas brought it to a preposterous head, a bridge too far.

Speaking of communism, many of my Catholic friends believe the present pope is not only communist but atheist. This makes sense, since communism and atheism are inseparable – and now rule the self-destructing donkey party in DC and its allies in Hollywood and yes, in the Vatican.

The racism card will simply not work anymore. Every *legal* immigrant to America has as much right and liberty as any other American, to have a dream and to work to attain it. America has always been different because ideas have consequences; Christianity and the Constitution forged our culture.

Every American who sits by while enemies destroy our foundations are forfeiting the last, best hope of man on earth. Our culture – not that of Mexico, Africa, or Israel – is America's root system. As Tocqueville put it,

"The sovereignty of the States rests on memories, habits, local prejudices; on the egoism of province and family; in a word, on all the things that make the instinct for native land so powerful in the heart of man…

"All peoples who…form a confederation have had a certain number of common interests that serve as the intellectual bonds of the association. But beyond material interests, man still has ideas and sentiments. For a confederation to last…there must be [as much] homogeneity in the civilization as in the needs of the diverse peoples who constitute it."

Lesson 21 Question for Parents

1. Can you name four or five things in your family's life that you consider cultural bedrock – things that keep American civilization alive and healthy in your family?

Lesson 22

Support Our Troops?

My first wish is to see this plague of mankind, war, banished from the earth. **General George Washington**

I hate war as only a soldier who has lived it can, only as one who has seen its brutality, its futility, its stupidity. **General Dwight D. Eisenhower**

Even now, the families of the wounded men and of the mentally broken and those who never were able to readjust themselves are still suffering and still paying...There are only two reasons why you should ever be asked to give your youngsters. One is defense of our homes. The other is the defense of our Bill of Rights and particularly the right to worship God as we see fit. Every other reason advanced for the murder of young men is a racket, pure and simple. **General Smedley D. Butler**

The world has achieved brilliance without wisdom, power without conscience. Ours is a world of nuclear giants and ethical infants. We know more about war than we know about peace, more about killing than we know about living. **General Omar Bradley**

America is in greater social and political upheaval than ever before; we face what can accurately be called a constitutional crisis. What we need is true, constitutional law enforcement because the Founding Fathers designed a system of law and order specifically designed to avoid or deal with exactly what we face today – whether rioting lunatics or natural disasters. That system of self-defense can be put back in place in an amazingly short period of time in your state.

But first we must deal with a very unpopular subject. As every politician and Country Western singer knows, the quickest way to cash is to 'support our troops', unquestioningly. If we are to restore our land and rule of law, we must return to the law itself, and enforce it – even if it means roasting a lawless, much-loved sacred cow, the war industry.

Most of the U.S. military is illegal, according to the Constitution. This monograph will give you basics and point to more resources. Every assertion herein is true. Any veteran reading this: it will make you furious — and then challenge you *not* to hang your head in shame but be a leader right here at home, rather than a hired killer abroad.

I hope to shock you awake and test your allegiance to the Constitution. Christ said that no man can serve two masters; every former or current military employee or family needs to choose their allegiance: the Constitution, or their industry? Every American should support our troops, but 'our troops' means two mutually exclusive things:

> 1) the U.S. Constitution defines 'our troops' as the Militias
>
> 2) the military industry and employees claim 'our troops' means *them*

Verify this in the U.S. Constitution, Article I, Section 8, Clauses 12-16. Those are the only references besides the Second Amendment that relate to national defense (please go to Appendix E to confirm it).

Constitutional Definition of 'Our Troops'

Okay, you can read right there that 'our troops' are defined in the U.S. Constitution as only a Navy (clause 13), and Citizen Militias *"to execute the Laws of the Union, suppress Insurrections, and repel Invasions"* (clause 15).

Representative Elbridge Gerry, on August 17, 1789 in debate on what later became the Second Amendment, wrote:

"What, sir, is the use of a militia? It is to prevent the establishment of a standing army, the bane of liberty. Whenever Governments mean to invade the rights and liberties of the people, they always attempt to destroy the militia, in order to raise an army upon their ruins."

Clause 12 stipulates that Congress can only fund Militia ground operations for two years at a time, whereas Clause 13 suggests that the Navy can be full-time to defend our shores.

So forget the Second Amendment and the century-old Dick Act; citizens owning and bearing *military grade* arms — semi-auto, selective-fire, and fully automatic is not only a right stipulated in the Second Amendment, it is a *duty* of every citizen in Militia, as stipulated in Article I, Section 8, Clause 15 of the Constitution.

The *Posse Comitatus* Act and the 1903 Dick Act only reiterate what the Constitution had already guaranteed, and what God had granted from the beginning.

As for the Coast Guard, that branch logically extends from the Navy and provides invaluable lifesaving service to Americans and others in U.S. waters every day. Air Force and space-based defense might even be said to be a modern-day equivalent of the US Navy defense perimeter concept of the 18th century. The Constitution has to be amended to make them legal, but in principle they're a defense shield; a high-tech extrapolation of the founders' intentions for the Navy: defending our coasts.

But this is not true of the U.S. Army or Marines; the idea of a standing army on American soil or plundering foreign lands for industry would have been anathema to every Founding Father. The Citizen Militia of the several States was the only armed force that they ever intended on American soil. The founders passionately believed that free citizens in Militia would keep America free, but paid government troops would destroy our republic.

But I am *not* against military employees. Let me repeat, *I have absolutely nothing against military employees.*

As I will explain below, I believe that most members of the United States armed forces are among the most honorable, dedicated Americans alive. But an even greater number of courageous, honorable Americans have never been in the military industry. We consider most military employees a valuable asset to the republic, though a few of them are sociopaths looking for a legal way to kill, even as some gang members satisfy that lust.

As horrible as their deployment(s) may have been on their spirit and mind, the military veteran can become a vital resource in America's near-term future. He can restore the righteousness of the duty he believed he was performing for his country. Read on.

Our Troops: arming for national defense NOW

Obama claimed to have taught constitutional law, so he has read Article I, Section 8, Clause 15 many times. He knew that the American people buying millions of firearms and tens of billions of rounds of ammunition while he was in the White House, were responding to his idiotic threats exactly as Clause 15 and the Second Amendment indicate that Americans should.

Like a giant organism, We the People respond as antibodies against a looming threat to our lives, liberties, property, and way of life. All during the 'Obamanation', Americans bought millions more firearms and billions more rounds of ammunition. The problem is, we are still doing no more than that. So we are not meeting the Founding Fathers' plan for national defense: the Militias of the Several States.

Civics & History Resources

First, anyone who still does not know how the military industry has evolved into possibly our greatest domestic threat, needs to learn some facts about the industry's history from 1890 to 2013. Consider Stephen Kinzer's book _Overthrow: America's century of regime change from Hawaii to Iraq_. No matter how much you may love employees of that industry; no matter how you may think it is 'defending liberty', by remaining ignorant of 20th century history, you support exactly what the Founding Fathers hated and warned against.

Kinzer demonstrates that not a single foreign action/invasion by the U.S. military has ever been conducted for the national defense of these sovereign States of America. _Not one._

Andrew Bacevich formerly taught at West Point and was a decorated officer in Vietnam. His book _The New American Militarism_ explains that the military built since Lincoln's time is _antithetical_ to everything the Founding Fathers fought for.

The smallest book on this subject but possibly the best, is a classic written by the most highly-decorated U.S. Marine in history, General Smedley Butler. In his classic little booklet called _War is a Racket,_ the repentant old war-horse writes…

"I helped make Mexico...safe for American oil interests in 1914. I helped make Haiti and Cuba a decent place for the National City Bank boys to collect revenues in. I helped in the raping of half a dozen Central American republics for the benefit of Wall Street....I helped purify Nicaragua for the international banking house of Brown Brothers in 1909-12. I brought electricity to the Dominican Republic for American sugar interests in 1916. In China, I helped to see to it that Standard Oil went its way unmolested." (pg. 10)

Secondly, presidents cannot initiate wars. As James Madison, Father of the Constitution, wrote...

"The declaring of war is expressly made a legislative function. The judging of the obligations to make war, is admitted to be included as a legislative function. Whenever, then, a question occurs whether war shall be declared, or whether public stipulations require it, the question necessarily belongs to the department to which those functions belong—and no other department can be in the execution of its proper functions, if it should undertake to decide such a question."

Some Troops Plunder...Others Keep Us Free

In my lifetime I've witnessed this domestic enemy that President Eisenhower, a former 5-star general, warned about. He dubbed it the 'Military-Industrial Complex' and it is *huge* business for overseas industries of every kind.

When I was a kid, those U.S. troops (unknowingly) defended the Rockefellers' rubber plantations and offshore oilfields in Vietnam; but for the past century the U.S. troops also provided free mercenary forces for the petrochemical industry in Central and South America and the Middle East. It is a perfectly symbiotic relationship: while providing free mercenary services for U.S. industry overseas, the war industry is a massive business in itself. Its supply train is long, wide, and complex, affecting almost every sector of industry.

For much more on this subject, read any book by Peter Dale Scott, especially <u>American War Machine</u> and <u>The American Deep State</u>. It will make your blood boil to learn how the Deep State fools millions of patriotic Americans into working *against* the U.S. Constitution and for their industry profits. (The criminal operations of the CIA and NSA are also covered in great detail in many of Scott's books, but that subject is beyond the scope of this essay.)

Contrary to the military industry's propaganda, U.S. military employees deployed overseas and every foreign military base operated by that industry is illegal and has *nothing* to do with keeping us free.

Not only that, but the war industry, beyond destroying the lives of countless American veterans and their families, have made large parts of Southern Iraq, Afghanistan, Kuwait, and Saudi Arabia uninhabitable for the rest of history, by firing over 1,300 tons of depleted uranium munitions in those areas. If you want to learn the horrific extent of the cancers, deformities and other maladies just from the depleted uranium treachery, watch this full-length documentary <u>Beyond Treason</u>, by the late Captain Joyce Riley, founder of The Power Hour.

You will never again think of presidents Reagan, Bush I, Clinton, Bush II, or Obama the same way again (Trump was much better, and Biden was never a president; only a lawless puppet of an organized crime occupation).

Resources for Those Suffering From PTSD

For a detailed analysis of how we are taught to kill other human beings, read the book *On Killing* by Lt. Col. Dave Grossman, explaining why we are naturally unwilling to kill, except in self-defense or the defense of home or family. The Founding Fathers designed our military around the Citizen Militia, a purely defensive force, because this is the only ethical national defense. Americans are now programmed from early childhood by the 'entertainment' and computer gaming industries to love the act of killing. The war industry uses this programming to 'deploy' you to kill in homes and neighborhoods on the other side of the world, with no declaration of war. This is not only illegal; your moral soul fights it all the way.

One last book, by psychotherapist Edward Tick, is *War and the Soul: Healing our Nation's Veterans From Post-traumatic Stress Disorder.*

That's the bad news. It is America's dirtiest big secret and it has been making life a living hell for America's vets. They're only human; having killed others has made them want to kill themselves. For God's sake, *they must seek help*.

Drugs are all they get from the VA; they want to get people processed. The spiritual need is greater than anything – and their training can become a profound blessing for their fellow Americans and a meaningful new career for the vet.

I've shaken a veteran's foundations with truth: they were defrauded by their employer. They believed their indoctrination, as Major General Butler said: *war is a racket*. To live the rest of life with restored sanity they must face the truth, learn how they were abused – and then forgive themselves.

Let me repeat that: the first thing a vet must do is forgive himself. God knows our heart; we all sin, sometimes worse than others. But what they did in ignorance, having been defrauded by a ruthless industry, God will never hold against them. They should go to God in repentance for any lives they took, and know that God is in the business of forgiveness.

The Duty of Every Oath Keeper: Be a National Resource

Oath Keepers tries to convince military employees not to turn against their sovereigns, the American people. I think we must do much more than keep public servants with firearms from abusing citizens.

The Army and most of the operations of the U.S. Marines are technically unconstitutional, as I demonstrated. But vets were paid by the taxpayers to 'defend the Constitution from enemies foreign and domestic', and that is still in their DNA.

Eight of the past ten presidents and their congresses have cut deeply at the Constitution's roots. Bush II, Obama, and *Resident* Biden were finally the bridge too far. Their open disdain for the sovereign People and the Constitution placed We The People on high alert. Yet we are unprepared to defend the Republic. Trump did what Reagan did; added fuel to the war industry fires and waved the flag, with no interest in the Constitution's stipulated limits on federal military. Every politician and country singer knows that if you wave the flag and 'support the troops', you will be popular.

Tens of millions of Americans have fine firearms, even almost military-grade equipment. But most of us could not serve effective militia duty to save our souls. Americans need Militia training and by law, our state is supposed to provide it. But not a single state does.

Veterans, especially those with recent or specialist training, will be among the most valuable citizens in this Republic. If they're still a federal employee, they should *retire*. Then they can serve this republic as never before.

Restoring the Citizen Militias

We should have Militia officers in every community, and county Militia ordinances meeting the intent of Article I, Section 8, Clause 16 of the U.S. Constitution, because the states are derelict. This is not a debatable political issue; it is the highest American law, and We The People must get our county governments to do what state governments refuse to do. Everything from hurricanes and raging wildfires to lunatic social justice warriors and Antifa fascists or Nazis in the streets, demands reinstatement of the Militias.

Today's so-called militia groups have no accountability beyond their inner circle, which is true of every street gang or vigilante group.

Some of the officers must be tactical firearms trainers; others might train members in logistics, communications, emergency response, first aid, survival techniques, anti-terrorism drills, riot control and suppression, emergency infrastructure, heavy equipment operations, and the like. Every community has unique challenges due to geography, topography, climate and culture. Moreover, there are vast differences between urban, suburban, small town and rural environments, culture and infrastructure.

Within a few months, those who are called and interested, like Volunteer Fire Department duty, will have the first constitutional Militia in their community in over 150 years.

Our sovereign States abdicated their duties because We the People first abdicated ours. To restore the 'Homeland Security' of our Founding Fathers (Militias), the first step is Tactical Civics™ chapters helping newly-forming County Militia units to push through our proposed County Militia Ordinance.

I say to the veteran, stop hanging your head in shame. I've been tough on you not because I don't appreciate your sacrifice, but because you've been fighting for the wrong cause, unwittingly violating the Rule of Law you swore to defend.

Please consider helping your fellow citizens by using the leadership skills you learned at their expense to now rebuild the Founding Fathers' constitutional homeland security force. The greatest military veteran stories are yet to be told. Yours needs to be one of them. Americans by the millions are waiting to be trained to do our duty as citizens. Will you stand in the gap of history?

Today's Nonsensical Second Amendment Debate

After every mass shooting, gun-grabbers and armed citizens go at it again. This is nothing new; the body of our free republic is healing itself. It is defending itself as antibodies do against infection. But we're asking the wrong questions and fighting the wrong battle.

To help you understand why the Second Amendment is not even the right battle to fight, Lesson 23 will explain how the gun lobby works against restoring Citizen Militia required by law. In 25 years of arguments about the Second Amendment, we have not heard anything about America's constitutional military defense, the Militia. Our book, *Time to Start Over, America,* provides the most complete, concise education on the subject available today.

American veterans are vital to the next phase in our history. Almost every country on earth faces turmoil and upheaval in our day, but no other people can lawfully, peacefully do what Americans can do through Tactical Civics™. The duty of well-trained veterans will be to prepare *every* American to be always ready to defend our homes and Republic against all enemies foreign and domestic.

There are over 70 million armed citizens in these sovereign States. According to the Constitution, *all of us* are the U.S. military and have a duty for Militia. By working wisely and diligently at this critical time in history, we can *all* keep America free, by the grace of God.

Lesson 22 Questions for Parents

1. Why do you think Militia has such a terrible stigma?

2. Had you realized that several decorated generals and other officers had blown the whistle against the Military Industrial Complex over the past 80 years? If you believe that D.C. military deployed all over the world 'keeps us free', please explain how it does that.

3. I have said many times that America's homeschooling Moms are doing *far more* to actually keep America free, than all D.C. troops 'deployed' worldwide. If you agree, please explain.

Lesson 23
Shooting Second Amendment Blanks

With every real and false-flag shooting in this republic, statists and liberals rekindle their heated attacks on 'our rights under the 2nd Amendment'. The constant reversion back to that Amendment instead of to the authority and duty we have under Article 1 of the Constitution, is a self-destructive habit. Led by gun organizations supposedly on our own side, we keep handing the gun-grabbers easy victories by simply not knowing the *powers* and *duties* of We The People that we codified in the Constitution.

TACTICAL CIVICS™ is a new way of life that can finally put full-spectrum popular sovereignty in the hands of every American who will accept that responsibility. If only half of 1% of the American people will take our duty and authority seriously, we turn the tables forever on Washington D.C.'s Deep State and collusive media.

Firearms are necessary – but not sufficient

We The People are arming ourselves as never before. That's fine; but free republics and their rule of law are maintained by *wisdom*, not primarily by force of arms. Imagine: We The People, the sovereigns over the Constitution and the government we created and limited by that law, have never attempted to enforce the Constitution; *not a single time.* Why start shooting lawless public servants when we haven't yet taken the first law enforcement step?

Notice that in real life and even on television, only criminal defense lawyers appeal to the Constitution; the prosecution never does. That is because We The People never created a mechanism to *enforce* our highest law. As we stipulate in Amendment X, we *retain the power* to do it at any time. TACTICAL CIVICS™ is the only solution in the republic today designed for that purpose.

No mere armed citizens can perform this law enforcement mission in total alignment with the Founding Fathers and our Constitution.

National Firearms Act of 1934 is Unconstitutional

We explained that *We The People are the U.S. military according to the Constitution.* It is grossly illegal for Congress, with the National Firearms Act of 1934, to have forced manufacturers and dealers to use the 'military and law enforcement use only' designation for all the best firearms and equipment. There is no *constitutional* limit to the type, caliber, fire-control system, or optics of the arms that citizens can and should own. The 1934 act forces tactical arms and equipment manufacturers to tip the scales against the constitutional citizen Militia stipulated in Article I Section 8.

Today, millions of citizens argue with gun-grabbers who remain on the offensive, infringing on magazine capacity, barrel length, pistol grip stocks, bump stocks, noise suppressors, flash hiders, and fire control systems. We fell to this ludicrous position because we cower in the face of Congress' 79-year-long violation of the Constitution. The military industry and local police departments side with their career interests, against the People's authority, duty and liberty.

Congress making any law infringing on the right of citizens to buy, build, repair, trade, sell, carry and use *military-grade* weaponry for Militia use is precisely the situation the Second Amendment was meant to avoid. But because We The People first abdicated our *authority, power* and *duty* that we stipulate in Article I, Section 8, Clause 15 and we refuse to make our state governments obey their duty that we stipulate in Clause 16, it is *not* a Second Amendment *rights* issue but an Article I People's law enforcement *powers* and *duties* issue.

The Gun Rights Lobby is Peddling Fear Porn

Had it wanted to, the NRA could easily have restored constitutional Militia anytime over its 150-year existence; but it refuses to do so. As Adam Winkler explains in his book <u>Gun Fight</u>, the NRA was a *gun control* organization before it became a gun rights lobby group. The ancient, self-serving behemoth institution with its huge headquarters and careerist staff first creates 'crises' in DC and then pretends to end them. Actually, NRA is only playing footsies on The Hill.

As we explained in Lesson 17, every non-profit and conservative talker is part of a mammoth industry that is very active on the Right. Fear Porn raises billions in tax-exempt donations and advertising revenues each year.

If you think they are actually trying to *solve* the problems they complain about, you don't understand the revenue model: feed a regular stream of fabricated crises to keep the member/donor/listener afraid and coming back for more.

The brain's limbic system is the target for pornography, horror movies, violent sports, and murder mysteries featuring execrable villains. As they daily exercise their followers' limbic system of the brain with doses of fear and anger, they create addicts; and addicts come back daily. Advertising, product sales, and donation revenues rise.

This is why the NRA will never solve any of the crises; if the problems are ever solved, the victims stop giving. Rush Limbaugh spun this along for over 35 years, but the NRA has done so for over 150 years!

I was an NRA member for decades; the only thing it has *never* been is an effort to restore the Militias as stipulated by We The People in the Constitution. Gun Owners of America is no better; at best, it pays lip service to Militia.

It does not even frame the enemy in the right terms. Notice this GOA bumper sticker sending exactly the NRA 'gun rights' message…

It's a Right... Not a Privilege!

A *right?* In the U.S. Constitution Article I, Section 8, Clause 15, We The People stipulate that *'to execute the Laws of the Union, suppress Insurrections, and repel Invasions'* is the *duty* and the *power* of the Militia. No police forces, sheriffs, or standing army are stipulated in the law; only Citizen Militia as law enforcement.

Especially enforcing the Constitution itself against organized crime in our legislatures; but also riot control against thugs in Antifa, neo-Nazi and Black Lives Matter hordes. And especially these days, border security against current invading hordes of Muslims and Latin American drug mules, gang-bangers, illegal workers, and welfare queens.

The Basic Civics

Forget Second Amendment 'rights' until you first exercise our Article I power and duty. In the first three words of the Constitution, We The People stipulate that we are the highest power in government, creating it. In Article I Section 8, we gave them only 17 powers that standardize our public services such as mail service, coining gold and silver money, copyrights, naturalization laws, etc.

In the Tenth Amendment, We The People stipulate that *we retain every imaginable power for ourselves and only grant our servants the powers we enumerate.*

Our arrogant servants puffed themselves up as we sat by and watched for five generations. They arrogated hundreds of illegal powers to themselves over the past 150 years. Now the best we can do instead of law enforcement is to beg our criminal employees for *rights?*

Partial List of Our Servants' Felonies

Our servants in the U.S. Congress now take it on themselves almost weekly to attack the retained sovereign powers of We The People and these sovereign States. Every member of both houses took a solemn oath, then violates it on a regular basis.

Every member is constructively, even if only by ignorance or professional negligence, violating the Constitution with respect to infants' right to life, our stipulations for lawful money, honest banking, the very limited land that federal government can claim or use, and our stipulation of a well-trained Militia of the Several States.

Before Trump, the Deep Axis tried a fake 'war on terror' and Islamic jihad or Iranian saber-rattling kindled and reinforced by the CIA; then the saber-rattling little North Korean, who could be taken out tomorrow by U.S. Special Forces but instead was goaded by the globalist war industry because it's good for them.

The truth is: *the arrogant organized crime operation known as The Deep State now makes the U.S. Congress the most pressing, potent enemy of these sovereign States and People.*

It is long overdue that We The People begin to 'execute the Laws of the Union' against this Democrat/Republican machine that:

- Invites enemies across our borders as cheap labor for its patrons in industry
- Refuses to throttle the lawless courts under its aegis
- Continues to run the largest counterfeiting operation on earth (FED cartel)
- Continues to operate earth's largest extortion/payroll-skimming (IRS)
- Continues the largest gaslighting operation in our history (COVID scam)
- Swept under the rug the first openly stolen election (stole *our government*)
- Continues to load its sovereigns down with rules, regulations, fees, and programs that it does not have to live under
- Continues to engage in felony insider trading every day, making millions by buying and shorting stocks of industries that it regulates or supports
- Pays itself whatever it decides, from *our* payroll accounts, including *fat benefits and pensions to the grave, even after we kick them out of office* – while we struggle to make ends meet!

I could go on for pages; but you get the idea. We The People are now at that point in the movie where we have the opportunity to trap the mafia kingpins and finally bring them to justice. TACTICAL CIVICS™ has developed the best solution in American history.

Going on Offense in Our Counties

If we want to obey the Constitution *over which we ourselves are the highest authority*...first, we need to pass our model County Militia Ordinance in every county possible, because *every state legislature is violating the stipulation for constitutional Militia;* Article I, Section 8, Clause 16 of the U.S. Constitution. There is no higher law in America! It stipulates that *every* state must appoint its Militia officers and set regular training of State Militia, but not one State is doing so.

Obviously, we have a long way to go before our state legislatures are obeying the Constitution – the supreme Law of the Land. So now, along with revitalizing our Grand Jury in every county via our County Grand Jury Ordinance, the County Militia Ordinance will finally put teeth back in the U.S. Constitution.

Instead of demanding that Congress and our State legislatures stop violating these major stipulations in law, gun rights organizations have trained generations of

Americans to instead argue about a last-ditch Second Amendment 'right' when we are not performing the only *duty* that We The People demand of ourselves in the entire Constitution!

Once we have seen to it that our counties recognize well-regulated, properly-officered Militias, then We The People ourselves will *'execute the Laws of the Union, suppress Insurrections and repel Invasions'* (Clause 15).

Making Militia Cool, Fun, and Affordable

We need to restore our constitutional Militias, rather than allowing liberals and statists, after every shooting, to make new arguments about red flag laws, barrel length, magazine capacity, pistol-grips on shotguns, open carry rules, full-auto or select-fire, flash-hiders, noise suppressors, bump stocks and more.

Instead of complaining about out-of-control cops and biting our fingernails over 20 Muslim training camps scattered across rural America, millions of Americans should be mustering, training, and gathering as neighbors and friends once did in America. When we have *thousands* of constitutional Militia units, Second Amendment talk will become a relic. There are over 32,000 municipalities and towns in our Republic so there should be over 32,000 Militia training camps across America. Militia training should be as common as baseball games; as popular, cool, fun, and enjoyable as golf, hunting, or fishing.

Wake up; It's Morning in America!

The most effective step Americans can take is to go on tactical *offense* today. So-called 'militia groups' are operating outside the Constitution's stipulations that We The People set for ourselves. They will never be legitimate until they get over their mere desire to train in the field without re-training their attitude as responsible to oversee government.

Exactly the same problem plagues the so-called 'common law grand juries' attempting to appoint themselves. Before we had a Constitution, the two fundamental institutions of American law enforcement were the Militia of the State or community, and the Grand Jury of the county. Those two fundamental institutions must work in tight coordination as we explained in Lesson 7. Putting all the pieces together is the mission of TACTICAL CIVICS™.

There has never been a better time to be alive in America, than today. Americans have never been more ready to take our lives back, but what we need to do is far more than any president can do. We The People must turn the tables ourselves.

We were warned by General Smedley Butler in the 1930s, by General and President Dwight Eisenhower in 1961, by criminologist Donald Cressey in 1969, and by Professor Thomas DiLorenzo in 2012, that our most dangerous enemy is Washington D.C. – an independent, lawless, ruthless city-state that fell under the control of evil men and corporations long ago.

Now, We The People must begin to 'execute the Laws of the Union', not with a last-ditch right stipulated in the Second Amendment, but using a full-spectrum tactical plan, most of which does not involve force. By God's grace, we begin turning the tide of history just when the evil ones thought they had won.

And we will do it not only by using arms, but by using *brains.*

Lesson 23 Question for Parents

1. If the County Militia had a monthly family day including training exercises but also including a family meal and fellowship, would your family participate?

2. The Second Amendment reads, *A well-regulated Militia being necessary to the security of a free State, the right of the People to keep and bear arms shall not be infringed.* With five million members and $250 million annual revenues, NRA could restore America's Militias within mere weeks if it decided to do so. Why do you think it doesn't?

Lesson 24
Fake History = Fake News

Teaching fake history as truth is even more dangerous than 'reporting' fake news. For instance, besides teaching that the sheriff is the highest constitution enforcement officer in each county, KrisAnne Hall doesn't even get basic civics correct. She says,

"The Declaration of Independence is the Sixth liberty charter in the long history of British law. It catalogues the grievances of the colonists and lay out [sic] *the principles upon which they separate from Great Britain. It is rooted in the principle of sovereignty – that no one is naturally the ruler of another. This principle is at the heart of individual liberty. Walk through this foundational document and learn the precise foundation that was laid for our future. See that the singular principle of liberty permeated all of our founders' motivations. Arm yourself with the truth that you need to counter the dispersion's* [sic] *about our Republic's origins."*

With all due respect, KrisAnne continues wrongly citing the provenance of our Anglo-American rule of law, as we've informed her for many years. All she had to do was corroborate what we have told her, many times.

The TRUE Origins of our Rule of Law

Our Anglo-American rule of law, or liberty charters as KrisAnne calls them, originated in the *Compact of Ethelred* in 1014 A.D., when the English people forced a king to meet their demands. For the first time, kings could not do as they pleased. The rest of our Constitution's genealogy (liberty charters)...

#2 *Charter of Liberties* (1100 A.D.)

#3 *Magna Carta* (1215 A.D.)

#4 *Provisions of Oxford* (1258 A.D.)

#5 *Declaration of Arbroath* (1320 A.D.)

#6 *Mayflower Compact* (1620)

#7 *Petition of Right* (1628)

#8 *Grand Remonstrance* (1641)

#9 *English Bill of Rights* (1689)

#10 *Declaration of Independence* (1776)

Those were all established by Englishmen, over there and over here. Then, the two purely *American* entries in the ancient lineage of our Anglo-American rule of law...

#11 Articles of Confederation (1781)

#12 U.S. Constitution (ratified 1789)

Like our People's ancient law enforcement institutions, Grand Jury and Militia, this rule of law was born and matured in England, but now exists **only** here in America. So our rule of law is called *Anglo-American,* but the people of England allowed it all to crumble on their side of the pond.

KrisAnne is still teaching her fans/customers, and former sheriff Richard Mack (founder of the group CSPOA, Constitutional Sheriffs and Peace Officers Association) is still teaching his fans/customers that the sheriff is the highest constitutional enforcement officer in America. *That is a dangerous falsehood.*

You can learn the true history of sheriffs in our books and articles in the TACTICAL CIVICS™ Training Center; but in brief, the sheriff **cannot** be the highest constitution enforcer, because...

A) We The People don't authorize (or even mention!) sheriffs in the Constitution;

B) The *shire reeve* was the king's tax collector/enforcer against the People; and

C) *Today's sheriffs still perform that same duty in every county.*

Think about it: We The People cannot actually *own* property in this Republic. Sheriffs and tax collection lawyers make that impossible. So, like all communists, even after we pay off the mortgage, we can only *rent* our home, business, or farm from those taxing authorities who are living high on the hog...on our backs.

Anyone who believes that they own the farm or home that they paid off years ago, should just not pay the next property tax bill on that farm or home! The sheriff will sell it at a foreclosure sale on the courthouse steps, and put the family on the street. It was never their property because *private property doesn't exist anymore in America.* Organized crime cartels wearing the label, 'government' or 'school district' embezzle all private property and the so-called owners have no voice in the transaction. That's life in America under God's judgment.

So one duty of the friendly, neighborhood sheriff is to assure that you pay bureaucrats their pound of flesh for the privilege of living in a home. Another major activity of the sheriff is running his mouth about being a 'constitutionalist' during re-election campaigns.

In Times of Universal Deceit

...telling the truth will be a revolutionary act". That was one of George Orwell's zingers, and it fits our lawless era just beautifully. Plain truth sounds *very* harsh today.

We are no scofflaws at TACTICAL CIVICS™; our mission educates, supports, and organizes the willing remnant of the People to again exercise our authority and *duty* of law enforcement in every county. Even very Marxist or atheist counties. *Law is law.*

This is basic history and civics that every homeschooler can learn, but government schools cannot teach, or they'd have to stop taxing Americans through the nose to pay for opulent new school buildings, bureaucrat goodies, and salaries.

America is corrupt because Americans have been lazy and ignorant. Now, by the grace of God, some of us are reforming ourselves. We are teaching hard truth to *very* lazy people; so of course it's not popular. But truth followed by repentance in action are the only way to restore our land, now under God's judgment.

When comparing 'save America' organizations, the first consideration should be: *does the organization offer a comprehensive, long term plan of action with projects on the ground to execute on the plan...or is it all just more talk?*

The second consideration: *what is the background of the organization's founder; could they have a former career bias?* For instance, KrisAnne Hall's prior career was a state assistant prosecutor. Richard Mack's prior career was county sheriff. My prior career was architectural engineer with side jobs as cattleman, homebuilder, missionary pilot, Tax Honesty author, and founder of K-12 classical Christian schools. I never took a dime from taxpayers, and I never will.

We don't wish to besmirch a fellow Christian (Hall) or even a Mormon (Mack). But our mission is often compared to theirs and that's *preposterous.* They are teaching the *opposite* of history as *fact.* And presentation style aside, truth is terribly important just now.

Lesson 24 Questions for Parents

1. Had you ever considered that the county sheriff still fulfills the same role as the Sheriff of Nottingham in the classic book, Robin Hood?

2. Do you think your sheriff would support a constitutional County Militia?

Lesson 25
'Rights' is Wrong

If upset parents of lawless, even criminal children, pout and insist to the children, *"I have rights!"*, would that make sense?

Our Three Ugly Babies

As soon as you turn 18 years of age, if you wish to take responsibility for government, you become one of 'We The People' – and collectively, we are the 'parent' of government. We gave birth to our federal government in an era of relative honor and morality, but in the past 160 years it became a lawless, wicked, massive monster. Still, the basic relationship of sovereign-to-servant is set out in our highest law.

No one can deny the birth process...*We The People...do ordain*...and then following that Preamble in the U.S. Constitution come Articles I, II, and III. Our three servants, newborn and innocent.

The Anti-Federalists Were Right

Alas, James Madison seems to have been saying, *"Now, be sure to check on one another, children!"*, with his checks-and-balances so *absurd* today. I suppose that the idea was rational back then to the Federalists. But the 'Anti-Federalists' saw red flags.

I can understand Madison's confidence: bracketed by that Preamble and our open-ended reservation of powers in Amendment X, there is, *'Militia, to execute the Laws of the Union'*. What could go wrong? Most honorable, diligent folk of that time could not foresee the collapse of norms and nobility that began with Lincoln, Marx, and Darwin, and grew to full-throated D.C. treachery through the 20th century.

The so-called 'Anti-Federalists' *did* foresee it. But because they were the political minority, they were voted down, and we got this Constitution with its 'elastic clauses'. But I will say in defense of both this Constitution and of the Federalists: they assumed that We The People would always do our part as the collective sovereign; a responsible parent. Old Ben Franklin had his reservations, answering Lady Powell, *"A Republic, Madam, if you can keep it."*

It's unfortunate but understandable that the Founding Fathers used the term *rights* so often. They knew what it was to be a subject of a monarch from whom you had to beg rights. But we are only subjects of our own indolence. Having been born in a century grown long of tooth and claw, we irresponsible parents should *never* have expected our three children to check and balance one another. Our ancestors for generations should have known better! *But they didn't.*

Well, *we* certainly know better *now*, don't we? In this surreal, hijacked condition (I am writing in 2021, in Marxist-occupied America) everything good is called evil by Communists and atheists and they will do or say *anything* to win. While we won't stoop so low, we do need to watch our language when it comes to civics. Remember, the simple definition of civics is, *Who is Boss?*.

To put it bluntly: Communists and atheists will steal your words, twist and harden them, gut you with them, then decapitate you and urinate down your windpipe.

The forces of evil are determined that American Communism not die.

And we are determined to kill it.

The overthrow of our laws, creating 'sanctuary' cities and states openly violating our laws is only one of many crimes of late-stage American Communism.

'Rights' is Wrong

This is not a 'kinetic' war (armed conflict), but a plunder-and-occupation scheme waged with words and ideas. The 'enemy', predators and parasites of society, have been winning for generations. They lie and cheat, and are masters at gaslighting. *Yet most Americans allow them to train up their children.*

We tell the truth and play by the rules. By the grace of God, the rules are on our side. But the predators and parasites don't intend to slack off, so neither can we.

We The People have *authority* over the Constitution; so use *that* word.

We have a *duty* to enforce it, as we stipulate in that law; so use *that* word.

But please, fellow American Christian, never speak of *rights* again.

Lesson 25 Question for Parents

1. Have you ever noticed that no federal cases are ever fought for the *prosecution* side of the Constitution; only to 'defend our rights' under that Law?

2. Instead of 'our right to firearms', what is the constitutional issue there?

3. Property taxation abolished private property in America. There is no 'right' to private property; Americans only *rent* from taxing entities. In this light, what *duty* do Americans have, to restore true private property in these States?

Lesson 26

The Greater Magistrate (Part I)

The framers of our Constitution knew the Scriptures. The memories and traditions were still fresh in their minds, of being subjects of the British throne. And they were also intimately familiar with the command in Romans 13:

Let every soul be subject to the higher powers. For there is no power but of God; the powers that exist are ordained by God. Whosoever therefore resists the power, resists God's ordinance; and they that resist shall receive to themselves damnation. For rulers are not a terror to good works, but to the evildoer. Would you wish to not have fear of the power? Do that which is good, and you shall have praise from the same, for he is the minister of God to you for good. But if you do that which is evil, be afraid; for he bears not the sword in vain. He is the minister of God; an avenger to execute wrath on him that does evil. (Rom 13:1-4)

The magnificent law they wrote, the highest and most authoritative human law in this Republic, in opening with the words, *We The People...do ordain and establish this Constitution...*, set out the most liberating, powerful, unique human law in the history of this planet. Having won their war for our independence from the tyrant monarch across the Atlantic, those men took their wish lists and went for broke, crafting a written Constitution for our blessed, unique Republic.

Hey Pulpit-man: America Isn't Rome Under Caesars

These states are a unique republic because, in the opening three words of our highest law, We The People ourselves, as long as American People still exist, grant ourselves the hardest and most liberating authority that men have ever granted themselves: the duty to govern our governors; the authority to assure that the servants we create through that Constitution, will obey it or we "execute the Laws of the Union". Law enforcement at the highest level.

Among all the governments ever created on earth, only in this Republic of sovereign States are the People themselves the actual Big Boss. *By law.*

Forever.

But only if we know the Constitution and enforce it, as Romans 13 says that God ordained us to do. Collectively, we are supposed to be "the higher powers". If you don't believe that God ordained that our original founders should arrive here in Jesus' name, and that He inspired our systems of law, economics, ethics, government and family structure for at least the first 250 years of this experiment, then you don't know American history. Those are our spiritual roots.

As to civil government and law, as I demonstrated above, We The People are the Big Boss. The higher powers. We The People — collectively, not individually as anarchists — are, in the words of the 16th century German confessions, the *Greater Magistrate* above our federal, state, county, and local governments.

They're *lesser* magistrates. Our *servants*. We elect and pay them to perform *only* the functions that we enumerate in our constitutions and in our county and city charter documents.

Do not misunderstand. We are not suggesting that every *individual* American is sovereign in our system of government. Only *collectively;* only as community. That is why we have government in the first place: to avoid the every-man-for-himself attitude of the anarchist and libertarian. Those who peddle the 'sovereign individual' fantasy have no foundation under their feet. They have no examples. No history, no law, no tradition or custom. And no *Constitution.*

On the other hand, the Romans 13 command, *be subject to the higher powers* applies to each of us individually, as it does to every public servant. Yes, even Trump. And even the treacherous Roberts, the chief robe of that black robe set which has for generations been lining its own high nest as it steadily chipped away at our Rule of Law.

To sit in the Big Boss position of the Greater Magistrate, you do it as a member of either your County Grand Jury or Militia. Only in those two primordial law enforcement institutions of Western civilization do you occupy the office of the Big Boss in your county.

And only during good behavior.

And only when that Grand Jury or Militia *are not making it up as they go along.*

Our mission to America is called TACTICAL CIVICS™ because this new way of life restores basic civics and teaches Americans tactics that make up Popular Constitutionalism. We show you what the Constitution requires of you as an American – especially when you serve in Militia and Grand Jury. We show you the lies we have been programmed in, and the powerful truth and solemn duties in the Constitution. Soon, you have enough good news and solid foundation to tell others in your circle of contacts, giving them hope.

Until a critical mass of Americans take responsibility and learn, train, and muster for duty, the Greater Magistrate that God ordained for our Republic will stay sound asleep or hiding in a corner while the lesser magistrates and criminals of every description take turns running the tables on one another.

Big Boss is Clueless

The conventional wisdom programmed into every American by government schools, Marxist colleges, the treacherous Deep State, and the 20 million career government employees is that that voting is the extent of the People's power to seize or reform criminals in public office.

Others, like the clever 'Q' psyop, just tried to keep us in our cages by assuring us that Barr and Durham, or some other lesser magistrates, will start indicting bad guys very soon. They said for years…*trust the plan.* This conventional wisdom is taught by every political party, law school, Political Science course, and 'reform' book, course, national speaker, think tank, or website.

But it's not what we read in the plain language of the Constitution, is it?

No indeed; in that law, We The People do not authorize any FBI, DOJ, police, or sheriffs. We don't even *mention* any of those. And the only place we mention an army (Article I, Section 8, Clauses 12-16), We The People limit it to two years' existence, then these 'armies' raised by Congress must go back to the duties as State Militias.

Isn't that amazing? Believing the nonsense fed to us in government schools and colleges staffed by Marxists, atheists, and unionists, We The People have allowed our servants and lesser magistrates to create their own lawless fiefdoms, in total violation of the Constitution.

So. That's the bedrock of our Constitution. We The People, in Grand Juries and in Militias duly established, task *our own selves* as the *Greater Magistrate*. We're supposed to *ordain,* as we stipulate in America's oldest, highest law.

But we don't, because we're busy playing golf, or keyboard warrior. Or paying for a fancier house than we need. Or…well, you get the idea. So here we are, the collective Big Boss, just doing as commanded by every petty, blue-light bureaucrat in D.C. or in our state palace, county palace, or city palace.

The criminals are so sure of themselves that they even get us to pay for every agency, bureau, program, regulation, fancy building, vehicle fleet, junket, or fat pension package they design for themselves. No matter how unconstitutional — in other words, *criminal* — all these things may be, Taxpayers just keep paying.

In 2020-21, at Trump's insistence and the imperious commands of dozens of rubber-sword emperors in state palaces, Americans by the tens of millions became masked zombies and took dangerous, unproved 'vaccinations' just to keep their jobs, buy groceries, eat at a restaurant, or go to any public venue. Can't be different than the flock. Must comply.

This was (and is) the most chilling, astounding mass reconditioning experiment in history. Blatantly unconstitutional and demonstrably fraudulent, yet the Masters of the Universe, today's gatekeepers of the public square, will cancel and destroy the career of any truth-teller even if they've published peer-reviewed medical reports.

The latest of three massive racketeering and attempted coup operations has been the most effective. Democrats and Communist Chinese are much smarter than conservatives are. And all governors love power trips; it's why they became governors. Meanwhile, the Higher Magistrate remains clueless of our authority and *duty* to arrest this ongoing hijacking of an entire civilization and economy. The 9/11 debacle was experiment #1; this was experiment #2, and actually far more chilling in terms of mass reconditioning of a formerly self-governing People, into fearful, compliant zombies.

It's bizarre. How foolish can the collective Greater Magistrate be? I'm not sure yet; my fellow Americans continually shock me. Trump surprised me, too; either he's on the enemy's side with Bill Gates and the vaccine industry, or he was perhaps punch drunk after all the daily attacks he endured. I wouldn't blame him, except for the fact that his staff knew perfectly well the several inexpensive, effective antidotes for the China virus. Why did Trump still push that monster Fauci on us? Why did he push Bill Gates' and Big Pharma's vaccine on hundreds of millions of Americans? And why did his fans accept it?

God's judgment is a tough place to live, but repentance is always an option. We pray for a great wave of real repentance in American hearts. In our American system of government, repentance must include learning your Greater Magistrate duties, and performing them. So let's review some civics.

Nullification and Interposition

After the ratification of our Constitution, James Madison and Thomas Jefferson posed two contesting principles on how to respond to our federal servants when they violate the supreme Law that We The People laid down, and by which we created those servants' offices. Jefferson favored *nullification* by the States of any lawless federal act or pronouncement. Fans of nullification still abound today; but two facts stand in the way of Jefferson's preferred solution.

First, each of the 50 States is running a unique racket in its state palace. Some have grown much longer in the tooth than others (often corresponding to how Roman Catholic the State's population is) but all are running rackets for people and industries with money. So it is beyond naïve to think at this hour of the day that *any* of the 50 state palaces will begin operating as servants, with We The People their boss. So the first problem with nullification is that the crooks in state governments just won't do it.

Secondly, if each of the 50 States make up their own response every time our *federal* servants become outlaws, we'll have worse coast-to-coast confusion than what we already have. Nullification won't fix the mess; it will add to it.

James Madison favored another principle, called *interposition,* which is this idea: when federal servants go rogue, the State must interpose between the bad guys in federal government and the People who are targeted by the bad guys. Other than pointless resolutions and other political tomfoolery, it has never worked.

As a practical matter, exactly *who* in the State would do the interposing, depended on the nature of the threat from federal rogues. The interposition force might have been an attorney and his staff from the state palace. (Have you ever seen a state attorney general preen in front of the camera? It's as theatrical as when governors or sheriffs do it.)

Or it might have been, as Alexander Hamilton posited in the 28th Federalist, the State military who would interpose. According to We The People in our highest law, that is we ourselves, serving in the Militia of our State.

Madison's analysis of the much-despised Alien and Sedition Acts, provided justification for such ultimate interposition. As Christian Fritz writes,

The people of the states "as co-parties to and creators of the constitution" could exercise their ultimate authority by amending the Constitution or finding other ways to express their constitutional understanding. Madison later conceded that the resolutions and his Report lacked specifics about "what mode the States could interpose in their collective character as parties to the Constitution." However, given "the object and reasoning" of those documents, specifics were "not necessary." "It was sufficient to show that the authority to interpose existed, and was a resort beyond that of the Supreme Court of the United States." If the sovereign people invoked their ultimate right to intervene, how they did so was their "own choice."

Madison knew that We The People had totally open options, because he led the committee that drafted and finalized the Bill of Rights.

Incidentally, there are 12 articles, not 10, in the 'Bill of Rights'. Our original First Right is still not fully ratified. The original Second Right was not finally ratified by three-fourths of the states until 1992…a 203-year-long ratification process!

So. Back to our law enforcement options. In the original 'Article the Twelfth', what we know today as the Tenth Amendment, We The People stipulate,

"The powers not delegated to the United States by the Constitution, nor prohibited by it to the States, are reserved to the States respectively, or to the People."

Or in modern language:

We The People, as the Big Boss, retain every power imaginable, except those that we delegated to the servants in our Constitution. What powers those may be, and in what form, and how executed, <u>is entirely up to us</u>.

Lesson 26 Question for Parents

1. Can you ever see yourself working with others in your county, as the collective Greater Magistrate, to assure that all of the lesser magistrates will no longer 'do that which is evil'?

Lesson 27

The Greater Magistrate (Part II)

Some pastors today claim that the Magdeburg Confession's 'Doctrine of the Lesser Magistrate' is how Madison's interposition idea works out today. To them, when your *high*-level lawless servant attempts to take the People's rights, the People's only recourse is to get a *lower*-level servant to stand between the People and the bad guy!

The first serious problem with this idea of lesser magistrates doing our job for us, is that it references the Magdeburg Confession of 1555 instead of the U.S. Constitution which is America's highest law today.

The second problem with this so-called doctrine of the lesser magistrate is that too many people, especially pastors who even dare preach about our murderous, lawless, ruthless civil government, always change the subject from our servants perpetrating criminal acts, to the servants just taking our rights.

No mature parents beg their rebellious, bratty 6-year-old for their rights; they lay down the law in the home. Societies only hold together as long as everyone plays by the same set of rules. We The People need to *enforce* our Constitution, just as we stipulate in that law. It's our *duty* to future generations and to God; *rights* have nothing to do with it.

Pulpit CEOs Are to Blame

Virtually every famous pastor in America being ignorant of basic American civics, it would be useful for seminaries to require a semester of true civics, not government programming, in their curriculum. We'd supply Tactical Civics™ books at no charge to any seminary, but I won't hold my breath. The career pastor and religious franchise industry is an unbiblical sham. Paul made and repaired tents; when he raised money from churches, it was usually for the support of other churches. Charles Finney once said,

"If Satan rules in our halls of legislation, the pulpit is responsible for it. If our politics become so corrupt that the very foundations of our government are ready to fall away, the pulpit is responsible for it."

I say to you today, Joe Farah, Chuck Baldwin, John McArthur, Hugh Hewitt, Bill Bennett, John Hagee, Max Lucado, Dinesh D'Souza, John Whitehead, Rick Warren, Os Guinness, Charles Stanley, Chuck Swindoll, Dave Ramsey, James Dobson and dozens more who have made your names into national brands: I have *begged* you. But you do nothing and say nothing in support of our mission to wake and teach Americans to do their chores. As an American, none of you Christian so-called leaders can use the excuse "It's not my ministry," nor can you plead ignorance. Satan rules in our halls of legislation, state and federal, and *you* are responsible for it.

Referring to a January 20, 2020 armed march in Richmond, VA by over 15,000 Americans including a great many self-proclaimed 'militia' members against an attempted gun grab by Governor Ralph 'Blackie' Northam, one pastor framed the problem like this,

The fundamental divide in America right now can be characterized as a difference over the nature of rights. What <u>are</u> rights? How are we to understand them? When we understand that, and not until then, we can understand gun rights. … The legislature cannot have the authority, and does not have the authority, to alienate the rights of the people from the people. Any attempt to do so is, by definition, a <u>lawless attempt</u>.

See? There's that silly talk about *rights* again. I challenge pastors to stop being so silly and lazy in their civics. The American People still hold pastors in high regard. The sheep *believe* pastors' nonsense. Programming in churches by incompetent shepherds is even *more* effective than corrupt government, in keeping Americans from our duties to enforce the law.

NRA Seminary

See, the problem is that 'Lesser Magistrate' pastors are posing the wrong questions and framing the wrong issues because apparently, they don't know the basic principles of American civics. By simply espousing a nonsense principle, *as the NRA has done for almost 150 years,* you can have your followers and fans chasing their tails for five lifetimes. The NRA, countless think tanks and conservative groups, and America's pastors, by teaching their followers to get the U.S. Constitution exactly backwards, allow massive criminal activity by our servants to continue for yet another generation, along with the flow of donations.

Take the fiery Chuck Baldwin, who decamped from a good gig in Florida to a safer good gig in Montana. For decades, I followed and listened in rapt attention to Chuck. Then I noticed that he was preaching great sermons while avoiding *duty,* just like the National Rifle Association, one of the largest, longest-running hoaxes in American history, second only to Congress' FED cartel and IRS heists, or the myth that Abraham Lincoln was a great president.

Anyone who doubts the truth about Congress' tax scam should read my free PDF book, *A Tax Honesty Primer.* I sent (14) IRS operatives home, empty-handed over a decade and they left me alone after that. Apparently, they agreed that being a law-abiding Nontaxpayer is lawful; merely inconvenient for their embezzlement operation.

And anyone who doubts that Lincoln was the hijacker of lawful American money, Militias, and our Constitution, should review Lesson 4 of this tutorial, then read one or more of the six books and one website linked there, exposing the true character and treachery of Dishonest Abe and the elites' true goal in that war.

Next lesson, in the third and final part of this series, we shift our spotlight from backwards civics in pulpits to feckless, destructive American academia where History, Government, Political Science, and Constitutional Law courses within two generations became palpable malpractice.

These colubrine professors lead students down blind alleys, always away from the central fact of American civics: We The People are the *Greater Magistrate*.

It is long, long overdue that We The People begin executing our authority and duties, before it's too late.

Lesson 27 Question for Parents

1. Have you ever noticed that American pastors often preach about the sins and crimes being committed all around us, but avoid teaching 'their' flock about our *duties* in the community?

2. What simple, effective steps would you recommend to your pastor, to end his avoiding 'unpopular' subjects?

3. Do you think churches should just stick to preaching Scripture and stay out of addressing 'government', no matter how lawless and destructive it becomes?

Lesson 28

The Greater Magistrate (Part III)

Before we move on to illustrate academia's similar malpractice, one last illustration of a pastor retrenching; trying to apply 16th century German law to our constitutional Republic. He writes,

One of the things that happened in the Reformation is that in various countries, the Protestants came into conflict with the magistrates who were wanting to suppress the reform efforts. Places where this conflict could be seen in high relief were France, the Netherlands, and Scotland. And when the magistrates took to the sword and stake, one of things that resulted was a theology of Protestant resistance…a three-step theology of resistance. The first was prophetic denunciation of the civic evil. When the magistrate is defying God, then courageous men in the pulpit should be authoritatively naming what is happening, and denouncing it…

A fat lot of good 'courageous men in the pulpit' have done (if that's not an oxymoron). Yet, this pastor continues digging himself in:

The second stage is for the believers to flee the persecution. Jesus said to do this — when you are persecuted in one city, flee to the next…

By which I can only assume he will soon lead an exodus to Canada? Yet he digs:

The third and final stage is to take up arms defensively…it is not permissible to undertake a revolution whereby the rebels seek to overthrow the existing authority. But taking up arms defensively is an option. And stating that you will refuse to comply if required by the tyrants to is also an option…

That is the logical and ethical equivalent of parents taking up defenses against their bratty children, telling them that they (the parents) refuse to comply with the brats' demands. Finally, this 'Reformed' pastor reaches his teacher's desk, invoking Calvin to twist American civics into 16th century German shape:

In his magisterial Institutes, John Calvin gave us another layer of protection against lawless anarchy. He taught that when the supreme ruler is resisted, it should be undertaken by the lesser magistrate, and that the people…should resist tyranny from the central government by means of submission to local authorities who are fulfilling their oath of office. Every lesser magistrate has the obligation (not the right, the obligation) to disobey unlawful orders from above. And, when they do this, the people have an obligation to rally behind them.

The governor wants to seize as many weapons as he can, and this is where we see Calvin's doctrine of the lesser magistrate on display… At this time of writing, over 90% of Virginia's counties have declared themselves to be Second Amendment sanctuaries. They have said to the state government that they will not comply with the usurpation of this unjust law.

Oh, Thou Pretty Resolution!

Actually, by passing toothless, non-binding political 'resolutions' (a very different thing from a binding city or county law, called an ordinance), 90% of Virginia's county governments simply took the quickest route to dispersing the crowds in late 2019 and early 2020, before the Communist Democrat machine found in its China Virus hoax a much more effective way to keep citizens from meeting in public or private, or even going to work or school – and the perfect way to manufacture *millions* of fake mail-in ballots.

These crimes will be exposed eventually, but don't hold your breath. Still, do we Christians have to be *this* gullible? We homeschoolers do not.

Blind Men in Frocks

The point to notice here is this universal practice by American preachers, of twisting Romans 13 into a total refutation of American civics. They preach and write as though we do *not* actually have a written Constitution; as though We The People do *not* clearly stipulate in that highest law that collectively, we are the top level of government and 'the higher authorities'.

The preacher we quote above simply refuses to grasp that 'submission to authorities' is not what the Greater Magistrate is supposed to do when the lesser magistrates turn to lives of crime:

And so this means that the rally in Virginia's capital — and which included a number of Virginia sheriffs — was not simply a mob. It was more than a crowd. It was not simply a protest. These were citizens were assembling in their state capital, declaring their intention of submitting to the existing authorities…They were citizens in submission to the law and to their authorities…

He even unwittingly plugs TACTICAL CIVICS™:

Some might complain…[about] a gun rights rally like this… [but] this is how it is to be done. We should all do it more…everyone take note. This is how it is to be done. As it happens, in order to respond as an informed citizenry, the citizens have to be instructed, taught, catechized. They have to know what their rights are, how they are to be protected, and what the response should be whenever they are threatened. But this requires civics classes…

Back to Grade School

As we have reiterated from the beginning of this article series, American civics – specifically, the law enforcement that We The People stipulate in the U.S. Constitution – is not about citizens' *rights,* but about our *authority* and *duties* as the Greater Magistrate. I reiterate: We The People (our haughty servants dismissively call us 'the general public') are the only human authority, collectively, *over* the U.S. Constitution.

I should not have to point out to preachers that the unique foundation of American civics, right in the opening three words of our highest law, is third grade civics. Yet they refuse to grasp it, though I've instructed and catechized them for years. In the aforementioned pastor's case, over 20 years; and he ends his discombobulated civics lesson with delicious irony:

It requires Christian leaders to write about this stuff. And it requires, when they write about this stuff, that they get it right. When that starts to happen, we can then be — as the meme has it — the America that Hong Kong thinks we are.

This fellow founded his own church, denomination, and Christian college. *Sigh.*

Don't upbraid me for my tough treatment of blockhead pastors. I stumble behind our King, Jesus Christ of Nazareth. Of all the people Jesus spoke and preached to, the only people He was truly tough on were those lofty, sniffy religion-men. If a pastor is teaching dangerous, backwards civics but learns the truth, he has the duty to make it clear to his followers that the People do indeed have authority over the hired help, and we are to exercise it *now*, before it is too late. *That* is reformation, Mr. 'Reformed faith'! But no; this pastor has refused, for years.

Preening, Puzzled Professoriate

This is not to say that religious careerists are the only demographic group working for the enemy while pretending to be on our side in the public square. It is now generally accepted that American education from kindergarten to graduate school has been deep-captured by godless Marxism, now having haughtily removed its mask. Parents who send their children into those places will reap the whirlwind for sending their children to Pharaoh for training.

I will not waste space even dignifying the openly godless, destructive practices of K-12 and post-secondary teachers today; there are many books on the subject. And because this tutorial is already long enough, I will only illustrate one example of dozens I could cite, of professors *supposedly* on 'our side' of American civics.

Christian Fritz teaches at the University of New Mexico School of Law. His book *American Sovereigns: The People and America's Constitutional Tradition Before the Civil War,* is a classic case of hundreds of pages of academic blather that misses basic civics. In a 2012 article about Interposition and Nullification, Fritz writes,

Political arguments frequently use history for justification. Invariably, such efforts are less about taking the past on its own terms than the desire to make symbolic historical references that resonate with modern audiences in order to achieve particular political objectives, whether liberal or conservative.

A fine kettle of fish; a professor pointing out one of the daily tactics of every member of his guild! But Fritz appears to be truly confused about who is boss in our system of government:

Who were "the people" that underlay the national constitution, and how could that sovereign act, and be recognized in action?... Madison's views about the constitutional implications of governments resting on a collective sovereign were easily overlooked then just as they are today.

Indeed; overlooked by law school professors writing about American constitutional history. But like the pastor above, Mr. Fritz doggedly keeps digging his students a trench.

We are no admirers of Alexander Hamilton; yet in his 28th Federalist we see the basic principle: whether the federal or state servants ran afoul of the Constitution, We The People would simply employ the non-offending servant, state or federal, to bring the other one back in line:

The obstacles to usurpation and the facilities of resistance increase with the increased extent of the state, <u>provided the citizens understand their rights and are disposed to defend them</u>. The natural strength of the people in a large community, in proportion to the artificial strength of the government, is greater than in a small, and of course more competent to a struggle with the attempts of the government to establish a tyranny. But in a confederacy the people, without exaggeration, may be said to be entirely the masters of their own fate. Power being almost always the rival of power, the general government will at all times stand ready to check the usurpations of the state governments, and these will have the same disposition towards the general government. <u>The people, by throwing themselves into either scale, will infallibly make it preponderate. If their rights are invaded by either, they can make use of the other as the instrument of redress</u>. [Underlined emphasis mine.]

See Mr. Fritz walk up to the water's edge repeatedly, but always refusing to drink:

The right to monitor the constitutional operation of government was a central issue of American constitutionalism after the adoption of the Constitution in 1787. The struggle over that right revealed a fundamental disagreement among Americans over the puzzle at the heart of the new federal system: What did rule by a collective sovereign mean under a national constitution when the people who held this sovereignty were also the sovereign of their individual state governments? ... In America, the people were the sovereign. A half-century after Americans established their governments on this principle, the concept remained as elusive as it was when it first energized the Revolution ... For purposes of the national government, all agreed that the people were the sovereign, but how could they exercise their sovereignty? ...

As the Constitution's sovereign creator, the people were not subordinate to their creation, the national government. The people had a final authority. The Constitution was merely "a description of those powers which the people have delegated to their Magistrates, to be exercised for definite purposes."

For Madison... the sovereign who gave life to the Constitution did not limit its own powers as the sovereign in adopting the Constitution. ...Simply because there were physical difficulties in manifesting an authentic action by that collective sovereign did not preclude the power of that sovereign to act on constitutional questions.

As he does in his 400+ page book *American Sovereigns,* Mr. Fritz surveys different events in early American history when We The People attempted to amend, change, or ignore the Constitution. He constantly reiterates that We The People are the sovereign in this Republic, yet he never concludes with action. Like far too many pastors in our day, the professor talks a great deal but *never acts.*

Summary

At this point, I'd forgive you for considering me a pompous ass. But truth is vital at this stage in America's self-destruction, so if one knows the truth on a tactically and strategically vital point of life, one had better put it out there, regardless how many people call you a judgmental know-it-all.

The pulpit and university have lost their former credibility because the blind have been leading the blind into a trench for generations. So while I do not pretend to have these men's credentials, to quote Erasmus of Rotterdam, *in the land of the blind, the one-eyed man is king*.

We close by reiterating the most fundamental principle of American civics, putting Romans 13 in proper context for every American:

We The People, collectively, are the Greater Magistrate over all other levels of government.

In his career writing and speaking about constitutional law and history, Mr. Fritz has never cited a single case in over 230 years where We The People *enforced* the law by which we created those lesser magistrates. That is because we, the Greater Magistrate, have *never once* attempted to enforce it.

To recruit, support, equip, and organize We The People to enforce it finally, and for the rest of American history, is the mission of TACTICAL CIVICS™.

Lesson 28 Question for Parents

1. What part do you think American professors have played in creating the present condition of American society and government?

2. Do you think that distance education at least for undergraduate degree studies, is preferable to on-campus college? If so, why? If not, why not?

Lesson 29

Some Days, the World Just Changes

June 15, 2021 was the 806th anniversary of the day that King John of England sealed Magna Carta, one of the most important documents in the history of western civilization.

TACTICAL CIVICS™ teaches that an earlier law is more fundamental: the Compact of Ethelred (1014 A.D.), wherein the People demand concessions of King Ethelred in order to return to his throne. Still, that day in the valley Runnymede, when John sealed Magna Carta (the image above is inaccurate; he did not sign but sealed the new law with his ring, in wax) was a day when the world changed.

America has very often been called an experiment, and surely it is that. From their writings and transcribed speeches, we know that the so-called Founding Fathers, including the framers of the U.S. Constitution, believed in an ineffable, all-powerful God and in the basic sin nature of mankind.

The evidence of that belief is found in the limits and *disabilities* of servant government expressed and implied in the U.S. Constitution. The framers had a visceral distrust of governments, that was expressed in Ben Franklin's axiom as he left the Philadelphia convention. When Lady Powell asked, *"Doctor Franklin, what kind of government have you given us?"*, Franklin's cogent reply was, *"A republic, madam…if you can keep it."* On the day (Sept 25, 1789) that the Constitution was finally sent to the States to be ratified, the world changed again.

Losing Our Phlogiston

Around the time of our War for Independence, the consensus of the science community relative to combustion held that all matter had an indeterminate amount of an almost weightless substance, *Phlogiston*. Some materials like metals were supposed to be rich in Phlogiston; others, like soil, were considered to have very little of the substance.

Phlogiston theory stated that combustion released phlogiston from a material, resulting in the diminished weight of the remaining product. *The fire comes, the phlogiston disappears…pouf!* was combustion science in George Washington's era.

Then, a Frenchman named Antoine Lavoisier wrote a treatise in 1777 that eventually earned him the title, 'father of modern chemistry'. Demonstrating that Phlogiston theory was hogswallop, in his treatise Lavoisier humbly proposed,

"I claim to substitute for it [the theory of 'Phlogiston'] *not a rigorously demonstrated theory, but only a more probable hypothesis which presents fewer contradictions…*[it] *explains with marvelous ease almost all of the phenomena of physics and chemistry."*

Lavoisier's simple experiments burned material with and without carbon, measuring the difference in the weights of the remaining product. His hypothesis was demonstrated in the tests; material burned in the presence of carbon produced *carbon dioxide,* proving that the process of combustion did not *lose* material (so-called phlogiston), only *rearranged* it into airborne products of combustion.

Lavoisier's work led to chemist John Dalton and others eventually discovering the atomic nature of matter, and beginning to understand how elements combine. But someone had to take that first radical step that 'changed the world' in chemistry and materials science, and that someone was Antoine Lavoisier.

Plato Had it Right

Plato was a philosopher and mathematician in Classical Greece; the first and most important mind to develop our philosophy in Western civilization and its first institution of higher learning. It was in Athens; he called it the Academy. One of my favorite Plato aphorisms is, quote, *"There are two things at which a person should never be angry: what they can help, and what they cannot."*

I'm amazed at the level of anger we see from conservatives today, because we can *help* it; we can *change* things. That's what Tactical Civics™ is all about. It's *exciting* even though very few people know about it yet. Do you know why?

It's a Remnant Thing

First, because these united States are a *very big* republic. And second, ever since Plato and Cicero complained about it centuries before Jesus came, most human beings are clueless and very *happy* to stay that way. That's not an elite statement; just a *fact of life* that has nothing to do with wealth or social standing. Some of the wealthiest people are also the stupidest. Remember, *ignorance* is the lack of information; *stupidity* is *avoiding* information or not *acting* on the information that you have because it may change your comfortable circumstances.

So if you feel angry at the stupidity of your fellow Americans, listen to Plato and give it up! As we say in our mission: be joyful in Christ, because however crazy things look presently, God always has His remnant, and repentance will always bring restoration. It just takes time, diligence – and most of all, faith.

Some Days, The World Just Changes

I am a whale about aphorisms; little ditties that convey a vital truth about life. With respect to this new way of life, I think of Tactical Civics™ as an extended family, or a church, or a school. We are the body of Christ, attempting to glorify Him by doing the chores. And I always say that the mission will take off when God has ordained it should take off, and almost certainly not by anything we do.

While God certainly doesn't want us sitting on our hands, the mission will take off by God's amazing grace, despite our floundering around. So my aphorism is, *"Some days, the world just changes"*.

For instance, there was a time in America – a period lasting almost three generations – when the steamboat was all that stood between life and death for countless American villages and towns. In the winter, the last steamboat deliveries before the river or bay became un-navigable, iced in – that steamboat brought all that you would see of the outside world until late spring.

The first steamboat whistle of late spring brought men, women and children, pig-herds and pastors, millers and matrons, running to the docks to greet their iron and thread; their fabric and rifles; their tea and coffee and sugar; their oil lamps and lumber and civilized books and magazines. No one in those generations could imagine life without the steamboats.

But! Then came the railroad to town, pushing the steamboats off the pages of history as surely as Spring pushes Winter out of our lives; as though the snows and cold had never been, and new life is everywhere. The railroads carried civilization to a whole new level.

Those steam-and-then-diesel-driven behemoths became like rolling villages on rails, transporting people and commodities and animals over mountains and across the great plains, shrinking America as the steamboats in their fixed, watery courses could never have done. The railroads were king, as summer seems to engulf all of life with its seemingly endless heat and humidity. Surely nothing could ever beat the mighty railroads?

But! Then came the automobile, with its increasing web-work of paved roads across the republic from sea to sea, and gasoline stations and tire stores and the ubiquitous American invention, the motor hotel, or 'motel'. No longer constrained by railway schedules, the traveler could go where he pleased when he pleased, stay as long as he pleased, and then move along with total liberty of travel. No official stations full of crowds; no ticket-punching officials poking their head in your room. For ease and speed of travel, nothing could supplant the automobile.

There was just one fly in the ointment, and that was, to travel beyond our shores, Americans still faced the crowds in loading areas, with their ticket-punchers and then a long, slow steamship or later diesel-burning cruise ship voyage.

But! Then came the commercial airliner; the final season, as it were, in human travel and shipping commodities. Now you can be in Europe in a matter of hours, although we still have to face the indignities of ticket-handlers, and far worse at the hands of the TSA Gestapo.

My point is, no one would think of using a steamboat for their daily needs or travel anymore because…*some days, the world just changes.* Yet back in the days of the steamboat, no one could imagine something better, faster, simpler and safer. Someone had to *invent* it and do the hard, risky work of executing on that vision. It happened in transportation, manufacturing, power generation, medicine, agriculture…*every area, except government.*

This seems bizarre, because government is the most crucial area of life. It impacts our lives, liberty and property more than any other area of human endeavor. Yet for two and a half centuries, one arrogant, lawless city-state, the District of Columbia, has ruled our lives as an emperor rules his subjects…since well before the steamboat era until today, in our era of space travel.

But! Then came Tactical Civics™.

Lesson 29 Question for Parents

1. Inventing a new widget is one thing; it's a very different thing to teach and convince Americans to live responsibly, overseeing public servants and doing Grand Jury and Militia duty. Do you think it rational to equate Tactical Civics™ with new modes of transportation or communication?

Will *you* change your life to take up these responsibilities? Will you expect your children to do so?

Lesson 30

Follow the Money

The FED is a crime cartel.

Most conscientious Americans know this or at least sense it, and many books describe that operation and its history in detail. But many people still believe that the 'federal reserve' cartel of bankers is part of federal government, because congress and its counterfeiting outsourcing cartel commit fraud every day against the American People. Let me explain the fraud; it's much larger than any other felony fraud operation. In any country. In any age.

Defraud the Boss; He'll Never Notice

Textbook fraud: the FED cartel of banks came up with a very 'governmenty'-sounding name, and created a seal that appears to be that of a federal government agency, to print on its worthless paper slips. Textbook counterfeiting: they foist them on the American People in place of lawful (silver) U.S. dollars, *which are defined in our oldest federal law on money, and demanded by us, specifically, in the Constitution, our highest law.*

It should be a felony crime to thus impersonate a federal agency and defraud the citizens for *trillions* of dollars. But it's not, because the servants who we charge with writing federal laws *designed* the conspiracy and bankers have incredible clout in society. When congress wrote the 'law' creating the cartel, since it violates the U.S. Constitution, the Federal Reserve Act was never law in the first place: '*All laws which are repugnant to the Constitution are null and void.' Marbury vs. Madison, 5 US (2 Cranch) 137, 174, 176, (1803)*

This lesson will tell the back story in brief; it is vitally important to know.

First, They Needed a Distraction

Wars are always bonanzas for bankers; they create crises that predators and parasites can glom on to. The runaway collapse of the worthless paper 'Continental dollar' (inflation) after our War of Independence caused the delegates at the Constitutional Convention to have We The People grant *only* to congress the power to *only coin* money, *not* any more worthless paper: '*To coin Money, regulate the Value thereof...' (Article I, Section 8, Clause 5, US Constitution)*.

The State Legislatures, Too

They put the same limit on the newly-independent, sovereign State governments that were printing paper bills and calling it money, too. The delegates had to bite the bullet and end the essentially criminal practice of runaway inflation by printing worthless papers and making their citizens honor it as money. This was anything but popular, because the shortage of silver specie and bullion at the time had farmers, merchants and of course speculators, short of funds with which to do their business.

But if potential crooks in congress couldn't counterfeit, the delegates reasoned, then neither could potential crooks in State legislatures, who were under great pressure from many demographic groups. So they added in the gold and silver clause, to end the flood of worthless 'bills of credit'...

'No State shall...coin Money, emit Bills of Credit; make any Thing but gold and silver Coin a Tender in Payment of Debts'. (Article I, Section 10, Clause 2, US Constitution).

In 1789, the States ratified the Constitution and it became our highest law, binding on all governments including the federal one that We The People created with the new law, and the State ones who were just as likely to be corrupted by bad men with big ideas. Like how to steal silver and give paper in return...and make it the law that the People must accept the crime!

Paper is illegal 'money'; rather, it is NOT lawful money and has never been lawful money under our Constitution.

Congress Once Was Honest

In 1792, congress passed the Coinage Act, of which Section 9 authorized the production of various coins...

'Dollars or Units—each to be of the value of a Spanish milled dollar as the same is now current, and to contain three hundred and seventy-one grains and four sixteenth parts of a grain of pure, or four hundred and sixteen grains of standard silver.'

Section 20 of the Act designates the United States dollar as the unit of currency of the United States...

'[T]he money of account of the United States shall be expressed in dollars, or units...and that all accounts in the public offices and all proceedings in the courts of the United States shall be kept and had in conformity to this regulation.'

That definition of a U.S. dollar has never changed. And Section 19 of the Act established the death penalty for debasing the gold or silver coins authorized by the Act.

For a while, America reverted to lawful, true money: gold and especially silver (you see that the only constitutional definition of a U.S. Dollar is a specified weight of silver).

Andrew Jackson had been able in the 1830s to beat back the Second Bank of the U.S., but he was not able to end the openly criminal counterfeiting operations of congress, protected after Lincoln's war by the corrupt SCOTUS.

Another Deadly Distraction

However, those bankers are shrewd, and many predators used Lincoln's war to bifurcate the American People into two equal, eternally-warring halves while they could increase their plunder and the People would be powerless to respond.

After the devastation of that *War to Enslave the States* (the only proper label for that war) in a series of preposterous opinions openly violating the Constitution, collectively known as the Legal Tender cases, the U.S. supreme court became an open, cynical co-conspirator. In the last such case, *Juilliard v. Greenman,* SCOTUS essentially ruled the Constitution void, and its opinions now the law of our land.

Finally in 1913, the banking families had their henchmen meet on Jekyll Island, Georgia and with several deeply corrupt senators fronting the deal, congress turned over its counterfeiting operations to the new FED cartel. We describe that crime in our documentary video, *AmericaAgain!- The Movie,* and of course there are a plethora of books, videos, papers, blog articles, and podcasts exposing that massive financial crime.

Death...and Taxes

The other half of congress' largest financial crime was evil genius. Since counterfeit paper 'dollars' would again lead to runaway inflation as it always did before, in 1913, the criminals in congress pushed through the 16th Amendment, creating the lawless monster that I expose in my book *A Tax Honesty Primer.*

You see, each year, congress siphons almost $4 TRILLION off of the American economy, with about half of that coming from individual payroll accounts. This sops up the excess liquidity that would accrue from printing all those fake 'dollars' (federal reserve paper notes), thus keeping inflation at bay despite counterfeiting.

We Have the Antidote

As you know, at Tactical Civics™, we teach this real history and economics and Constitution to adults and youth. Even better news: Tactical Civics™ has a detailed reform law (Reform Law #18 in the AmericaAgain! Declaration) to end this largest, longest financial crime in world history. That reform law was drafted by Dr. Edwin Vieira, the foremost authority on the history of the U.S. Dollar.

His 2-volume, 1600-page work, *Pieces of Eight: The Monetary Powers and Disabilities of the United States Constitution,* is the most detailed, definitive history of our money but it does have a misleading title. The title refers to the powers that We The People grant to congress for our money, and the disabilities we impose on them, against counterfeiting. But as everyone knows, they counterfeit anyway.

Our proposed reform law speaks of transitioning back to a silver U.S. dollar, and some people immediately respond, "But there's not enough silver!" because they do not know the story of how the U.S. military captured over 288,000 metric tons of gold in World War II from Japan (Yamashita's gold) and Germany (the Black Eagle gold) and the U.S. government (or possibly the thieves at the FED?) are still holding that gold, which is worth over *$17 trillion* at today's market price. In our <u>Sunday night podcast of November 11, 2018</u> (just click on those words for the link) we told that story, and explained how it was the reason for the 9/11 operation. Mystery solved. One more mega-crime for D.C.; nothing new.

If we (gradually) monetize it and convert it to silver dollar, $5, $10 and $20 coins, and keep some of the gold for $50 and $100 coins, we will have the most valuable, stable money in the world. This was true of gold bezants, that became standard money accepted worldwide for almost five centuries.

So! The bad guys are in control for now; evil is enjoying its last days in the dark and thousands of billionaires and millions of bureaucrats are teaching their children and grandchildren to follow their lead. The only antidote is truth and rule of law. And that means *repentance*…the detailed, full-spectrum mission of Tactical Civics™.

Bancroft's Plea, and Mine

The George Bancroft essay *A Plea for the Constitution of the United States, Wounded in the House of Its Guardians* is one of those works of American history that is never mentioned or taught in schools, colleges, or law schools. For obvious reasons; it is a (supposedly) scathing indictment of congress, for openly counterfeiting the U.S. dollar using worthless paper.

If you read it, keep Tactical Civics™ in mind and you will be able to find the hole in Mr. Bancroft's goblet, from his stream of pearl-twisting nonsense pouring out.

The Hole in the Goblet

I can't take a thing away from Mr. Bancroft as an historian. But perhaps historians should not write treatises on constitutional law.

Set aside Bancroft's far-too-deferential view of congress throughout the pamphlet, and just note the *title* he gave it. Give the man an A+ for evocative articulation, but he refers to congress as the *guardians* of the Constitution? We The People not only clearly stipulate that *we* are its guardians, but I find it impossible to believe that George Bancroft, the most noted writer of American history of his generation, could not comprehend the plain words of Article I of that law, wherein We The People *create* congress, *define* it, and *severely limit* its powers.

I discovered the same lacuna in another renowned historian, Edmund S. Morgan. In his floridly-written, historically accurate, thoroughly confused book, *Inventing the People*, the renowned atheist historian could not find the constitutional law handle on *'We The People…do ordain…'*, so he spent hundreds of pages in circumlocution, arriving at an hypothesis that 'We The People' is just a useless turn of phrase.

I've written many times about the book *American Sovereigns* by UNM Law School professor Christian Fritz, who comes to substantially the same conclusion by simply asking the wrong question for 425 pages. He surveys three historic occasions when mobs *demanded changes* in the Constitution; but never an occasion where the People simply *enforced* it. He clearly states, many times, that we have the *authority* to do so; but as he admits, he can't think of *how* we can do so.

Chisel Off the Nonsense (See Chisolm)

I don't know about you, but as I read the Constitution, I instantly see that *We The People* is the term for *the creator party* of the Constitution. It's right there in black letters, the opening three words.

Then in Article VI, Section 2 of our highest law, we stipulate in plain language that this law will be America's highest law over all others (supreme Law of the Land). Finally, in Amendments IX and X, the People lash everything down tight, saying that *we reserve to ourselves every power you can imagine*, that we didn't delegate to the servants in this Law.

America's highest law is not difficult to read. And it's not a joke; yet it's being treated like toilet paper by our arrogant, lawless servants. Our generation needs to start the maturation process; start acting like the *Enforcers and Guardians* of this law, which we are!

It's in the black-letter Constitution: *We The People are the collective sovereign of this government.* This most elementary fact of constitutional law was first acknowledged to the world by chief justice John Jay in *Chisolm v. Georgia* (1793), the first great constitutional case decided by the supreme court. That case addressed the most fundamental question in American civics: *Who is sovereign, the People or the State?* The *Chisolm* court denied that the State of Georgia was a sovereign, entitled like a king to assert immunity from a lawsuit brought by a citizen. Chief justice Jay ruled that in our constitutional system, *sovereignty inheres only in The People.*

Of course, we don't need a judge to tell us that; I reiterate that We The People stipulate it in plain English, at an 8th grade comprehension level. As former Stanford Law dean Larry Kramer explained on page 248 of his masterful book *The People Themselves:* "*The supreme court is not the highest authority in the land on constitutional law. We are.*"

In Times of Deceit, Honesty Looks Like Brilliance

So you see that unlike historians, at least a very few law professors get it. Here's another one, Randy Barnett at Georgetown Law School, who opined years ago:

"Chisolm is not among the canon of cases that all law students are taught. Why not? ...Constitutional law is taught by doctrine rather than chronologically...law professors follow the lead of the Supreme Court and...the Supreme Court has deemed its first great decision too radical in its implications."

In the inbred, overpopulated demographic of self-referencing, self-adulating mechanics of mendacity – courts, judges, law schools, all the lawyers who populate them, and all those who serve the lawyers – the rare honest ones among them bemoan 'the corrupt system' but they offer no solutions.

So on our original subject, America's counterfeit money, we come full circle, back to the criminals who are *supposed* to make laws but have been *violating* our *highest* law instead, counterfeiting our 'money' for 160 years and siphoning off the inflation threat by skimming America's payroll accounts through the IRS state-sponsored terror agency.

Apparently, historians and professors of law can't (won't dare?) figure out how to end all this criminality. But We The People, serving on our county Grand Juries, can show them how it's done; in fact, *it was always our job to do so.*

Let us pray – no; more than that, *let us work* – to hasten the day that we return to our chores.

Lesson 30 Questions for Parents

1. Have you ever heard about the 288,000 tons of gold that U.S. troops seized from the Japanese and Germans in World War II? For a very detailed historical account of this massive *embezzlement* by our own servants, beginning with Harry Truman, of the property of the American People, read the book *Gold Warriors,* by Sterling and Peggy Seagrave.

2. Certainly a $17 trillion crime is worth knowing about, and ending as soon as possible. We The People have been so deceived by literal embezzlers and criminals in government for over 75 years because of government 'education'. Do you now see why this book, and homeschooling more generally, are vital to American liberty and justice?

Lesson 31

A New Way of Life Begins

Unlike most 'subjects', the tutorial that you have now completed furnishes you the basic materials for a new way of life…including the 72 books and resources listed in Appendix A. Together, those would comprise a Liberty Library for any American of high school age or older, and can easily be read in three years.

After you turn 18, your duties as an American include taking responsibility for our servants in every level of government. It is critical to understand that the founders meant what they wrote in the opening words of the U.S. Constitution: *We The People…do ordain*.

Things are a mess today. We The People have no one to blame but ourselves, unless we blame our parents and grandparents who never taught us this basic civics. But we can't blame *them*, because *their* parents and teachers never taught *them*…because *their* parents and teachers didn't know it, either.

When you trace it back, you find it all began when Dishonest Abe and the 37th Congress finally pulled off the hijacking of America that the elites had been trying ever since Alexander Hamilton was their errand boy on this side of the Atlantic. So as we have reiterated many times in this tutorial: the hijacking of our lawful money, Militias, and Constitution did not begin with Obama or 'resident' Biden. It began in the generation of Lincoln, Marx and Darwin.

Americans could never find the time in their busy lives to stop and study our condition; to see that *this is all organized crime, not politics*. Criminals in public office and private industry have been running our lives for five generations, while We The People have met Albert Einstein's definition of insanity: *Repeatedly doing the same thing, and always expecting a different result*.

God has shed His grace on our generations who are alive today; we now know that we must forget politics; it is an evil distraction. Popular constitutionalism is for the few who take responsibility. Many of us have begun doing this together, in counties from coast to coast. Just a few people in each county at first, as is true of all new things that are designed to last.

This amazing mission will not mature overnight, but you can now become part of the true, lawful, peaceful, full-spectrum solution – and it is *not* politics.

It will not be easy but it will be exciting and fulfilling. And it will eventually change the world by God's grace, again. Your final essay and oration assignment in this tutorial is: give an honest assessment of this course. Will it change your way of thinking or living? If so, in what particulars will it do so?

Lesson 31 Question for Parents

1. Even if you personally do not agree with all of its lessons, do you see merit in this tutorial, for your child? For yourself?

2. What is the single most valuable concept you took from this tutorial?

3. What lesson or concept in this tutorial do you find most offensive, or most disagree with?

Appendices

Appendix A
Recommended Reading – A Liberty Library

When asked, *"Can you give me an essential reading list for Christians and other TACTICAL CIVICS™ members?"*, our staff could list several hundred books. But we will be selective and explain a little about books that I call 'vital titles'.

Besides obvious bedrock – the Bible, Shakespeare's Complete Works, *Pilgrim's Progress,* C.S. Lewis's *Chronicles of Narnia* and other great novels, this Liberty Library introduces 72 works that transformed my thinking; that shocked me at the lies I had believed all my life. This is a great reading compendium for any 14-18-year old homeschooler who plans a career in his own business or trade but also wants the equivalent of an undergraduate Liberal Arts or Political Science degree, just get to the marrow of our civilization.

Edmund Burke's dictum, *"(t)he only thing necessary for the triumph of evil is that good men do nothing"*, keeps repeating itself because as philosopher George Santayana said, *"Those who refuse to learn the lessons of history are doomed to repeat them."* With our civilization crumbling at every turn, where will it all end? Our members know my dictum, *The tombstone of a civilization may be laid at that point where truth is no longer defended, because it cannot be known.*

The U.S. Constitution is the Supreme Law of the Land, yet D.C. organized crime considers itself untouchable. Much of the world hates us, and we can't figure out why. The rich get richer, and the productive American increasingly joins the ranks of the poor and unemployed.

In this tutorial, you learned how the Deep Axis has run our republic for at least six generations, with complete secrecy. <u>Regardless of elections</u>. To restore America, We The People must take informed, coordinated tactical action. That means first we need basic education – such as this tutorial! This is no longer available in most schools or colleges. But we need more; we need to expose the lies on which the 'culture war' is being waged, because truth <u>can</u> be known.

This reading list makes an excellent reading program for an intensive 3-year regimen or a more leisurely 5-7 year pace. Reading the classics is fine; but our times call for more practical education. Having read all of the books listed here, an American will be in the top one-tenth of 1% of our population in American history, ethics, economics, geopolitics, political economy and more. *The Harvard Classics cannot do that.*

During the 20th century, our republic was transformed into a plundering empire populated by historically clueless 'voters' who commute to their jobs every day to pay the bills, their apathy granting legitimacy to staggering international crimes.

Since most people will not read 72 works over the next few years, I list the 16 most vital works first (15 books and an online pamphlet and white paper). Pick the work that most intrigues you, and read it with highlighter in hand; when you finish that one, read another. Move at your own pace and you will find these great books growing on you.

As you later review highlighted passages, life lessons emerge and a pattern comes together as you begin to see through media propaganda and grasp the lies that steer American policy – especially Washington DC organized crime, and its wars.

So again, set the classics aside for now. Given the duty before us, these 72 works will vault you over walls of ignorance about our history and Constitution; about money, credit, and banking; about how Israel and the Deep State used the boogeyman of communism and Islamic jihad to run America from behind the scenes with the help of mega-church pastors. You will begin to clearly see the fallen state of our Republic and the gullible, powerless Christian church. These books won't make you a pencil-necked geek; *they will impart real wisdom.*

If you believe that the Internet is all we need because it is opening minds and threatening tyrants all over the world, Egyptian dictator Mubarak proved in 2011 that government can shut down a country's Internet access. It has not happened fully yet in America, but see how far Big Tech has gone in that direction already, and as Tim Wu explains in the book *Master Switch*, Big Tech can go much further still. As the movie *The Book of Eli* suggests, when civilization falls, printed books will become our most valuable treasures.

For less than the cost of two college courses, this Liberty Library will place you among that rare species: *the informed, self-governing American.*

The 15 Most Vital Books (and Two Online Resources)

<u>The American Deep State</u> is Peter Dale Scott's best book yet, of over 40 books published over 40+ years, exposing the Deep State. The author has spent his adult life laying a trail of primary-source evidence for the shocking, revealing assertions in his books. The Deep State refers to the banking, war, and oil industries together with the 'intelligence' industry in all its secret agencies. Every foreign war the USA has fought has been instigated by, and directly benefited, the Deep State. This shadow government is unelected, unaccountable, invisible to productive Americans, and ruthless. It first sought to hijack the Constitution through Hamilton and Clay, finally succeeding with Lincoln and ever since. *If you read only one book on the list, make it this one.*

<u>The Sovereign Individual</u> by James Davidson & Lord William Rees-Mogg explains the shake-up of nations introduced by the Internet, much like the impact that the movable-type printing press had in medieval times. Even now, 18 years after the first edition of this book, the world's institutions have not come to grips with the Internet. But the news is daily illustrating the acceleration of revolution against wicked and bloated industries, institutions, and governments. As institutions attempt to deal with newly-liberated humanity, the authors posit that informed

individuals and small businesses will win, and fascism (big governments plus industry) will lose. AmericaAgain! Trust agrees with this assessment, and the TACTICAL CIVICS™ Training Center is our antidote to anything the evil ones can throw at our civilization.

I will here clarify that we do not subscribe to the anarchist school of thought touting 'sovereign citizen' nonsense. We The People are only <u>collectively</u> the sovereign of this republic, and <u>only</u> as we operate within the stipulated bounds that we ourselves set in the U.S. Constitution.

<u>Hamilton's Curse: How Jefferson's Arch Enemy Betrayed the American Revolution – and What it Means for Americans Today</u> by Thomas J. DiLorenzo (2009) is a long-overdue correction of the record about Alexander Hamilton. Although a courageous hero of our War for Independence, Hamilton was a wily tactician in laying the foundation for America's corrupt banking industry, and perhaps the most destructive 'founding father'. DiLorenzo debunks the long-held legends that deify Hamilton, exposing the man for what he was: a conniving, self-absorbed con artist. In the final chapter, *Ending the Curse,* I find nothing upon which to disagree with the author except that, like most authors offering reform proposals, he fails to offer a mechanism to *enact* his solutions.

<u>The Problem With Lincoln</u> by Thomas J. DiLorenzo debunks the legends offered as reasons for Lincoln's war. The author exposes why Lincoln suspended *habeas corpus,* why he imprisoned thousands of Northern war dissenters, and why he shut down hundreds of opposition newspapers. He also exposes Lincoln's real economic agenda. If you wonder why schools don't teach this, understand that the uber-wealthy love their riches more than God, and are as ruthless as they are treacherous, smiles and all.

<u>Lincoln's Marxists: Marxism in the Civil War</u> by Walter D. Kennedy and Al Benson, Jr. is another of those books that convinced me that I was cheated even in my expensive private education. The book exposes Union army generals that were Marxists, and the Marxist ideas that informed the Lincoln administration. I voted GOP for 25 years because I thought the GOP was the party that would conserve the Constitution. How little I knew about the history of the GOP's founding and its Red Roots! Rather than the party of individual liberty, it has always been the power center for American mercantilists and bankers.

<u>A Century of War</u> by John Denson; an exhaustively-documented account of how Lincoln deliberately suckered the South into war at the behest of Northern mercantilists, directly against the unanimous counsel of his cabinet. Denson omits the crucial Spanish American War – where America was transformed into a world empire – but <u>The War Lovers</u> (see below) offers that vital story.

<u>Overthrow: America's Century of Regime Change from Hawaii to Iraq</u> by veteran news correspondent Stephen Kinzer is the best single-volume historical survey I can find covering the U.S. government's attempts at empire. This fast-moving little book is a series of vignettes of U.S. government takeovers of Hawaii, Guam, the Philippines, Puerto Rico and countless others including botched invasions of

Mexico, Venezuela, Panama, and sweet spots around the globe, all long before the present invasion of Iraq and Afghanistan. Bottom line: for 125 years, small nations and islands of the world have been mere real estate assets for American corporations and military, violating our Constitution every time.

Drugs, Oil and War by Peter Dale Scott is a more narrowly-focused explanation of how the Deep State planned and executed American foreign policy and wars since World War II. Many Americans on the left and right are finally realizing that the bankers and war industry are joined at the hip. But in this book, Scott adds the missing pieces, demonstrating how the oil industry and CIA-spawned drug cartels from Latin America to Southeast Asia, and then the Middle East, made the trap complete.

The New American Militarism: How Americans Are Seduced by War is unlike 'anti-war' books, which I do not generally care for. Andrew Bacevich is a former U.S. Army colonel, Vietnam veteran, West Point professor of history and international relations. This Christian offers a logical, historically accurate analysis of what President Eisenhower dubbed the Military-Industrial Complex. Patriotic Christians, especially active military or veterans, can discover that while the U.S. military industry outspends all other militaries on earth combined, it also opposes the positions of Washington, Jefferson, and Madison. Bottom line: veterans and civilians need to reconsider what they were taught; the Deep State programs America's military subculture to violate our Supreme Law as it directs the foreign policy of our republic.

Against Our Better Judgment by Alison Weir is only 93 pages of body text, followed by 107 pages of endnotes. With most professional academics being paid shills of the Deep State and its private foundations, a reader should not look for truth and authors' credentials to necessarily jibe. This book is copiously documented, with almost 375 references. Does Israel control Washington DC? Read, and decide.

JFK-9/11: 50 Years of the Deep State I disagree with his dismissal of Old Testament Scripture, but Frenchman Laurent Guyenot is a Renaissance man with degrees in engineering and Medieval Studies who worked in the arms industry and also authored a study on the psychological and social damage of mass pornography. In this book, Guyenot offers an even better analysis of 9/11 than Ruppert's book, in that he demonstrates the Deep State sponsorship of both the JFK assassination and the 9/11 attacks. Bottom line: the smoking gun of both Deep State actions leads to the Israeli Mossad and the CIA.

The Fourth Turning: What the Cycles of History Tell Us About America's Next Rendezvous With Destiny by William Strauss and Neil Howe is a smaller, more exciting 1998 follow-up to their 1991 book *Generations: The History of America's Future*. In this national bestseller, Strauss and Howe illustrate the historical 80- to 100-year cycle called a *saecula,* further divided into five 20-year periods/generations. The authors call each transition between these generations, a *turning*. Thus in 1998, the authors accurately predicted the fourth turning of our saecula; a crisis period from 2005-2015.

This was partially fulfilled in the Ron Paul Revolution, TEA Party movement, 'Great Recession', staggering collapse of the U.S. Dollar, and increasing mistrust of institutions leading to the election of Trump. Tracing 'heroic' generations back to pre-colonial times, the authors conclude that by 2015, Americans in the 'Baby Boomer' and 'Thirteener' generations would step up to meet the crisis. They thought they did, by electing Trump, but didn't know enough civics to realize that presidents can't do the People's job. The bottom line of this book is still correct: today's Chicken Little refrain is dead wrong, and we believe that TACTICAL CIVICS™ is the most likely contender for the major, long-term return to responsibility that Strauss & Howe predicted.

The Lost World of Genesis One: Ancient Cosmology and the Origins Debate by John H. Walton, who has a PhD in Hebrew and is a professor of Old Testament Theology at Wheaton, is one of the most liberating books I have ever read! I mean this sincerely. This book smashes the Young-Old Earth Creation debate; smashes it flat, into irrelevance, for begging the question of material origins. His thesis consists of a series of propositions, culminating in the hypothesis that the creation account in Genesis is a description of the universe's construction as a temple of God, not as material 'stuff'. A few high points…

First: There is no reason that God would have communicated 'scientifically-correct' data about His creation to simple, ancient people. In other words, no statement in the Bible conveys scientific truth that the biblical writers would not have already known.

Second: Some statements in the Bible convey cosmological and physiological notions that do not comport with science; for instance, 'domed' cosmology has no scientific merit but it worked well for primitive ancients. Some of the words translated as 'mind' in English actually mean 'entrails' in the Hebrew; people in those days (and for centuries after) believed that emotions and feelings derived from the guts. Walton suggests that God didn't correct them; there was no point, in their place and time. We would not waste our time today trying to argue that our guts are the seat of our thoughts and emotions, yet that is how Young Earth creationists and Intelligent Design apologists defend the creation account!

Third: Walton explains how the ontology of the creation account is not material but *functional*. To illustrate, he compares a chair to a corporation; a chair is 'created' by the nature of its *material* status, but a corporation is 'created' by its *functional* status; on pg. 26: *"In a functional ontology, to bring something into existence would require giving it a function or a role in an ordered system, rather than giving it material property."* Because the entities created in the Genesis account are material entities, we presume that Genesis must be a material ontology. This is a senseless assumption, as Walton explains with contextual evidence of many ancient Near Eastern creation accounts and analyzing Hebrew words like *bara*. Bottom line: the whole Origins debate is a false dilemma.

Constitutional Income: Do You have Any? by former Idaho state representative and structural engineer Phil Hart is the meticulously-documented story of how from 1909-1913, Congress conspired to create the largest, longest-running financial crime in history. Featuring facsimile copies of congressional floor debate, private memoranda, and newspaper articles of the period, this book will make every Taxpayer furious, and give ammunition to every law-abiding Nontaxpayer among today's estimated 67 million non-filers. Bottom line: all of that corruption and pork isn't magic; follow the money.

A Tax Honesty Primer is my little book and TaxHonestyPrimer.com site. Having read the Internal Revenue Code, countless court rulings and cases, seven books on Tax Honesty, and dozens of websites over two years, I then became a law-abiding Nontaxpayer in 1994. I couldn't find in one place enough information to take action and expose the corruption, so I created *A Tax Honesty Primer* as the first step in Taxpayer due diligence, so that others can avoid years of wading through tax protester theories. The book is not my opinion or 'position'; it's a compendium of easily verifiable facts, court rulings, Tax Code sections, federal regulations, jury verdicts, IRS commissioner and IRS employee statements, and well-settled law. On the site, I do not sell anything or accept donations.

Tax Honesty is wonderful defense for the self-employed (it's all but impossible if you work for someone else, especially a large company); but playing defense will never arrest Congress' crimes. Until our Indictment Engine™ becomes our permanent citizen mechanism to arrest organized crime in Congress, at least Tax Honesty offers short-term relief. It is something like household secession from Congress' corruption.

The Official Counterfeiter is a 36-page free cartoon booklet created in 1969 by Vic Lockman; the clearest explanation I've ever read, of Congress' money and banking crimes on behalf of the corrupt banking industry.

http://scripturalscrutinydotcom.files.wordpress.com/2012/01/the-official-counterfeiter-biblical-economics.pdf

War, Oil, Drugs, Banking, and The Deep State

The Devil's Chessboard by David Talbot is the story of the Dulles brothers (Allen and John Foster), creators and evil masterminds of the CIA. As Talbot exposes the characters of these two sociopath brothers and their evil, world-shifting chicanery, you begin each chapter asking yourself how the American People failed to stop these criminals. But you cannot stop what you do not see. You begin to understand that the very existence of the CIA – like the FBI, DOJ, NSA, DIA and others – is criminal. Nowhere authorized in the Constitution, and in fact, a 'shadow government', as described in countless whistleblower books exposing the criminality of these agencies.

Gold Warriors by Sterling and Peggy Seagraves is one of the most fascinating books I have ever read. After years and years of painstaking journalistic investigations and collecting scores of first-person testimony and actual photographs of the caves filled with gold bars and crates upon crates of gold bonds, the intrepid couple present the story of the most fascinating story in history of gold and war.

After World War II, the DC government captured and seized 288,000 metric tons of gold, plundered from Europe and China by Japan and Germany, called 'Yamashita's Gold' and 'Black Eagle Gold', respectively. How was it located, and by whom? How was it transported, and to what location? What happened to this astounding hoard of gold after the DC cabal seized it? What have congresses done about it, since this is the constitutional purview of Congress? A fascinating detective story, illustrating that Washington DC is truly the most ruthless, lawless city-state in modern world history.

The Transparent Cabal: The Neoconservative Agenda, War in the Middle East, and the National Interest of Israel by Stephen Sniegoski, is a more detailed dive into the American war industry's operations in the Middle East. If you first read Alison Weir's book, *Against Our Better Judgment* (see above), you will understand who created the modern political state of Israel, that also created a domestic PR campaign in thousands of American churches, twisting Scripture to make the case that the anti-Christian -- indeed atheistic -- political state of our day in Israel, is actually the remnant of God described in the New Testament.

Sniegoski goes much deeper into mechanics of geopolitical crime, and the DC cabal's operations. If you want to understand how and why powerful pro-Israel neoconservatives in the U.S. misled Americans and used the complicit Dubya Bush (of the Bush oil family!) to order the U.S. invasion of Iraq in 2003, and how they persuaded the U.S. Congress to give Dubya the (supposed) authority to order the invasion, read this outstanding book. Prepare to be very angry...but as with dozens of the books on this list: once you know the players and discover their massive financial motivation, the history of America's foreign wars (ALL of them) turns out to be just a series of pirate stories.

Myths, Lies and Oil Wars by William Engdahl is probably the best book if you want to learn about the theory of 'Abyssal Abiotic Petroleum Origins' (i.e., petroleum doesn't come from dead plants and dinosaurs – so-called 'fossil fuel' – but from deep in the earth and is practically limitless) and to grasp U.S. military industry geopolitics in the Middle East, Russia and China over the past few decades.

The Deep, Hot Biosphere: The Myth of Fossil Fuels by Dr. Thomas Gold was plagiarized from the Russian-Ukrainian theory of Abyssal Abiotic Petroleum Origins – the theory that there exists an enormous store of hydrocarbons upwelling from deep within the earth that can provide us with gas and petroleum for as long as man lives on Earth. In this 1999 book, Dr. Gold copied the original work of the Ukrainian and Russian pioneers to debunk the myth that petroleum had its genesis in dinosaurs and old plants. The theory is thus called the theory of 'abiotic oil' and includes three controversial, potentially earth-shattering positions:

First: Below the surface of the earth is a biosphere of greater mass and volume than the sum of all living things on all continents and in all oceans.

Second: The inhabitants of this subterranean biosphere are not plants or animals but heat-loving bacteria that survive on hydrocarbons (natural gas & petroleum).

Third: Most hydrocarbons on Earth are not the byproduct of biological debris ('fossil fuels'), but were a common constituent of the materials from which Earth itself was formed.

If all of these scientists are correct, the implications are astounding, and disastrous for the oil industry. This would also explode the environmentalist so-called 'Peak Oil' theory – which went the way of the dinosaurs in 2012 with the GAO reported that the Green River Formation alone contains more recoverable petroleum than the entire previously-known world oil reserves.

Further down in this list, I link to a white paper by J.F. Kenney, senior geologist at Gas Resources Corporation in Houston, listing most of the Russian and Ukrainian scientists that hypothesized abyssal abiotic petroleum origins' long before Dr. Gold plagiarized their work to claim in the American scientific media that it was his own. Besides the Ukrainian and Russian originators of the theory, a growing body of supporting evidence is being produced by American scientists like Jean Whelan at Woods Hole Oceanographic Institute; Mahlon Kennicutt, Professor of Chemical Oceanography at Texas A&M; Giora Proskurowski, professor of Oceanography at University of Washington, and others.

Crossing the Rubicon: The Decline of the American Empire at the End of the Age of Oil by Michael Ruppert is the only 9/11 book I include, and this will be a long synopsis because the 9/11 debacle is important – not for the tragedy itself, but because of the major shift in government and media propaganda that took place over the 20 years since that 'New Pearl Harbor'.

Erasmus of Rotterdam said, *"In the land of the blind, the one-eyed man is king"*. We needn't know everything about the 911 debacle; what we do know is more than sufficient to know it was a massive government fraud on the American people.

A fifth grader in possession of the facts grasps this general concept: powerful men and institutions have influenced governments throughout history. The 160-year pattern in America since Fort Sumter is: first we experience a catalyst attack either of unexplained origin or out of proportion to the war that follows. Next, federal government and its industry allies ratchet their power; government gains new ground against its own population, then holds the new ground to gain further illicit powers. This is the one-way advance of tyranny.

Ruppert's book is the most credible of twenty-two books and three videos I reviewed over nine years relating to the 9/11 debacle. I no longer spend time on this issue; as I said above, I only include this book because that hoax catalyzed American domestic and foreign policy for the foreseeable future. The government's official story and its media hacks must be hooted off the stage!

We did a podcast in 2018 called *Collateral Damage (Beyond Treason)* discussing a report by E.P. Heidner, the only surviving member of the Office of Naval Intelligence task force that was investigating George Bush Senior's shady deal with Russian oligarchs that Heidner shows was the most likely reason for the 9/11 operation. Heidner's ONI task force's offices just happened to be located precisely where that cruise missile hit the Pentagon on 9/11. Just coincidence!

Yet it's pointless to argue about 9/11 itself; TACTICAL CIVICS™ can empower the American people to beat the predator-parasite horde at last: self-governing citizens and resurgent sovereign States can *enforce* the Constitution and arrest the long pattern of government-corporate-military corruption using a legal choke-collar on each individual member of Congress. As we work on a new long-term arrest mechanism, there's no sense arguing about one of the criminals' last in a 120-year series of frauds, since 9/11 was followed by the Russiagate-Sham-peachment-BLAntifa-Chinavirus-Election Steal overthrow of anything even *resembling* legitimate government. Those who still don't get it, are beyond help.

Whoever our domestic enemies are, they use Congress for financing and legislative enablement. The typical globalist player's goal is always to become insanely wealthy, and Congress is their key. After every war, they get us arguing among ourselves for decades about who caused the fire so we won't stop to think about trapping the kingpins who hired the arsonist.

I am one of several hundred engineers, scientists, and architects who signed on at *Architects and Engineers for 911 Truth* not because I care to argue about this latest in a long pattern of war-sparking hoaxes, but because the official story is so preposterous in structural forensics, physics, and materials science. As a professional engineer having performed structural design for 28 years, I became interested in the story when I witnessed video of the collapses of WTC 1 and 2 and especially WTC Building 7, that day. To assert that the first three instances in history of fire-induced collapse of steel multistory buildings occurred in one city, in one day (one of them with no aircraft collision) is ludicrous. Of countless raging fires in steel structures around the world, some have lasted far longer than the WTC fires, yet none led to plastic collapse, much less to the pulverizing (pyroclastic-style) destruction and free-fall-velocity collapse seen thrice on 9/11 but never seen before or since. *Except in every controlled demolition.*

Occam's Razor holds that the simplest explanation is most likely; put another way, if evidence contradicts an explanation that adds a pile of unlikely assumptions, that explanation is likely not true. On the morning of July 28, 1945, a fully-fueled B-25 Mitchell *bomber* lost in fog over Manhattan slammed into the 79th floor of the *Empire State Building. The* structure sustained no lasting damage, much less did it collapse in the free-fall-velocity, symmetrical implosion failure seen in steel structures *only* in controlled demolition.

Geopolitical forces in play in the world's mega-events need phenomenal amounts of money, logistics, and coordination that only major financial players enjoy. The idea that 9/11 was done by a handful of Muslims with the U.S. defense system fully engaged, is preposterous. It is one thing to believe legends about 'Honest Abe' because you were indoctrinated in school; it is another thing to believe a ludicrous story that defies logic and evidence simply because a few in the 'truther' camp happen to be eccentric.

Just listen to the analysis we did in 2018, read Heidner's report, and apply Occam's Razor.

Bottom line: from the assassination of JFK in 1963 to the 9/11 debacle, Russiagate, Shampeachment, the Chinavirus shutdown of America, and Election Steal 2020 – the Deep State will continue to destroy our economy, flood our borders with illegals, commit murders of presidents or of thousands of civilians foreign and domestic until We The People learn to focus on _our_ target: their power source and their puppet institution, *Congress*.

Churchill's Folly: How Winston Churchill created modern Iraq by Chris Catherwood, is the story of Britain's dissection of the Persian Empire into the petrodollar bloodbath we've seen ever since. Ralph Raico's *Rethinking Churchill* chapter in the book *Reassessing the Presidency* removed my blinders about the old Bulldog whose clever turns of phrase had always captured me. Bottom line: this book will teach you just what a scheming monster Churchill actually was.

Considerations About Recent Predictions of Impending Shortages of Petroleum Evaluated From the Perspective of Modern Petroleum Science by J. F. Kenney, is an online white paper that smashes the unfounded 'Peak Oil' scare trotted out along with the equally unsupported 'anthropogenic Climate Change' theory. These false prophets, ironically, helped drive oil prices through the roof for years; without a shred of evidence from petroleum science, they are useful puppets for Big Oil. The old 'fossil fuels' hypothesis originated in the 18th century; it held that petroleum miraculously evolves from decayed biological material – plants and animals – which would mean it is limited. The fossil fuels hypothesis has been replaced over the past four decades by the Russian-Ukrainian theory of 'Abyssal Abiotic Petroleum Origins' which establishes that petroleum is a primordial material that erupts from great depth and is practically unlimited in abundance, only depending on extraction technology and exploration competence. The white paper is found at http://www.csun.edu/~vcgeo005/Energy.html

It's the Crude, Dude: Greed, Gas, War, and the American Way by Linda McQuaig is a well-documented history of America's role in the game played first by the British and French in the sands of Araby. She lists individual deals, companies, sheikhs, and contracts over the past century. As bloody as we think Mohammedans are, this book proves that the Deep State, using *both* sides, causes these wars. Bottom line: we should feel sorry for any Middle East population as long as the Deep State owns Congress.

Reassessing the Presidency: The Rise of the Executive State and the Decline of Freedom is a 791-page lesson about how American history has been steered by our presidents; edited by John V. Denson. Each chapter can be read on its own to grasp a particular presidency or period. Bottom line is the book's recurring theme: as Madison and Jefferson, both presidents themselves, constantly reminded us that presidents are not to be trusted; the People must stay in control and remain always vigilant.

The Costs of War: America's Pyrrhic Victories is another compendium edited by John Denson. A treasure-trove for those who want to learn why our wars were fought. The book is worth buying for Raico's *Rethinking Churchill* chapter alone; it finally puts the butcherous Bulldog of Britain in the hall of infamy alongside Lincoln, Teddy Roosevelt, and FDR. But read Denson's *A Century of War* first.

War is a Racket is the small, powerful classic by the most-decorated officer in the history of the US Marine Corps, General Smedley Butler. He describes how the military industry – all the branches – conditions young minds to do its will, right or wrong; how he, as a decorated officer, did the bidding of banks, oil companies, sugar companies and military contractors, plundering foreign countries. General Butler spent many years after leaving the military, trying to warn America just as former 5-star general President Dwight Eisenhower did 25 years later in his farewell address when he coined the term 'Military Industrial Complex'. Bottom line: top military brass exposed the Deep State 80 years ago!

Truth is a Lonely Warrior by James Perloff is something like a Cliff's Notes version of half a dozen of the books I mention here. For lots of American history in one small book, this one is a winner.

The War Lovers: Roosevelt, Lodge, Hearst and the Rush to Empire, 1898 by Evan Thomas is the amazing story of how America was transformed from a non-interventionist economic giant into the world's foremost military plundering and invading power, knocking England from its hegemonic throne. Teddy Roosevelt was a romantic fraud; a sickly child who overcompensated by bullying the world. With his best friend, powerful warmonger Henry Cabot Lodge – and the timely help of America's most powerful newspaper man of the time – these men literally *created* the Spanish-American War to plunder the Philippines, Guam, Puerto Rico and others. Bottom line: as the Deep State used Lincoln to hijack our Constitution and occupy America, they used Teddy Roosevelt to spawn the worldwide Military-Industrial Complex that plagues the whole world to this day.

Wilson's War: How Woodrow Wilson's Great Blunder led to Hitler, Lenin, Stalin & World War II by Jim Powell is an excellent primer on Tom 'Woodrow' Wilson, highlighting the milquetoast do-gooder's colossal blunders from Mexico to Venezuela to America joining Europe's two world wars for huge military industry profits. Reading this account of presidential incompetence that many other presidents have since displayed, I finally understood that Wilson's chief weakness wasn't incompetence so much as useful wickedness. Bottom line: how Wilson knowingly dragged America into Europe's mega-wars.

FDR's Folly: How Roosevelt and his New Deal prolonged the Great Depression is the second primer on America's world-war presidents by historian Jim Powell. As he does with Wilson, the author illustrates how mendacious, bungling and evil FDR was. The hero of my parents' generation was also a good friend of Stalin, who killed 20 million of his own people. Another Deep State tool.

Roosevelt's Secret War: FDR & World War II Espionage is the story of FDR's creation of America's intelligence industry. Author Joseph Persico says, *"Few leaders were better adapted temperamentally to espionage than FDR; (he) compartmentalized information, misled associates, manipulated people, conducted intrigues, used private lines of communication, scattered responsibility, duplicated assignments, provoked rivalries, held the cards while showing few, and left few fingerprints."* And this from an author who *likes* FDR, referring to him as a principled Machiavellian who hoped to achieve clear ends (getting America into WWII) although most Americans wanted nothing to do with it.

Day of Deceit: The Truth about FDR and Pearl Harbor is Robert B. Stinnett's copious proof showing that Pearl Harbor was no surprise to FDR, just the 9/11 that the devious president needed to prime a multi-billion-dollar war machine on both sides of the ocean. *Millions of new jobs! What's a few tens of thousands dead?* Like Persico, Stinnett is still supportive of FDR; yet by simply reporting what he found, Stinnett's smoking guns expose FDR as a puppet of the Deep State 30 years before Eisenhower coined the term 'military-industrial complex'.

The Great Oil Conspiracy: How the U.S. Government Hid the Nazi Discovery of Abiotic Oil from the American People by Dr. Jerome Corsi is much like Thomas Gold's book, building on the Ukrainian and Russian theory of Abyssal Abiotic Petroleum Origins without giving due credit to the Ukrainian and Russian scientists that developed the theory long before the rise of a German variation of the theory.

Reset: Iran, Turkey, and America's Future is another master work by Stephen Kinzer. It is likely that 99.99% of Americans have never heard of the popular revolutions against Islamic rule by the people of Iran and Turkey a century ago. The 'Young Turks' – led by Mustafa Kemal Ataturk – succeeded, while the Persian (Iranian) people were enslaved in Mohammed's system. *Fascinating* read.

Unrestricted Warfare by Qiao Liang and Wang Xiangsui cannot be readily found in book form, but look it up online and you will find it in PDF format, over 200 pages, a 1999 publication by two Chinese politicians and military officers. Those who do not see the bigger picture (God's dealing with mankind on earth) often worry these days that China will conquer the world. Perhaps this is understandable...

First, because this 22-year-old book perfectly explains the Chinese bioweapon created and released, with funding and direction for gain-of-function viability research from bats to humans, by the diabolical Anthony Fauci. Late in 2019, the virus was allowed to infect a number of Chinese, who carried it from the laboratory in Wuhan province. The Chinese Communist Party took prophylactic precautions in China while allowing a few virus carriers to travel to Europe and America as human bioweapons. A brilliant, demonic strategy, perfectly fitting the thesis of Unrestricted Warfare.

Secondly, Americans should be afraid because of the sheer intellectual and strategic prowess of the two officers. A reader cannot fault the impressive and extensive knowledge of western history and culture displayed by these two Chinese military men. To read this 1999 treatise and compare it to anything published by any American author – especially an American politician or military officer – the reader chillingly understands that those Chicoms are not the boorish robots we believe they are. One wonders how many such brilliant minds exist in the Chinese Communist Party.

Read the book. I read it for my own education and edification, and learned a great deal of military history, East and West, and strategic thinking, besides. All I can say is: the CCP is here already, in force, especially in our universities and corporations. They are brilliant, godless, and ruthless; with that unnerving smile and superficial graciousness that puts the target at ease before they slip the stiletto under your ribs.

The New Empire of Debt by Bill Bonner and Addison Wiggin is the second edition of a work that traces America's past 120 years of world conquest, measuring blood and money with a mix of humor and morose fact that keeps you turning the pages to find out how stupid we can get before Congress' Deep State puppeteers bankrupt us entirely. Bottom line: illustrates exactly how America has become so hated around the world, and so bankrupt as well.

Two More on Lincoln, America's First Deep State Puppet

Forced Into Glory: Abraham Lincoln's White Dream is a 662-page shocker by Black author and history scholar Lerone Bennett Jr. This is from the back cover of this courageous African-American's book: *"Every American schoolchild knows the story of "The Great Emancipator" who freed Negroes with the stroke of a pen out of the kindness of his heart. (But) Lincoln wasn't the great emancipator…(he) was a conservative politician who said repeatedly that he believed in White supremacy. Not only that, he believed Blacks and Whites would be better off separated, preferably by the Atlantic Ocean…(his) Emancipation Proclamation…freed few if any of the slaves, and he called for the deportation of African-Americans and the creation of an all-White country."*

Bennett's scholarship is impeccable, his indictment of Lincoln, withering. Are all men created equal, as the Declaration of Independence holds? Not according to Lincoln, Bennett writes on page 315: *"Large chunks of Lincoln's debate speeches…are taken from Henry Clay's mouth…Lincoln said he had never tried to apply the principles of the Declaration of Independence to slavery or the political rights of Blacks in America. On at least fifteen occasions, he said publicly that the principles of the Declaration didn't require him or anybody else to do anything about slavery in the South and Jim Crow in the North."*

Bottom line: A racist monster was the best salesman ever in the White House.

America's Caesar: The Decline and Fall of Republican Government in the United States of America by Greg L. Durand probes more deeply than does DiLorenzo into the personal and religious aspects of Lincoln's character, using primary-sources to prove that Lincoln was a cross between Bill Clinton and Saddam Hussein: a godless butcher with a slick public persona. After you read these quotes from his friends, contemporaries, and Lincoln's own pen, you'll know that we all had a *propagandist* education.

Studies in the U.S. Constitution

The Tactical Civics™ Ready Constitution is a spiral-bound, super-handy desk copy of the U.S. Constitution with a unique design. It features Mike Holler's numbering system for each clause in the Constitution, making it easy to start memorizing where your favorite clauses are. Amendments are integrated in context where they affect the law. You can buy this handy spiral-bound edition in our Training Center. I use it every day.

Free, Sovereign, and Independent States: The Intended Meaning of the American Constitution by John Remington Graham explains the U.S. Constitution clause by clause, tracing legislative history from the kings' courts and parliaments of Great Britain to our Constitutional Convention. This ready reference on every clause in the Constitution is a masterful briefing on the origins of America's Supreme Law. Bottom line: this is the concise, historically complete explanation of every sentence in the U.S. Constitution.

The Founders' Constitution by editors Kurland and Lerner is a 5-volume massive reference set offering a more in-depth treatment than Graham's. It includes extracts from leading works of political theory, history, law, and constitutional argument that the Framers and their contemporaries used and produced. Available in paperback and CD-ROM, I find the electronic edition considerably handier. Bottom line: this is a far more in-depth background on the U.S. Constitution than Graham's book above, but Graham's work is more comprehensive regarding the provenance (legal roots) of every clause.

The People Themselves: Popular Constitutionalism and Judicial Review by Larry D. Kramer, former dean of Stanford Law School, is no dry tome filled with legal jargon. It is a refreshing look at why We The People have more lawful power than the U.S. Supreme Court. Dean Kramer discusses why it is critical that We The People begin to exercise that power peacefully and lawfully – or we will lose that power, and rule of law with it. Unfortunately, Dr. Kramer is now the president of a very liberal Silicon Valley foundation, but his thesis in this work still holds true. Bottom line: We the People have more power and authority than any U.S. supreme Court; we just never took advantage of it. *Until now!*

Founding Fathers and Roots of Our Condition

The First American Republic 1774-1789 by Thomas Chorlton is similar to an out of print book called *President Who?: Forgotten Founders* by Stanley Klos. George Washington called Payton Randolph "the Father of our country" because Randolph was the first President of the United States in Congress Assembled, and 14 presidential administrations existed prior to George Washington's! Read this one and you'll agree that most of us were cheated in our education.

The Republic of Letters: The Correspondence Between Jefferson and Madison 1776-1826 a 3-volume compendium of 50 years' correspondence between the two giants among America's founding fathers. Series editor James Smith makes segues from their correspondence to their historical context, helping the reader grasp these founders' development over their lifetimes. I learned more about Madison from these letters than from seven Madison biographies. To grasp a man's mind, read his letters.

Democracy in America by Alexis deTocqueville is a classic work of economics, sociology, and political science. Although the young Frenchman did not grasp the republican form of government guaranteed in our Constitution, he was prescient about *democracy* in America. Our founders created a representative constitutional republic of sovereign States specifically to *avoid* democracy, majority rule that always degenerates into warring mobs, grabbing for goodies from the all-knowing Nanny State.

From his limited view as a foreigner, Tocqueville accurately predicted that democracy in America would degenerate into soft despotism and 'tyranny of the majority' as Madison predicted 50 years earlier. Tocqueville said that majoritarian tyranny would spring from the confluence of two corrupting factors: dependence on government for material security, and the growing prejudices of an increasingly ignorant mass, against one another's factions and groups.

He was correct. After 150 years of government education, most Americans are European socialists, unfit to rule our passions and unwilling to oversee our servant government; instead, making it their master by begging security and provision from it.

Hull's Wall Chart of World History

Technically this is not a book, but a very long, folded pictographic chart of incredible intricacy. First published in the Victorian era, Edward Hull's superb *Wall Chart of World History: From Earliest Times to the Present* (the Dorset Press Edition if you can find it, dated 1989) is one of the most fascinating and entertaining resources I've ever used. I have bought half a dozen of them over the past 20 years, and only have one remaining. Several went to my children and grandchildren.

This wall chart is perhaps 18-20 feet long, but it folds up so that it can be read as a (large) book on your lap or table top. It's more fun to lay it out on the floor as I've done with children; you can spend hours teaching and learning world history. It is a jam-packed compendium of key people, facts, and dates in a whole new way of seeing them…as a visual flow of 'roots' from one generation to the next.

It covers all the major civilizations in the world, arranged chronologically. So you can easily see, for instance, what was happening in England, France, Germany, China, Italy, Egypt, et al, when Henry VIII was on the throne. Most people think of Henry VIII as the fellow who launched the 'Protestant' Church; but of course

Martin Luther was turning the Vatican on its head at the same time and the first 'Protestant' Council took place in Augsburg.

Simultaneously, you can see that during Henry's reign, Ivan the Terrible was marauding, Michelangelo was creating his sublime works to edify mankind, the Vatican seated six successive popes, and Suleiman 'the Magnificent' had plundered and ravaged to carry the Ottoman Empire to new heights. Meanwhile, you see that Portugal had begun plundering and colonizing India, while Charles I of Spain became king…of Germany!…as China rumbled on in isolation under the Ming Dynasty.

I have never found a more powerful teaching and learning tool for world history. Buy one if you can find the Dorset 1989 edition. *Do not* buy secular, revisionist imitations of Hull's priceless gem. There are knockoffs, but they leave out many important people and events, and add many unimportant trifles.

Economics, Money and Banking

Economics in One Lesson by Henry Hazlitt is a classic economics primer for people who would never read economics subjects but want to know how labor, money, government and credit operate in society to cause wars, inflation, depressions, and such.

The Mystery of Banking by Murray N. Rothbard, a student of Ludwig von Mises, a founder of 'Austrian School' classical economics. Rothbard shows where the bodies were buried as bankers and Washington D.C. debased and despoiled our currency and engage daily in fraud, theft, and counterfeiting. More importantly, on pages 262-268 the author provides a concise plan to restore lawful currency and banking in America that, together with the work of Professor Huerta de Soto (see below), TACTICAL CIVICS™ is using to draft our Lawful United States Money and Banking Act.

Blood Money: The Civil War and the Federal Reserve by John Remington Graham is a little booklet explaining that the Federal Reserve scam actually began generations before the Jekyll Island gang and Congress teamed up in 1910-13.

Barbara Villiers or, A History of Monetary Crimes by Alexander del Mar is a tiny book with a misleading name. Villiers was a favored mistress of an English king, for whose personal benefit coinage laws were passed. If you think this bizarre, read Rothbard's history, cited above; American monetary legislation since Lincoln's time has been the same kind of deals but with many 'mistresses'.

The Case Against the Fed by Murray Rothbard is a small book with a practical goal: to show how to shut down history's longest-running counterfeiting scam. This work forms the basic guide for the design of our proposed reform legislation, the *Lawful American Money and Banking Act*.

Money, Bank Credit, and Economic Cycles in the second English edition (2009) by Professor Jesus Huerta de Soto is the finest single volume in print on practical economics. Like the late Murray Rothbard, this author also explains the criminal nature of the fractional reserve banking scam throughout history; how all business boom-and-bust cycles have been created by the Federal Reserve crime families. Like Joseph Salerno is his book *Money: Sound & Unsound,* the author explains how the theories of Keynes and Marx are still used by central banks and the banking industry generally to defraud us. In his final chapter, Professor de Soto offers a simple, powerful plan to restore honest money and banking.

Pieces of Eight: The Monetary Powers and Disabilities of the United States Constitution by Edwin Vieira, Jr. is the definitive explanation of lawful U.S. money as stipulated in our Supreme Law, and also the definitive history of the U.S. Dollar. Out of print for about a decade, the huge two-volume hardbound set (over 1,700 pages) is available again through Amazon.com and at $200 is a bargain if you need definitive legal citations regarding U.S. money.

Unaccountable: How the accounting profession forfeited a public trust by Mike Brewster takes you from ancient clay tablets in Sumeria up to the breakup of the Big Eight, in a fast-moving tale of deceit and unprofessionalism, making 'the dismal profession' a riveting read.

For background on how deeply Congress has been involved in financial crimes this century, *AmericaAgain! – The Movie* is the best start. But here are a few good resources regarding banking:

The Best Way to Rob a Bank is to Own One by UMKC Law professor and former federal bank regulator William Black explains how at the end of last century the S&L crisis was a tremor of things to come. Many more recent books expose the grifters' games today; three good ones are:

It Takes a Pillage: Behind the Bailouts, Bonuses and Backroom Deals From Washington to Wall Street by Nomi Prins

The Great American Stickup: Greedy Bankers and the Politicians Who Love Them by Robert Scheer

Griftopia: A Story of Bankers, Politicians, and the Most Audacious Power Grab in History by Matt Taibbi

If you're not much of a reader, learn how staggeringly corrupt the banking industry is (and how it controls Congress and presidents) by watching the Academy-Award winning documentary *Inside Job.* You'll never feel the same walking into your bank.

Crumbling and Corrupt Civilization

Ideas Have Consequences by Richard M. Weaver is a little classic which proposes that language, virtue, maleness, femaleness, and ancient mores have almost gone out of our world. I disagree with Weaver's somber note at the end, but this book caused me to think about truth, goodness, and beauty outside my religious categories.

Amusing Ourselves to Death by Neil Postman is the most trenchant, helpful guidebook for ridding your home of television. Written in 1985, Postman's work is in many ways an extension of the thoughts of Walter Ong in his classic *Orality and Literacy*. There are clear reasons why the American mind degenerated as it has; to know why these things happened and how they are happening still, read Postman. Then sell your televisions and start buying good books; you'll be wealthier in spirit.

The Beast on the East River: The U.N. Threat to America's Sovereignty and Security by Nathan Tabor, the founder of The ConservativeVoice.com, is the best analysis of the U.N. threat that I have read. We used this work to draft the sections of the AmericaAgain! Declaration that deal with ending our U.N. debacle.

The Master Switch by Columbia University professor Tim Wu explains several things that I had always wondered about. How did the big radio corporations of the early 20th century become big television and media empires by the end of the century? How do media content empires fit together with the distribution empires to determine what Americans see and hear? Is the Internet really the open sea of information for everyone to dip into as we imagine, or do certain entities control what we can get access to, and how it's presented? We've seen Facebook and Twitter answer that question! And of course, what about Microsoft, Apple, and Google, the 800-pound gorilla on the block, whose motto was "don't be evil"? Each corporation is more powerful than most governments on earth; we now see them working with corrupt government to be evil; controlling the content of what we think is the Internet world. The author probes all this, and more.

The Mechanical Bride by Marshall McLuhan, is a useful book on *noetics* (knowing how we know), orality, and the impact of the written word on a world lit only by fire. This revolution of writing vs. speaking was far more fundamental to the human spirit than the modern reader might imagine. McLuhan gets a bit weighty and also more than a bit flighty at times; but if you stay with him, I think it pays off in the end.

Christians, Muslims, and Jews

A Wind in the House of Islam by David Garrison is the story of the nine geocultural variants of Islam around the world – what the author calls 'rooms in the House of Islam' – and how the Wind of God's Spirit is blowing through every one of them. Garrison spent three years travelling 250,000 miles through every corner of the Muslim world to investigate reports of Muslims turning to faith in Christ.

The researcher collected the stories of over 1,000 formerly-Muslim Christians, asking them the question: "What did God use to bring you to faith in Jesus Christ? Tell me your story." The result is an unprecedented look into the greatest turning of Muslims to Christ in history; stories of men and women who have sacrificed everything – home, family, even their lives – to follow Jesus. You hear from men and women from Africa to Indonesia and everywhere in between; how

God is at work through answered prayers, and through dreams and visions and through technology (Internet, satellite television, video and audio tools). The reader gains insight into each of the nine geo–cultural 'rooms' within Islam and, most importantly, learns how we can be part of the greatest turning of Muslims to Christ in history, both overseas and in our own communities.

The three main takeaways: 1) Christianity is growing today as never before on earth; 2) There is a great need for sound Biblical teaching among new converts; syncretism and pseudo-Christianity are always a danger; and 3) Most importantly, conservative Americans need to lose our hatred of all Muslims.

Similar books surveying the sudden growth of Christianity in the Middle East today are such books as *Jesus in Iran* by Eugene Bach; *Too Many to Jail: The Story of Iran's New Christians* by Mark Bradley; *Muslims, Christians and Jesus* by Carl Medearis; *The Coming Fall of Islam in Iran* by Reza Safa; *Seeking Allah, Finding Jesus* by Nabeel Qureshi and many others.

The Next Christendom by Philip Jenkins, Penn State University professor, suggests that the rapid growth of primitive and Pentecostal Christianity – both within and alongside existing traditions – is reshaping the world. 'Southern Christianity', Jenkins proposes, is Pentecostal, evangelical, and politically and morally conservative, pushing aside the cosmopolitan, unbelieving northern sensibilities that marked the senescence of European and American mainline denominations that now dismiss the basic teachings of the Bible in favor of enlightened, metrosexual life. (One caveat: Chapters 3&4 are his statistical and demographic thesis; slow, dry reading! I recommend reading the first two chapters, then jump to Chapter 5.)

Even as politically correct popes regurgitate Communism and Hollywood political correctness, the Next Christendom is draining the dying European denominations; for instance, openly challenging Anglicanism's apostasy. Jenkins posits that geopolitics, too, will be shaped by new Christians. 'Northern Christianity' and its secular political ideals are dying, as the opposite is happening in the southern hemisphere. With the gospel no longer shaped by a Eurocentric ethos and historical memory, the prophets of the 'post-Christian' world are wrong...*the Church is as alive as ever.*

Martyrs Mirror by Thielemann vanBraght is a hardbound compendium of 16 centuries of martyrs for the faith, from Christ's apostles through the 'Reformation', when believers who refused to sprinkle their babies and call it baptism were ruined, run out of town, jailed indefinitely and left to starve, drowned, or burned to death by Roman Catholics, Lutherans, and Calvinists. The purpose of reviewing these murders is to see that: a) Christians have been as savage as Muslims, for religion; b) the 'Reformation' was a *political* movement; and c) 'Reformed' folk run from these facts as Catholics run from the Inquisition. Ask me how I know this.

The Untold Story of the New Testament Church by Frank Viola explains how trying to read the Bible in the order we have it today is like re-arranging all the chapters of a novel, binding it back together, then trying to make sense of the story. Fascinating book.

Finding Organic Church: A Comprehensive Guide to Starting and Sustaining Authentic Christian Communities also by Frank Viola is a sequel to the amazing book, *Pagan Christianity?* – explaining how to gather with other believers in an organic fellowship without repeating the 501c3 lunacy of Christianity, Inc. or the opposite lunacy of most short-lived house church startups. Viola brings many years of hard experiences, as he has become a major figure in modern reformation.

The Great Christian Revolution by Otto Scott demonstrates that no matter how they may balk, even the most heathen anti-Christian in the West benefits from centuries of Christian foundation in every area of human endeavor.

Dismissing God by D. Bruce Lockerbie exposes the lives and work of the most influential writers of Abraham Lincoln's and subsequent generations. He explains how these angry humanists kicked out our moral underpinnings: Emily Dickinson, Walt Whitman, Ralph Waldo Emerson, Nathaniel Hawthorne, Herman Melville, Mark Twain, William Blake, Percy Bysshe Shelley, John Keats, John Ruskin, William Morris, William Butler Yeats, James Joyce, D.H Lawrence, Oscar Wilde, F. Scott Fitzgerald, Hemingway; the full lineup of perpetrators used by schools to *destroy* our Christian civilization.

Appendix B
28th Amendment Fact Sheet

Text of the 1789 Amendment

Article the First. – After the First Enumeration, required by the First Article of the Constitution, there shall be One Representative for every Thirty Thousand, until the Number shall amount to One Hundred; after which the Proportion shall be so regulated by Congress that there shall not be less than One Hundred Representatives, nor less than One Representative for every Forty Thousand Persons, until the number of Representatives shall amount to Two Hundred, after which the Proportion shall be so regulated by Congress that there shall not be less than Two Hundred Representatives, nor more than one Representative for every Fifty Thousand Persons.

Q: If we ratify this 28th Amendment with a U.S. population of 320 million, we'll have 6,600+ members of the U.S. House! Where would we put them all?

A: Which government places greater burdens on the American people – State or federal? The same 320 million Americans have 7,382 state legislators but only 535 federal ones. This is preposterous.

After ratifying the amendment, during the massive re-districting process in every state, AmericaAgain! will be pushing passage of the *Bring Congress Home Act* (BCHA) – a far more comprehensive version of HR287 filed by Eric Swalwell (D-CA) and Steve Pearce (R-NM) in 2013. Congress must move out of the 19th century.

Q: But won't the added cost be astronomical?

A: Total congressional operating budget would be approximately equal to the present $5.85 billion. Rather than the present 3-6 offices and staffs, U.S. congressmen under the BCHA would have a single office and paid staff of two. The BCHA will also end opulent perks and pensions and limit all members of Congress to two terms, either house.

Q: Doesn't the 20th Amendment say, "The Congress shall assemble at least once in every year, and such meeting shall begin at noon on the 3rd day of January"?

A: Yes. People attend meetings every day via teleconference and video-conference; Congress can do the same. It's time We The People ended Washington D.C. organized crime, and we begin with the 28th Amendment.

Q: It has been 223 years since the last ratification vote was held on this original First Amendment; hasn't the statute of limitations run out on this process?

A: No; unless there is a ratification deadline in the body of the article, a constitutional amendment has no expiration date for ratification. The original Second Amendment was not finally ratified by the required 38th state legislature until 204 years after Congress passed it on to the states for ratification in 1789.

Q: If this amendment was so important, it would have been ratified when Congress first passed it.

A: It *was* ratified when Congress first passed it! See page 3 of the draft Joint Resolution; the Connecticut House of Representatives in October 1789 voted to ratify; the CT Senate in May 1790 also voted to ratify. The House sought in 1790 to alter its vote due to a transcribing error, but the Senate rejected the idea, thus technically, Kentucky's 1792 vote was the twelfth vote among 15 states, more than three-fourths of the states.

Q: With 6600+ seats in the U.S. House, we will be faced with a massive redistricting project. Given our workload on budgetary and operational matters in our state, why should the State Legislature spend time on this frivolous political issue?

A: George Washington did not speak publicly at the 1787 Constitutional Convention until the final day of that historic four-month gathering. When he finally rose to speak on the last day of the convention, Washington's first words were to urge his fellow delegates to support apportionment of representation at one congressman per 30,000 people. As a practical matter, this is very simple: no committees, reconciliation bill, or governor's signature for a ratification vote, and we provided your draft Joint Resolution. This is not rocket science.

Q. Some people argue that the amendment has a fatal flaw in the last sentence, "*there shall not be less than Two Hundred Representatives, nor more than one Representative for every Fifty Thousand Persons.*" That should say, not *less* than one for every 50,000 persons; so if we ratify, we could have as few as 200 members in the U.S. House.

A. Read the amendment; as the 11 legislatures knew when they ratified the amendment, it is clear that the progression is 1: 30,000 then 1: 40,000 and finally

1: 50,000 people. Those who raise this objection either have ulterior motives or are ignorant of Article I, Section 2, Clause 4.

The 71st Congress, in restricting the House to only 435 districts, hijacked the Constitution. As explained on page 5 of the book *FEAR The People,* the Founding Fathers made this their first article of amendment because, as George Washington made clear during the Convention, adequate representation was paramount. It is time for our state legislatures to turn the tables on D.C., bring Congress home, and restore rule of law.

This first vital step in that process cannot be stopped by Washington D.C.; the amendment was passed by Congress, sent on to the state legislatures, and arguably already ratified once. **Now it is *your* duty to perform!**

Appendix C

Ratification Vote Model Resolution

House Joint Resolution
Original Constitutional Amendment #1 (28th Amendment)

Offered by Rep. _____

WHEREAS, The First Congress of the United States of America, at its first session begun and held March 4, 1789, sitting in New York, New York, in both houses, by a constitutional majority of two-thirds thereof, adopted the following proposition to amend the Constitution of the United States of America in the following words, to wit:

"RESOLVED, by the Senate and House of Representatives of the United States of America in Congress assembled, two thirds of both houses concurring, that the following (Article) be proposed to the Legislatures of the several States, … which (Article), when ratified by three fourths of the said Legislatures, to be valid to all intents and purposes, as part of the said Constitution, viz.: (An Article) in addition to, and Amendment of the Constitution of the United States of America, proposed by Congress, and ratified by the Legislatures of the several States, pursuant to the fifth Article of the original Constitution.

"Article the First. – After the First Enumeration, required by the First Article of the Constitution, there shall be One Representative for every Thirty Thousand, until the Number shall amount to One Hundred; after which the Proportion shall be so regulated by Congress that there shall not be less than One Hundred Representatives, nor less than One Representative for every Forty Thousand Persons, until the number of Representatives shall amount to Two Hundred, after which the Proportion shall be so regulated by Congress that there shall not be less than Two Hundred Representatives, nor more than one Representative for every Fifty Thousand Persons." And

WHEREAS, on the last day of the 1787 Constitutional Convention, delegate Nathanael Gorham proposed a change in Article I, Section 2, Clause 4 of the new U.S. Constitution, to limit the size of a U.S. congressional district to 30,000 people rather than 40,000 people – and this was the only subject about which President George Washington felt strongly enough to publicly address the Convention, urging the revision to smaller districts because 40,000 was too large; and

WHEREAS, of the first 12 amendments passed by Congress on September 25, 1789 the subject amendment was placed in first position for the reason given by Melancton Smith at the New York ratifying convention: "We certainly ought to fix in the Constitution those things which are essential to liberty. If anything falls under this description, it is the number of the legislature"; and

WHEREAS in one of the Anti-Federalist letters, the prophetic 'Cato' admonished: "It is a very important objection to this government, that the representation consists of so few; too few to resist the influence of corruption, and the temptation to treachery, against which all governments ought to take precautions..." and

WHEREAS, Article V of the Constitution of the United States allows the ratification of the proposed Amendment to the United States Constitution by the Legislature of the State of _____ , and does not dictate a time limit on ratification of an amendment submitted by Congress, and the First Congress specifically having not provided a time constraint for ratification of the above-quoted Amendment; and

WHEREAS, The Supreme Court of the United States in 1939 ruled in the landmark case of Coleman v. Miller that Congress is the final arbiter on the question of whether too much time has elapsed between Congress' submission of a particular amendment and the most recent state legislature's ratification of same if Congress did not specify a deadline on the proposal's consideration; and

WHEREAS, the Legislature of the State of _____ finds that the proposed Amendment is today even more meaningful and necessary to the United States Constitution than in the eighteenth century when submitted for adoption, given the level of corruption and lobbyist tampering resulting in multi-million-dollar U.S. congressional elections and inability of the United States Representative to meaningfully interact with the citizens he or she is supposed to represent; and

WHEREAS, the original First Amendment was designed to avoid precisely what we suffer today: multimillion-dollar campaigns for U.S. congressmen whose districts include up to 750,000 citizens and more — a population that they can never personally know, much less represent; and

WHEREAS, the proposed amendment to the United States Constitution has already been ratified by the legislatures of the following 11 states on the dates indicated, to wit: New Jersey on November 20, 1789; Maryland on December 19, 1789; North Carolina on December 22, 1789; South Carolina on January 19, 1790; New Hampshire on January 25, 1790; New York on March 27, 1790; Rhode Island on June 15, 1790; Pennsylvania on September 21, 1791; Vermont on

November 3, 1791; Virginia on December 15, 1791; and Kentucky on June 24, 1792; and

WHEREAS, the original First Amendment did actually receive sufficient votes for ratification once Kentucky's vote was recorded, due to the fact that the Connecticut House of Representatives in October 1789 voted to ratify Article the First, and the Connecticut Senate in May 1790 also voted to ratify it, and although the House sought by May 1790 to alter its vote due to a transcribing error, the Senate rejected the idea, thus technically, Kentucky's 1792 vote was the twelfth vote in 15 states at the time, the original First Amendment thus having been ratified by more than three-fourths of the states, making this present-day campaign truly a *re*-ratification of the People's original Right in the Bill of Rights; and

WHEREAS in 1993, the thirty-eighth State Legislature ratified the original Second Amendment, which had been ratified by the first State over 204 years earlier, at which time the Archivist of the United States declared it ratified as the Twenty-Seventh Amendment to the U.S. Constitution; and

WHEREAS this joint resolution only calls for the ratification vote of the original First Amendment to the U.S. Constitution under the stipulations of Article V thereof, and is not state legislation requiring committee deliberations, a reconciliation process or signature by the Governor; and

WHEREAS all due deliberation on this matter has been held on the floor of both Houses of this Legislature, it was found in the best interests of the people of _____ that the ratification vote be held without delay, and such vote having been held in favor of ratification;

THEREFORE, be it RESOLVED, BY THE HOUSE OF REPRESENTATIVES OF THE _____ LEGISLATURE OF THE STATE OF _____, THE SENATE CONCURRING HEREIN, that the foregoing proposed Amendment to the Constitution of the United States is hereby ratified by the Legislature of the State of _____; and be it further RESOLVED, that the Secretary of State of _____ shall transmit certified copies of this resolution to the Archivist of the United States, to the Vice-President of the United States, and to the Speaker of the United States House of Representatives with a request that it be printed in full in the Congressional Record.

Appendix D

Declaration of Independence

The Declaration of Independence as finally edited by Congress from Thomas Jefferson's draft, appeared on July 8, 1776 in The Pennsylvania Packet, a weekly newspaper.

The Unanimous Declaration of the Thirteen United States of America

When, in the course of human events, it becomes necessary for one people to dissolve the political bands which have connected them with another, and to assume among the powers of the earth, the separate and equal station to which the laws of nature and of nature's God entitle them, a decent respect to the opinions of mankind requires that they should declare the causes which impel them to the separation.

We hold these truths to be self-evident, that all men are created equal, that they are endowed by their Creator with certain unalienable rights, that among these are life, liberty and the pursuit of happiness. That to secure these rights, governments are instituted among men, deriving their just powers from the consent of the governed. That whenever any form of government becomes destructive to these ends, it is the right of the people to alter or to abolish it, and to institute new government, laying its foundation on such principles and organizing its powers in such form, as to them shall seem most likely to effect their safety and happiness.

Prudence, indeed, will dictate that governments long established should not be changed for light and transient causes; and accordingly all experience hath shown that mankind are more disposed to suffer, while evils are sufferable, than to right themselves by abolishing the forms to which they are accustomed. But when a long train of abuses and usurpations, pursuing invariably the same object evinces a design to reduce them under absolute despotism, it is their right, it is their duty, to throw off such government, and to provide new guards for their future security. –Such has been the patient sufferance of these colonies; and such is now the necessity which constrains them to alter their former systems of government. The history of the present King of Great Britain is a history of repeated injuries and usurpations, all having in direct object the establishment of an absolute tyranny over these states. To prove this, let facts be submitted to a candid world.

He has refused his assent to laws, the most wholesome and necessary for the public good.

He has forbidden his governors to pass laws of immediate and pressing importance, unless suspended in their operation till his assent should be obtained; and when so suspended, he has utterly neglected to attend to them.

He has refused to pass other laws for the accommodation of large districts of people, unless those people would relinquish the right of representation in the legislature, a right inestimable to them and formidable to tyrants only.

He has called together legislative bodies at places unusual, uncomfortable, and distant from the depository of their public records, for the sole purpose of fatiguing them into compliance with his measures.

He has dissolved representative houses repeatedly, for opposing with manly firmness his invasions on the rights of the people.

He has refused for a long time, after such dissolutions, to cause others to be elected; whereby the legislative powers, incapable of annihilation, have returned to the people at large for their exercise; the state remaining in the meantime exposed to all the dangers of invasion from without, and convulsions within.

He has endeavored to prevent the population of these states; for that purpose obstructing the laws for naturalization of foreigners; refusing to pass others to encourage their migration hither, and raising the conditions of new appropriations of lands.

He has obstructed the administration of justice, by refusing his assent to laws for establishing judiciary powers.

He has made judges dependent on his will alone, for the tenure of their offices, and the amount and payment of their salaries.

He has erected a multitude of new offices, and sent hither swarms of officers to harass our people, and eat out their substance.

He has kept among us, in times of peace, standing armies without the consent of our legislature.

He has affected to render the military independent of and superior to civil power.

He has combined with others to subject us to a jurisdiction foreign to our constitution, and unacknowledged by our laws; giving his assent to their acts of pretended legislation:

For quartering large bodies of armed troops among us:

For protecting them, by mock trial, from punishment for any murders which they should commit on the inhabitants of these states:

For cutting off our trade with all parts of the world:

For imposing taxes on us without our consent:

For depriving us in many cases, of the benefits of trial by jury:

For transporting us beyond seas to be tried for pretended offenses:

For abolishing the free system of English laws in a neigh-boring province, establishing therein an arbitrary government, and enlarging its boundaries so as to render it at once an example and fit instrument for introducing the same absolute rule in these colonies:

For taking away our charters, abolishing our most valuable laws, and altering fundamentally the forms of our governments:

For suspending our own legislatures, and declaring them-selves invested with power to legislate for us in all cases whatsoever.

He has abdicated government here, by declaring us out of his protection and waging war against us.

He has plundered our seas, ravaged our coasts, burned our towns, and destroyed the lives of our people.

He is at this time transporting large armies of foreign mercenaries to complete the works of death, desolation and tyranny, already begun with circumstances of cruelty and perfidy scarcely paralleled in the most barbarous ages, and totally unworthy the head of a civilized nation.

He has constrained our fellow citizens taken captive on the high seas to bear arms against their country, to become the executioners of their friends and brethren, or to fall themselves by their hands.

He has excited domestic insurrections amongst us, and has endeavored to bring on the inhabitants of our frontiers, the merciless Indian savages, whose known rule of warfare, is undistinguished destruction of all ages, sexes and conditions.

In every stage of these oppressions we have petitioned for redress in the most humble terms: our repeated petitions have been answered only by repeated injury. A prince, whose character is thus marked by every act which may define a tyrant, is unfit to be the ruler of a free people.

Nor have we been wanting in attention to our British brethren. We have warned them from time to time of attempts by their legislature to extend an unwarrantable jurisdiction over us. We have reminded them of the circumstances of our emigration and settlement here. We have appealed to their native justice and magnanimity, and we have conjured them by the ties of our common kindred to disavow these usurpations, which, would inevitably interrupt our connections and correspondence. They too have been deaf to the voice of justice and of consanguinity. We must, therefore, acquiesce in the necessity, which denounces our separation, and hold them, as we hold the rest of mankind, enemies in war, in peace friends.

We, therefore, the representatives of the United States of America, in General Congress, assembled, appealing to the Supreme Judge of the world for the rectitude of our intentions, do, in the name, and by the authority of the good people of these colonies, solemnly publish and declare, that these united colonies are, and of right ought to be free and independent states; that they are absolved from all allegiance to the British Crown, and that all political connection between them and the state of Great Britain, is and ought to be totally dissolved; and that as free and independent states, they have full power to levy war, conclude peace, contract alliances, establish commerce, and to do all other acts and things which independent states may of right do. And for the support of this declaration, with a firm reliance on the protection of Divine Providence, we mutually pledge to each other our lives, our fortunes and our sacred honor.

New Hampshire: Josiah Bartlett, William Whipple, Matthew Thornton

Massachusetts: John Hancock, Samuel Adams, John Adams, Robert Treat Paine, Elbridge Gerry

Rhode Island: Stephen Hopkins, William Ellery

Connecticut: Roger Sherman, Samuel Huntington, William Williams, Oliver Wolcott

New York: William Floyd, Philip Livingston, Francis Lewis, Lewis Morris

New Jersey: Richard Stockton, John Witherspoon, Francis Hopkinson, John Hart, Abraham Clark

Pennsylvania: Robert Morris, Benjamin Rush, Benjamin Franklin, John Morton, George Clymer, James Smith, George Taylor, James Wilson, George Ross

Delaware: Caesar Rodney, George Read, Thomas McKean

Maryland: Samuel Chase, William Paca, Thomas Stone, Charles Carroll of Carrollton

Virginia: George Wythe, Richard Henry Lee, Thomas Jefferson, Benjamin Harrison, Thomas Nelson, Jr., Francis Lightfoot Lee, Carter Braxton

North Carolina: William Hooper, Joseph Hewes, John Penn

South Carolina: Edward Rutledge, Thomas Heyward, Jr., Thomas Lynch, Jr., Arthur Middleton

Georgia: Button Gwinnett, Lyman Hall, George Walton

Appendix E

U.S. Constitution

*This edition of the Constitution contains the exact language of the original, including archaic spellings. For ease of reference, we have added an indexing system, appearing before each clause in bold numerals. For instance, Article I, Section 8, Clause 15 reads, "**1.8.15** To provide for calling forth the Militia to execute the Laws of the Union, suppress Insurrections and repel Invasions". This system allows the citizen to quickly reference and more easily memorize the Constitution.*

We the People of the United States, in Order to form a more perfect Union, establish Justice, insure domestic Tranquility, provide for the common defence, promote the general Welfare, and secure the Blessings of Liberty to ourselves and our Posterity, do ordain and establish this Constitution for the United States of America.

Article I

Section 1

All legislative Powers herein granted shall be vested in a Congress of the United States, which shall consist of a Senate and House of Representatives.

Section 2

1.2.1 The House of Representatives shall be composed of Members chosen every second Year by the People of the

several States, and the Electors in each State shall have the Qualifications requisite for Electors of the most numerous Branch of the State Legislature.

1.2.2 No Person shall be a Representative who shall not have attained to the Age of twenty five Years, and been seven Years a Citizen of the United States, and who shall not, when elected, be an Inhabitant of that State in which he shall be chosen.

1.2.3 Representatives and direct Taxes shall be apportioned among the several States which may be included within this Union, according to their respective Numbers, which shall be determined by adding to the whole Number of free Persons, including those bound to Service for a Term of Years, and excluding Indians not taxed, three fifths of all other Persons.

1.2.4 The actual Enumeration shall be made within three Years after the first Meeting of the Congress of the United States, and within every subsequent Term of ten Years, in such Manner as they shall by Law direct. The Number of Representatives shall not exceed one for every thirty Thousand, but each State shall have at Least one Representative; and until such enumeration shall be made, the State of New Hampshire shall be entitled to chuse three, Massachusetts eight, Rhode-Island and Providence Plantations one, Connecticut five, New-York six, New Jersey four, Pennsylvania eight, Delaware one, Maryland six, Virginia ten, North Carolina five, South Carolina five, and Georgia three.

1.2.5   When vacancies happen in the Representation from any State, the Executive Authority thereof shall issue Writs of Election to fill such Vacancies.

1.2.6   The House of Representatives shall chuse their Speaker and other Officers; and shall have the sole Power of Impeachment.

Section 3

1.3.1   The Senate of the United States shall be composed of two Senators from each State, chosen by the Legislature thereof, for six Years; and each Senator shall have one Vote.

1.3.2   Immediately after they shall be assembled in Consequence of the first Election, they shall be divided as equally as may be into three Classes. The Seats of the Senators of the first Class shall be vacated at the Expiration of the second Year, of the second Class at the Expiration of the fourth Year, and of the third Class at the Expiration of the sixth Year, so that one third may be chosen every second Year;

1.3.3   and if Vacancies happen by Resignation, or otherwise, during the Recess of the Legislature of any State, the Executive thereof may make temporary Appointments until the next Meeting of the Legislature, which shall then fill such Vacancies.

1.3.4   No Person shall be a Senator who shall not have attained to the Age of thirty Years, and been nine Years a Citizen of the United States, and who shall not, when elected, be an Inhabitant of that State for which he shall be chosen.

1.3.5   The Vice President of the United States shall be President of the Senate, but shall have no Vote, unless they be equally divided.

1.3.6   The Senate shall chuse their other Officers, and also a President pro tempore, in the Absence of the Vice President, or when he shall exercise the Office of President of the United States.

1.3.7   The Senate shall have the sole Power to try all Impeachments. When sitting for that Purpose, they shall be on Oath or Affirmation. When the President of the United States is tried, the Chief Justice shall preside: And no Person shall be convicted without the Concurrence of two thirds of the Members present.

1.3.8   Judgment in Cases of Impeachment shall not extend further than to removal from Office, and disqualification to hold and enjoy any Office of honor, Trust or Profit under the United States: but the Party convicted shall nevertheless be liable and subject to Indictment, Trial, Judgment and Punishment, according to Law.

Section 4

1.4.1 The Times, Places and Manner of holding Elections for Senators and Representatives, shall be prescribed in each State by the Legislature thereof; but the Congress may at any time by Law make or alter such Regulations, except as to the Places of chusing Senators.

1.4.2 The Congress shall assemble at least once in every Year, and such Meeting shall be on the first Monday in December, unless they shall by Law appoint a different Day. [Changed; see 20th Amendment.]

Section 5

1.5.1 Each House shall be the Judge of the Elections, Returns and Qualifications of its own Members, and a Majority of each shall constitute a Quorum to do Business; but a smaller Number may adjourn from day to day, and may be authorized to compel the Attendance of absent Members, in such Manner, and under such Penalties as each House may provide.

1.5.2 Each House may determine the Rules of its Proceedings, punish its Members for disorderly Behaviour, and, with the Concurrence of two thirds, expel a Member.

1.5.3 Each House shall keep a Journal of its Proceedings, and from time to time publish the same, excepting such Parts as may in their Judgment require Secrecy; and the Yeas and Nays of the Members of either House on any question shall, at the Desire of one fifth of those Present, be entered on the Journal.

1.5.4 Neither House, during the Session of Congress, shall, without the Consent of the other, adjourn for more than three days, nor to any other Place than that in which the two Houses shall be sitting.

Section 6

1.6.1 The Senators and Representatives shall receive a Compensation for their Services, to be ascertained by Law, and paid out of the Treasury of the United States.

1.6.2 They shall in all Cases, except Treason, Felony and Breach of the Peace, be privileged from Arrest during their Attendance at the Session of their respective Houses, and in going to and returning from the same; and for any Speech or Debate in either House, they shall not be questioned in any other Place.

1.6.3 No Senator or Representative shall, during the Time for which he was elected, be appointed to any civil Office under the Authority of the United States, which shall have been created, or the Emoluments whereof shall have been encreased during such time; and no Person holding any Office under the United States, shall be a Member of either House during his Continuance in Office.

Section 7

1.7.1 All Bills for raising Revenue shall originate in the House of Representatives; but the Senate may propose or concur with Amendments as on other Bills.

1.7.2 Every Bill which shall have passed the House of Representatives and the Senate, shall, before it become a Law, be presented to the President of the United States; If he approve he shall sign it, but if not he shall return it, with his Objections to that House in which it shall have originated, who shall enter the Objections at large on their Journal, and proceed to reconsider it.

1.7.3 If after such Reconsideration two thirds of that House shall agree to pass the Bill, it shall be sent, together with the Objections, to the other House, by which it shall likewise be reconsidered, and if approved by two thirds of that House, it shall become a Law.

1.7.4 But in all such Cases the Votes of both Houses shall be determined by yeas and Nays, and the Names of the Persons voting for and against the Bill shall be entered on the Journal of each House respectively. If any Bill shall not be returned by the President within ten Days (Sundays excepted) after it shall have been presented to him, the Same shall be a Law, in like Manner as if he had signed it, unless the Congress by their Adjournment prevent its Return, in which Case it shall not be a Law.

1.7.5 Every Order, Resolution, or Vote to which the Concurrence of the Senate and House of Representatives may be necessary (except on a question of Adjournment) shall be presented to the President of the United States; and before the Same shall take Effect, shall be approved by him, or being disapproved by him, shall be repassed by two thirds of the Senate and House of Representatives, according to the Rules and Limitations prescribed in the Case of a Bill.

Section 8

1.8.1 The Congress shall have Power To lay and collect Taxes, Duties, Imposts and Excises, to pay the Debts and provide for the common Defence and general Welfare of the United States; but all Duties, Imposts and Excises shall be uniform throughout the United States;

1.8.2 To borrow Money on the credit of the United States;

1.8.3 To regulate Commerce with foreign Nations, and among the several States, and with the Indian Tribes;

1.8.4 To establish an uniform Rule of Naturalization, and uniform Laws on the subject of Bankruptcies throughout the United States;

1.8.5 To coin Money, regulate the Value thereof, and of foreign Coin, and fix the Standard of Weights and Measures;

1.8.6 To provide for the Punishment of counterfeiting the Securities and current Coin of the United States;

1.8.7 To establish Post Offices and post Roads;

1.8.8 To promote the Progress of Science and useful Arts, by securing for limited Times to Authors and Inventors the exclusive Right to their respective Writings and Discoveries;

1.8.9 To constitute Tribunals inferior to the supreme Court;

1.8.10 To define and punish Piracies and Felonies committed on the high Seas, and Offences against the Law of Nations;

1.8.11 To declare War, grant Letters of Marque and Reprisal, and make Rules concerning Captures on Land and Water;

1.8.12 To raise and support Armies, but no Appropriation of Money to that Use shall be for a longer Term than two Years;

1.8.13 To provide and maintain a Navy;

1.8.14 To make Rules for the Government and Regulation of the land and naval Forces;

1.8.15 To provide for calling forth the Militia to execute the Laws of the Union, suppress Insurrections and repel Invasions;

1.8.16 To provide for organizing, arming, and disciplining, the Militia, and for governing such Part of them as may be employed in the Service of the United States, reserving to the States respectively, the Appointment of the Officers, and the Authority of training the Militia according to the discipline prescribed by Congress;

1.8.17 To exercise exclusive Legislation in all Cases whatsoever, over such District (not exceeding ten Miles square) as may, by Cession of particular States, and the Acceptance of Congress, become the Seat of the Government of the United States, and to exercise like Authority over all Places purchased by the Consent of the Legislature of the State in which the Same shall be, for the Erection of Forts, Magazines, Arsenals, dock-Yards, and other needful Buildings;—And

1.8.18 To make all Laws which shall be necessary and proper for carrying into Execution the foregoing Powers, and all other Powers vested by this Constitution in the Government of the United States, or in any Department or Officer thereof.

Section 9

1.9.1 The Migration or Importation of such Persons as any of the States now existing shall think proper to admit, shall not be prohibited by the Congress prior to the Year one thousand eight hundred and eight, but a Tax or duty may be imposed on such Importation, not exceeding ten dollars for each Person. [Nullified; now obsolete.]

1.9.2 The Privilege of the Writ of Habeas Corpus shall not be suspended, unless when in Cases of Rebellion or Invasion the public Safety may require it.

1.9.3 No Bill of Attainder or ex post facto Law shall be passed.

1.9.4 No Capitation, or other direct, Tax shall be laid, unless in Proportion to the Census or enumeration herein before directed to be taken.

1.9.5 No Tax or Duty shall be laid on Articles exported from any State.

1.9.6 No Preference shall be given by any Regulation of Commerce or Revenue to the Ports of one State over those of another: nor shall Vessels bound to, or from, one State, be obliged to enter, clear, or pay Duties in another.

1.9.7 No Money shall be drawn from the Treasury, but in Consequence of Appropriations made by Law; and a regular Statement and Account of the Receipts and Expenditures of all public Money shall be published from time to time.

1.9.8 No Title of Nobility shall be granted by the United States: And no Person holding any Office of Profit or Trust under them, shall, without the Consent of the Congress, accept of any present, Emolument, Office, or Title, of any kind whatever, from any King, Prince, or foreign State.

Section 10

1.10.1 No State shall enter into any Treaty, Alliance, or Confederation; grant Letters of Marque and Reprisal;

1.10.2 coin Money; emit Bills of Credit; make any Thing but gold and silver Coin a Tender in Payment of Debts;

1.10.3 pass any Bill of Attainder, ex post facto Law,

1.10.4 or Law impairing the Obligation of Contracts, or grant any Title of Nobility.

1.10.5 No State shall, without the Consent of the Congress, lay any Imposts or Duties on Imports or Exports, except

what may be absolutely necessary for executing its inspection Laws: and the net Produce of all Duties and Imposts, laid by any State on Imports or Exports, shall be for the Use of the Treasury of the United States; and all such Laws shall be subject to the Revision and Controul of the Congress.

1.10.6 No State shall, without the Consent of Congress, lay any Duty of Tonnage, keep Troops, or Ships of War in time of Peace, enter into any Agreement or Compact with another State, or with a foreign Power, or engage in War, unless actually invaded, or in such imminent Danger as will not admit of delay.

Article II

Section 1

2.1.1 The executive Power shall be vested in a President of the United States of America. He shall hold his Office during the Term of four Years, and, together with the Vice President, chosen for the same Term, be elected, as follows

2.1.2 Each State shall appoint, in such Manner as the Legislature thereof may direct, a Number of Electors, equal to the whole Number of Senators and Representatives to which the State may be entitled in the Congress: but no Senator or Representative, or Person holding an Office of Trust or Profit under the United States, shall be appointed an Elector.

2.1.3 The Electors shall meet in their respective States, and vote by Ballot for two Persons, of whom one at least shall not be an Inhabitant of the same State with themselves.

2.1.4 And they shall make a List of all the Persons voted for, and of the Number of Votes for each; which List they shall sign and certify, and transmit sealed to the Seat of the Government of the United States, directed to the President of the Senate.

2.1.5 The President of the Senate shall, in the Presence of the Senate and House of Representatives, open all the Certificates, and the Votes shall then be counted. The Person having the greatest Number of Votes shall be the President, if such Number be a Majority of the whole Number of Electors appointed;

2.1.6 and if there be more than one who have such Majority, and have an equal Number of Votes, then the House of Representatives shall immediately chuse by Ballot one of them for President; and if no Person have a Majority, then from the five highest on the List the said House shall in like Manner chuse the President. But in chusing the President, the Votes shall be taken by States, the Representation from each State having one Vote; A quorum for this Purpose shall consist of a Member or Members from two thirds of the States, and a Majority of all the States shall be necessary to a Choice. [Changed; see 12th Amendment.]

2.1.7 [Removed; see 20th Amendment.]

2.1.8 [Removed by the 20th Amendment.]

2.1.9 In every Case, after the Choice of the President, the Person having the greatest Number of Votes of the Electors shall be the Vice President. But if there should remain two or more who have equal Votes, the Senate shall chuse from them by Ballot the Vice President.

[Changed; see 12th Amendment.]

2.1.10 The Congress may determine the Time of chusing the Electors, and the Day on which they shall give their Votes; which Day shall be the same throughout the United States.

2.1.11 No Person except a natural born Citizen, or a Citizen of the United States, at the time of the Adoption of this Constitution, shall be eligible to the Office of President; neither shall any Person be eligible to that Office who shall not have attained to the Age of thirty five Years, and been fourteen Years a Resident within the United States.

2.1.12 In Case of the Removal of the President from Office, or of his Death, Resignation, or Inability to discharge the Powers and Duties of the said Office, the Same shall devolve on the Vice President, [Changed; see 25th Amendment.]

2.1.13 [See 25th Amendment]

2.1.14 and the Congress may by Law provide for the Case of Removal, Death, Resignation or Inability, both of the President and Vice President, declaring what Officer shall then act as President, and such Officer shall act accordingly, until the Disability be removed, or a President shall be elected.

2.1.15-18 [See 25th Amendment]

2.1.19 The President shall, at stated Times, receive for his Services, a Compensation, which shall neither be encreased nor diminished during the Period for which he shall have been elected, and he shall not receive within that Period any other Emolument from the United States, or any of them.

2.1.20 Before he enter on the Execution of his Office, he shall take the following Oath or Affirmation:—"I do solemnly swear (or affirm) that I will faithfully execute the Office of President of the United States, and will to the best of my Ability, preserve, protect and defend the Constitution of the United States."

Section 2

2.2.1 The President shall be Commander in Chief of the Army and Navy of the United States, and of the Militia of the several States, when called into the actual Service of the United States; he may require the Opinion, in writing, of the principal Officer in each of the executive Departments, upon any Subject relating to the Duties of their respective Offices, and he shall have Power to grant Reprieves and Pardons for Offences against the United States, except in Cases of Impeachment.

2.2.2 He shall have Power, by and with the Advice and Consent of the Senate, to make Treaties, provided two thirds of the Senators present concur; and he shall nominate, and by and with the Advice and Consent of the Senate, shall appoint Ambassadors, other public Ministers and Consuls, Judges of the supreme Court, and all other Officers of the United States, whose Appointments are not herein otherwise provided for, and which shall be established by Law:

2.2.3 but the Congress may by Law vest the Appointment of such inferior Officers, as they think proper, in the President alone, in the Courts of Law, or in the Heads of Departments.

2.2.4 The President shall have Power to fill up all Vacancies that may happen during the Recess of the Senate, by granting Commissions which shall expire at the End of their next Session.

Section 3

2.3.1 He shall from time to time give to the Congress Information of the State of the Union, and recommend to their Consideration such Measures as he shall judge necessary and expedient;

2.3.2 he may, on extraordinary Occasions, convene both Houses, or either of them, and in Case of Disagreement between them, with Respect to the Time of Adjournment, he may adjourn them to such Time as he shall think proper;

2.3.3 he shall receive Ambassadors and other public Ministers; he shall take Care that the Laws be faithfully executed, and shall Commission all the Officers of the United States.

Section 4

The President, Vice President and all civil Officers of the United States, shall be removed from Office on Impeachment for, and Conviction of, Treason, Bribery, or other high Crimes and Misdemeanors.

Article III

Section 1

The judicial Power of the United States, shall be vested in one supreme Court, and in such inferior Courts as the Congress may from time to time ordain and establish. The Judges, both of the supreme and inferior Courts, shall hold their Offices during good Behaviour, and shall, at stated Times, receive for their Services, a Compensation, which shall not be diminished during their Continuance in Office.

Section 2

3.2.1 The judicial Power shall extend to all Cases, in Law and Equity, arising under this Constitution, the Laws of the United States, and Treaties made, or which shall be made, under their Authority;—to all Cases affecting Ambassadors, other public Ministers and Consuls;—to all Cases of admiralty and maritime Jurisdiction;—to Controversies to which the United States shall be a Party;—to Controversies between two or more States;— <u>between a State and Citizens of another State</u>,—between Citizens of different States,—between Citizens of the same State claiming Lands under Grants of different States, <u>and between a State, or the Citizens thereof, and foreign States, Citizens or Subjects.</u> [Changed by the 11th Amendment.]

3.2.2 In all Cases affecting Ambassadors, other public Ministers and Consuls, and those in which a State shall be Party, the supreme Court shall have original Jurisdiction. In all the other Cases before mentioned, the supreme Court shall have appellate Jurisdiction, both as to Law and Fact, with such Exceptions, and under such Regulations as the Congress shall make.

3.2.3 The Trial of all Crimes, except in Cases of Impeachment, shall be by Jury; and such Trial shall be held in the State where the said Crimes shall have been committed; but when not committed within any State, the Trial shall be at such Place or Places as the Congress may by Law have directed.

Section 3

3.3.1 Treason against the United States, shall consist only in levying War against them, or in adhering to their Enemies, giving them Aid and Comfort. No Person shall be convicted of Treason unless on the Testimony of two Witnesses to the same overt Act, or on Confession in open Court.

3.3.2 The Congress shall have Power to declare the Punishment of Treason, but no Attainder of Treason shall work Corruption of Blood, or Forfeiture except during the Life of the Person attainted.

Article IV

Section 1

Full Faith and Credit shall be given in each State to the public Acts, Records, and judicial Proceedings of every other State. And the Congress may by general Laws prescribe the Manner in which such Acts, Records and Proceedings shall be proved, and the Effect thereof.

Section 2

4.2.1 The Citizens of each State shall be entitled to all Privileges and Immunities of Citizens in the several States.

4.2.2 A Person charged in any State with Treason, Felony, or other Crime, who shall flee from Justice, and be found in another State, shall on Demand of the executive Authority of the State from which he fled, be delivered up, to be removed to the State having Jurisdiction of the Crime.

4.2.3 <u>No Person held to Service or Labour in one State, under the Laws thereof, escaping into another, shall, in Consequence of any Law or Regulation therein, be discharged from such Service or Labour, but shall be delivered up on Claim of the Party to whom such Service or Labour may be due.</u> [Made obsolete by the 13th Amendment.]

Section 3

4.3.1 New States may be admitted by the Congress into this Union; but no new State shall be formed or erected within the Jurisdiction of any other State; nor any State be formed by the Junction of two or more States, or Parts of States, without the Consent of the Legislatures of the States concerned as well as of the Congress.

4.3.2 The Congress shall have Power to dispose of and make all needful Rules and Regulations respecting the Territory or other Property belonging to the United States; and nothing in this Constitution shall be so construed as to Prejudice any Claims of the United States, or of any particular State.

Section 4

The United States shall guarantee to every State in this Union a Republican Form of Government, and shall protect each of them against Invasion; and on Application of the Legislature, or of the Executive (when the Legislature cannot be convened), against domestic Violence.

Article V

Section 1 The Congress, whenever two thirds of both Houses shall deem it necessary, shall propose Amendments to this Constitution, or, on the Application of the Legislatures of two thirds of the several States, shall call a Convention for proposing Amendments,

Section 2 which, in either Case, shall be valid to all Intents and Purposes, as Part of this Constitution, when ratified by the Legislatures of three fourths of the several States, or by Conventions in three fourths thereof, as the one or the other Mode of Ratification may be proposed by the Congress;

Section 3 Provided that no Amendment which may be made prior to the Year One thousand eight hundred and eight shall in any Manner affect the first and fourth Clauses in the Ninth Section of the first Article; and that no State, without its Consent, shall be deprived of its equal Suffrage in the Senate.

Article VI

Section 1 All Debts contracted and Engagements entered into, before the Adoption of this Constitution, shall be as valid against the United States under this Constitution, as under the Confederation.

Section 2 This Constitution, and the Laws of the United States which shall be made in Pursuance thereof; and all Treaties made, or which shall be made, under the Authority of the United States, shall be the supreme Law of the Land; and the Judges in every State shall be bound thereby, any Thing in the Constitution or Laws of any State to the Contrary notwithstanding.

Section 3 The Senators and Representatives before mentioned, and the Members of the several State Legislatures, and all executive and judicial Officers, both of the United States and of the several States, shall be bound by Oath or Affirmation, to support this Constitution; but no religious Test shall ever be required as a Qualification to any Office or public Trust under the United States.

Article VII

The Ratification of the Conventions of nine States, shall be sufficient for the Establishment of this Constitution between the States so ratifying the Same.

Done in Convention by the Unanimous Consent of the States present the Seventeenth Day of September in the Year of our Lord one thousand seven hundred and Eighty seven and of the Independence of the United States of America the Twelfth In witness whereof We have hereunto subscribed our Names,

Go. WASHINGTON — Presidt.
and deputy from Virginia

New Hampshire
> JOHN LANGDON   NICHOLAS GILMAN

Massachusetts
> NATHANIEL GORHAM   RUFUS KING

Connecticut
> WM. SAML. JOHNSON   ROGER SHERMAN

New York
> ALEXANDER HAMILTON

New Jersey
> WIL: LIVINGSTON   DAVID BREARLEY
> WM. PATERSON   JONA: DAYTON

Pennsylvania
> B FRANKLIN   THOMAS MIFFLIN
> ROBT MORRIS   GEO. CLYMER
> THOS. FITZ SIMONS   JARED INGERSOLL
> JAMES WILSON   GOUV MORRIS

Delaware
> GEO: READ   GUNNING BEDFORD jun
> JOHN DICKINSON   RICHARD BASSETT
> JACO: BROOM

Maryland
> JAMES MCHENRY   DAN OF ST THOS. JENIFER
> DANL CARROLL

Virginia
> JOHN BLAIR   JAMES MADISON jr

North Carolina
> WM. BLOUNT   RICHD. DOBBS SPAIGHT
> HU WILLIAMSON

South Carolina
> J. RUTLEDGE   CHARLES COTESWORTH PINCKNEY
> CHARLES PINCKNEY
> PIERCE BUTLER

Georgia WILLIAM FEW   ABR BALDWIN

In Convention Monday, September 17th, 1787.

Present

The States of New Hampshire, Massachusetts, Connecticut, MR. Hamilton from New York, New Jersey, Pennsylvania, Delaware, Maryland, Virginia, North Carolina, South Carolina and Georgia.

Resolved,

That the preceding Constitution be laid before the United States in Congress assembled, and that it is the Opinion of this Convention, that it should afterwards be submitted to a Convention of Delegates, chosen in each State by the People thereof, under the Recommendation of its Legislature, for their Assent and Ratification; and that each Convention assenting to, and ratifying the Same, should give Notice thereof to the United States in Congress assembled. Resolved, That it is the Opinion of this Convention, that as soon as the Conventions of nine States shall have ratified this Constitution, the United States in Congress assembled should fix a Day on which Electors should be appointed by the States which have ratified the same, and a Day on which the Electors should assemble to vote for the President, and the Time and Place for commencing Proceedings under this Constitution. That after such Publication the Electors should be appointed, and the Senators and Representatives elected: That the Electors should meet on the Day fixed for the Election of the President, and should transmit their Votes certified, signed, sealed and directed, as the Constitution requires, to the Secretary of the United States in Congress assembled, that the Senators and Representatives should convene at the Time and Place assigned; that the Senators should appoint a President of the Senate, for the sole purpose of receiving, opening and counting the Votes for President; and, that after he shall be chosen, the Congress, together with the President, should, without Delay, proceed to execute this Constitution.

By the Unanimous Order of the Convention

Go. WASHINGTON — Presidt.
W. JACKSON Secretary

Amendments to the Constitution

On September 25, 1789, the First Congress of the United States proposed the first 12 amendments to the Constitution. The original 'Bill of Rights', all 12 Articles, is displayed in the National Archives Museum. Ten of the proposed 12 amendments were ratified by three-fourths of the states by December 15, 1791. In 1992, over 200 years after the first states ratified it, Article 2 was ratified as the 27th Amendment. Article 1 has been ratified by 11 states; **Our First Right** *is our effort to gain ratification by the 27 more states required to make it the 28th Amendment: no U.S. congressional district shall contain more than 50,000 persons.*

Congress of the United States begun and held at the City of New-York, on Wednesday the fourth of March, one thousand seven hundred and eighty nine.

THE Conventions of a number of the States, having at the time of their adopting the Constitution, expressed a desire, in order to prevent misconstruction or abuse of its powers, that further declaratory and restrictive clauses should be added: And as extending the ground of public confidence in the Government, will best ensure the beneficent ends of its institution.

RESOLVED by the Senate and House of Representatives of the United States of America, in Congress assembled, two thirds of both Houses concurring, that the following Articles be proposed to the Legislatures of the several States, as amendments to the Constitution of the United States, all, or any of which Articles, when ratified by three fourths of the said Legislatures, to be valid to all intents and purposes, as part of the said Constitution; viz.

ARTICLES in addition to, and Amendment of the Constitution of the United States of America, proposed by Congress, and ratified by the Legislatures of the several States, pursuant to the fifth Article of the original Constitution.

[The following is a transcription of the first ten amendments to the Constitution in their original form. Ratified December 15, 1791 they are restrictions on the servants, but are erroneously called 'Bill of Rights'.]

Amendment I

Congress shall make no law respecting an establishment of religion, or prohibiting the free exercise thereof; or abridging the freedom of speech, or of the press; or the right of the people peaceably to assemble, and to petition the Government for a redress of grievances.

Amendment II

A well regulated Militia, being necessary to the security of a free State, the right of the people to keep and bear Arms, shall not be infringed.

Amendment III

No Soldier shall, in time of peace be quartered in any house, without the consent of the Owner, nor in time of war, but in a manner to be prescribed by law.

Amendment IV

The right of the people to be secure in their persons, houses, papers, and effects, against unreasonable searches and seizures, shall not be violated, and no Warrants shall issue, but upon probable cause, supported by Oath or affirmation, and particularly describing the place to be searched, and the persons or things to be seized.

Amendment V

No person shall be held to answer for a capital, or otherwise infamous crime, unless on a presentment or indictment of a Grand Jury, except in cases arising in the land or naval forces, or in the Militia, when in actual service in time of War or public danger; nor shall any person be subject for the same offence to be twice put in jeopardy of life or limb; nor shall be compelled in any criminal case to be a witness against himself, nor be deprived of life, liberty, or property, without due process of law; nor shall private property be taken for public use, without just compensation.

Amendment VI

In all criminal prosecutions, the accused shall enjoy the right to a speedy and public trial, by an impartial jury of the State and district wherein the crime shall have been committed, which district shall have been previously ascertained by law, and to be informed of the nature and cause of the accusation; to be confronted with the witnesses against him; to have compulsory process for obtaining witnesses in his favor, and to have the Assistance of Counsel for his defence.

Amendment VII

In Suits at common law, where the value in controversy shall exceed twenty dollars, the right of trial by jury shall be preserved, and no fact tried by a jury, shall be otherwise re-examined in any Court of the United States, than according to the rules of the common law.

Amendment VIII

Excessive bail shall not be required, nor excessive fines imposed, nor cruel and unusual punishments inflicted.

Amendment IX

The enumeration in the Constitution, of certain rights, shall not be construed to deny or disparage others retained by the people.

Amendment X

The powers not delegated to the United States by the Constitution, nor prohibited by it to the States, are reserved to the States respectively, or to the people.

Amendment XI

Passed by Congress March 4, 1794. Ratified February 7, 1795.

Article III, section 2, of the Constitution was modified by amendment 11.

The Judicial power of the United States shall not be construed to extend to any suit in law or equity, commenced or prosecuted against one of the United States by Citizens of another State, or by Citizens or Subjects of any Foreign State.

Amendment XII

Passed by Congress December 9, 1803. Ratified June 15, 1804.

A portion of Article II, section 1 of the Constitution was superseded by the 12th amendment.

The Electors shall meet in their respective states and vote by ballot for President and Vice-President, one of whom, at least, shall not be an inhabitant of the same state with themselves; they shall name in their ballots the person voted for as President, and in distinct ballots the person voted for as Vice-President, and they shall make distinct lists of all persons voted for as President, and of all persons voted for as Vice-President, and of the number of votes for each, which lists they shall sign and certify, and transmit sealed to the seat of the government of the United States, directed to the President of the Senate; — the President of the Senate shall, in the presence of the Senate and House of Representatives, open all the certificates and the votes shall then be counted; — The person having the greatest number of votes for President, shall be the President, if such number be a majority of the whole number of Electors appointed; and if no person have such majority, then from the persons having the highest numbers not exceeding three on the list of those voted for as President, the House of Representatives shall choose immediately, by ballot, the President. But in choosing the President, the votes shall be taken by states, the representation from each state having one vote; a quorum for this purpose shall consist of a member or members from two-thirds of the states, and a majority of all the states shall be necessary to a choice. [And if the House of Representatives shall not choose a President whenever the right of choice shall devolve upon them, before the fourth day of March next following, then the Vice-President shall act as President, as in case of the death or other constitutional disability of the President. –]* The person having the greatest number of votes as Vice-President, shall be the Vice-President, if such number be a majority of the whole number of Electors appointed, and if no person have a majority, then from the two highest numbers on the list, the Senate shall choose the Vice-

President; a quorum for the purpose shall consist of two-thirds of the whole number of Senators, and a majority of the whole number shall be necessary to a choice. But no person constitutionally ineligible to the office of President shall be eligible to that of Vice-President of the United States.

*Superseded by section 3 of the 20th amendment.

Amendment XIII

Passed by Congress January 31, 1865. Ratified December 6, 1865.

A portion of Article IV, section 2, of the Constitution was superseded by the 13th amendment.

Section 1.
Neither slavery nor involuntary servitude, except as a punishment for crime whereof the party shall have been duly convicted, shall exist within the United States, or any place subject to their jurisdiction.

Section 2.
Congress shall have power to enforce this article by appropriate legislation.

Amendment XIV

Passed by Congress June 13, 1866. Ratified July 9, 1868.

Article I, section 2, of the Constitution was modified by section 2 of the 14th amendment.

Section 1.
All persons born or naturalized in the United States, and subject to the jurisdiction thereof, are citizens of the United States and of the State wherein they reside. No State shall make or enforce any law which shall abridge the privileges or immunities of citizens of the United States; nor shall any State deprive any person of life, liberty, or property, without due process of law; nor deny to any person within its jurisdiction the equal protection of the laws.

Section 2.
Representatives shall be apportioned among the several States according to their respective numbers, counting the whole number of persons in each State, excluding Indians not taxed. But when the right to vote at any election for the choice of electors for President and Vice-President of the United States, Representatives in Congress, the Executive and Judicial officers of a State, or the members of the Legislature thereof, is denied to any of the male inhabitants of such State, being twenty-one years of age,* and citizens of the United States, or in any way abridged, except for participation in rebellion, or other crime, the basis of representation therein shall be reduced in the proportion which the number of such male citizens shall bear to the whole number of male citizens twenty-one years of age in such State.

Section 3.
No person shall be a Senator or Representative in Congress, or elector of President and Vice-President, or hold any office, civil or military, under the United States, or under any State, who, having previously taken an oath, as a member of Congress, or as an officer of the United States, or as a member of any State legislature, or as an executive or judicial officer of any State, to support the

Constitution of the United States, shall have engaged in insurrection or rebellion against the same, or given aid or comfort to the enemies thereof. But Congress may by a vote of two-thirds of each House, remove such disability.

Section 4.

The validity of the public debt of the United States, authorized by law, including debts incurred for payment of pensions and bounties for services in suppressing insurrection or rebellion, shall not be questioned. But neither the United States nor any State shall assume or pay any debt or obligation incurred in aid of insurrection or rebellion against the United States, or any claim for the loss or emancipation of any slave; but all such debts, obligations and claims shall be held illegal and void.

Section 5.

The Congress shall have the power to enforce, by appropriate legislation, the provisions of this article.

Changed by section 1 of the 26th amendment.

Amendment XV

Passed by Congress February 26, 1869. Ratified February 3, 1870.

Section 1.

The right of citizens of the United States to vote shall not be denied or abridged by the United States or by any State on account of race, color, or previous condition of servitude.

Section 2.

The Congress shall have the power to enforce this article by appropriate legislation.

Amendment XVI

Passed by Congress July 2, 1909. Ratified February 3, 1913.

Article I, section 9 of the Constitution was supposedly (arguably) modified by amendment 16.

The Congress shall have power to lay and collect taxes on incomes, from whatever source derived, without apportionment among the several States, and without regard to any census or enumeration.

Amendment XVII

Passed by Congress May 13, 1912. Ratified April 8, 1913.

Article I, section 3, of the Constitution was modified by the 17th amendment.

The Senate of the United States shall be composed of two Senators from each State, elected by the people thereof, for six years; and each Senator shall have one vote. The electors in each State shall have the qualifications requisite for electors of the most numerous branch of the State legislatures.

When vacancies happen in the representation of any State in the Senate, the executive authority of such State shall issue writs of election to fill such vacancies: *Provided*, That the legislature of any State may empower the executive thereof to make temporary appointments until the people fill the vacancies by election as the legislature may direct.

This amendment shall not be so construed as to affect the election or term of any Senator chosen before it becomes valid as part of the Constitution.

Amendment XVIII

Passed by Congress December 18, 1917. Ratified January 16, 1919. Repealed by amendment 21.

Section 1.
After one year from the ratification of this article the manufacture, sale, or transportation of intoxicating liquors within, the importation thereof into, or the exportation thereof from the United States and all territory subject to the jurisdiction thereof for beverage purposes is hereby prohibited.

Section 2.
The Congress and the several States shall have concurrent power to enforce this article by appropriate legislation.

Section 3.
This article shall be inoperative unless it shall have been ratified as an amendment to the Constitution by the legislatures of the several States, as provided in the Constitution, within seven years from the date of the submission hereof to the States by the Congress.

Amendment XIX

Passed by Congress June 4, 1919. Ratified August 18, 1920.

The right of citizens of the United States to vote shall not be denied or abridged by the United States or by any State on account of sex.

Congress shall have power to enforce this article by appropriate legislation.

Amendment XX

Passed by Congress March 2, 1932. Ratified January 23, 1933.

Article I, section 4, of the Constitution was modified by section 2 of this amendment. In addition, a portion of the 12th amendment was superseded by section 3.

Section 1.
The terms of the President and the Vice President shall end at noon on the 20th day of January, and the terms of Senators and Representatives at noon on the 3d day of January, of the years in which such terms would have ended if this article had not been ratified; and the terms of their successors shall then begin.

Section 2.

The Congress shall assemble at least once in every year, and such meeting shall begin at noon on the 3d day of January, unless they shall by law appoint a different day.

Section 3.

If, at the time fixed for the beginning of the term of the President, the President elect shall have died, the Vice President elect shall become President. If a President shall not have been chosen before the time fixed for the beginning of his term, or if the President elect shall have failed to qualify, then the Vice

President elect shall act as President until a President shall have qualified; and the Congress may by law provide for the case wherein neither a President elect nor a Vice President elect shall have qualified, declaring who shall then act as President, or the manner in which one who is to act shall be selected, and such person shall act accordingly until a President or Vice President shall have qualified.

Section 4.

The Congress may by law provide for the case of the death of any of the persons from whom the House of Representatives may choose a President whenever the right of choice shall have devolved upon them, and for the case of the death of any of the persons from whom the Senate may choose a Vice President whenever the right of choice shall have devolved upon them.

Section 5.

Sections 1 and 2 shall take effect on the 15th day of October following the ratification of this article.

Section 6.

This article shall be inoperative unless it shall have been ratified as an amendment to the Constitution by the legislatures of three-fourths of the several States within seven years from the date of its submission.

Amendment XXI

Passed by Congress February 20, 1933. Ratified December 5, 1933.

Section 1.

The eighteenth article of amendment to the Constitution of the United States is hereby repealed.

Section 2.

The transportation or importation into any State, Territory, or possession of the United States for delivery or use therein of intoxicating liquors, in violation of the laws thereof, is hereby prohibited.

Section 3.

This article shall be inoperative unless it shall have been

ratified as an amendment to the Constitution by conventions in the several States, as provided in the Constitution, within seven years from the date of the submission hereof to the States by the Congress.

Amendment XXII

Passed by Congress March 21, 1947. Ratified February 27, 1951.

Section 1.
No person shall be elected to the office of the President more than twice, and no person who has held the office of President, or acted as President, for more than two years of a term to which some other person was elected President shall be elected to the office of the President more than once. But this Article shall not apply to any person holding the office of President when this Article was proposed by the Congress, and shall not prevent any person who may be holding the office of President, or acting as President, during the term within which this Article becomes operative from holding the office of President or acting as President during the remainder of such term.

Section 2.
This article shall be inoperative unless it shall have been ratified as an amendment to the Constitution by the legislatures of three-fourths of the several States within seven years from the date of its submission to the States by the Congress.

Amendment XXIII

Passed by Congress June 16, 1960. Ratified March 29, 1961.

Section 1.
The District constituting the seat of Government of the United States shall appoint in such manner as the Congress may direct:

A number of electors of President and Vice President equal to the whole number of Senators and Representatives in Congress to which the District would be entitled if it were a State, but in no event more than the least populous State; they shall be in addition to those appointed by the States, but they shall be considered, for the purposes of the election of President and Vice President, to be electors appointed by a State; and they shall meet in the District and perform such duties as provided by the twelfth article of amendment.

Section 2.
The Congress shall have power to enforce this article by appropriate legislation.

Amendment XXIV

Passed by Congress August 27, 1962. Ratified January 23, 1964.

Section 1.
The right of citizens of the United States to vote in any primary or other election for President or Vice President, for electors for President or Vice President, or for Senator or Representative in Congress, shall not be denied or abridged by the United States or any State by reason of failure to pay any poll tax or other tax.

Section 2.
The Congress shall have power to enforce this article by appropriate legislation.

Amendment XXV

Passed by Congress July 6, 1965. Ratified February 10, 1967.

Article II, section 1, of the Constitution was affected by the 25th amendment.

Section 1.
In case of the removal of the President from office or of his death or resignation, the Vice President shall become President.

Section 2.
Whenever there is a vacancy in the office of the Vice President, the President shall nominate a Vice President who shall take office upon confirmation by a majority vote of both Houses of Congress.

Section 3.
Whenever the President transmits to the President pro tempore of the Senate and the Speaker of the House of Representatives his written declaration that he is unable to discharge the powers and duties of his office, and until he transmits to them a written declaration to the contrary, such powers and duties shall be discharged by the Vice President as Acting President.

Section 4.
Whenever the Vice President and a majority of either the principal officers of the executive departments or of such other body as Congress may by law provide, transmit to the President pro tempore of the Senate and the Speaker of the House of Representatives their written declaration that the President is unable to discharge the powers and duties of his office, the Vice President shall immediately assume the powers and duties of the office as Acting President.

Thereafter, when the President transmits to the President pro tempore of the Senate and the Speaker of the House of Representatives his written declaration that no inability exists, he shall resume the powers and duties of his office unless the Vice President and a majority of either the principal officers of the executive department or of such other body as Congress may by law provide, transmit within four days to the President pro tempore of the Senate and the Speaker of the House of Representatives their written declaration that the President is unable to discharge the powers and duties of his office. Thereupon Congress shall decide the issue, assembling within forty-eight hours for that purpose if not in session. If the Congress, within twenty-one days after receipt of the latter written declaration, or, if Congress is not in session, within twenty-one days after Congress is required to assemble, determines by two-thirds vote of both Houses that the President is unable to discharge the powers and duties of his office, the Vice President shall continue to discharge the same as Acting President; otherwise, the President shall resume the powers and duties of his office.

Amendment XXVI

Passed by Congress March 23, 1971. Ratified July 1, 1971.

Amendment 14, section 2, of the Constitution was modified by section 1 of the 26th amendment.

Section 1.
The right of citizens of the United States, who are eighteen years of age or older, to vote shall not be denied or abridged by the United States or by any State on account of age.

Section 2.
The Congress shall have power to enforce this article by appropriate legislation.

Amendment XXVII

Passed by Congress Sept. 25, 1789. Ratified May 7, 1992.

No law, varying the compensation for the services of the Senators and Representatives, shall take effect, until an election of Representatives shall have intervened.

Appendix F
AmericaAgain! Declaration

When a government has ceased to protect the lives, liberty and property of We The People from whom its legitimate powers are derived, and for the advancement of whose happiness it was instituted, and so far from being a guarantee for the enjoyment of those inestimable and inalienable rights, becomes an instrument in the hands of evil rulers for their oppression;

When the federal republican Constitution, which they have sworn to support, no longer has a substantial existence – the whole nature of our servant government having been changed without our consent, from a restricted republic of sovereign States to a consolidated central despotism in which productive Americans are forced to work for imperious bureaucrats and government functionaries, favored industries, tyrannical and abusive Big Tech corporations more powerful than governments, and a growing parasitic population that has rendered our Republic fully Communist;

When, long after the spirit of the Constitution has departed, moderation is thrown to the wind by those in power, the semblance of freedom removed, and the forms of the Constitution discontinued as in the arrogant violation of the Second Amendment's proscription against any infringement of the right of the People to keep and bear arms (which Article I, Section 8, Clause 15 assumes is the duty of all able-bodied Americans);

When for five generations, We The People have suffered the general government's instigation, perpetration, funding, and defense of organized crime;

When, far from our petitions being regarded, citizens who show public concern for these infringements and usurpations are marked as 'terrorists' or arrested by tyrannical new city, state, and federal agencies hatched under the guises first of 'war on terror' then of a hoax 'pandemic';

When, with each new legislature, administration, and federal Supreme Court, the public servants of We The People more openly and arrogantly burden us and encroach on our privacy; on our liberty to travel freely; on our ability to enjoy our own property freely or to raise our children as we see fit; on our ability to actually own our property free and clear; to operate our farms, shops, or businesses as we see fit without posing any harm to others; on our ability to even open our small businesses, eat in restaurants or even gather in our own homes and churches! – all under the threat of a proven Chinese-engineered hoax 'pandemic'; and now have colluded in both corrupt political parties to openly, cynically steal a national election in which one candidate received easily 80 million true votes, yet was 'defeated' by a nearly senile puppet candidate whose gaslighting operation enlisted a massive, Communist-style phalanx of state-owned media (Google, Twitter, YouTube, Facebook, ABC, MSNBC, CBS, CNN, NPR, Fox News and others);

In consequence of such acts of malfeasance and abdication on the part of the servant government, anarchy threatens to dissolve civil society into its original elements, the first law of nature and the right of self-preservation, the powers reserved by We The People as stipulated in the U.S. Constitution, Amendment X, enjoins not only our right but a sacred obligation to our posterity, to enforce the specific limits of federal power as enumerated in that supreme Law of the Land, by all the lawful and necessary means provided in that Constitution, including but not limited to the Courts of our sovereign States and such federal legislative reforms as We The People may effect, to secure our welfare and happiness.

Nations, as well as individuals, are amenable for their acts to the public opinion of mankind. A statement of a part of our grievances is therefore submitted to an impartial world along with the peaceful, lawful, and legitimate enforcement steps that We The People of these United States now intend to take, to which the nations of the earth are witness.

We The People of the fifty sovereign States of America, creators of the U.S. Constitution, acknowledge the duty of every American to preserve, protect, and defend that Supreme Law. We hereby announce to a watching world our intention to restore the original form, purpose, and enumerated limits of our government, superintending from this day forward our State courts and federal servants so that we may once more secure the Blessings of Liberty to ourselves and to our posterity.

These United States have a solemn duty to serve their citizen masters by enforcing our supreme Law of the Land when one or more branches of federal government violate it. When the States neglect this duty, our Declaration of Independence establishes that this duty and the power to execute it return to the people at large for their exercise. The three branches of federal government are creatures — things created by us in the U.S. Constitution, the highest law in this Republic.

In the Constitution, We the People clearly enumerate the powers of federal government. We retain any powers not specifically enumerated therein, to ourselves and our sovereign States. Any exercise of power by government beyond those listed powers is an egregious violation of the Supreme Law.

President Jefferson said that *"in questions of powers…let no more be heard of confidence in man, but bind him down from mischief by the chains of the Constitution"*. Such "binding down" can be peaceably accomplished by binding the federal purse and by We the People and sovereign States enforcing that Law of Limitation for the first time in American history.

The present $3.9 trillion annual federal revenue – and the far larger mountain of financial derivatives that Congress allows the financial industry to create from thin air and our labor – have spawned a brood of corruptions as unlimited oceans of money always do. This ocean of illicit D.C. cash has spawned unconstitutional federal powers, cabinet departments, agents, agencies, programs, projects, offices, regulations, and financial industry 'assets' that for sheer number are impossible to list here but that threaten our liberties, property, livelihood, posterity, and public morals, making a joke of our Supreme Law.

In Federalist #28, Alexander Hamilton said that by merely exercising our power as creators of the federal government, we can prevail: *"the larger the American population would become, the more effectively we can resist federal government tyranny… Power being almost always the rival of power, the general government will at all times stand ready to check the usurpations of State governments, and these will have the same disposition towards the general government. The People, by throwing themselves into either scale, will infallibly make it preponderate. If their rights are invaded by either, they can make use of the other as the instrument of redress..".* The mission of AmericaAgain! is to make good on the guarantees offered in the Federalist Papers to our fore-fathers.

All three branches of our federal creature have ceased to check-and-balance one another, instead colluding over the past 150 years abusing the "necessary and proper", "general welfare", and "interstate commerce" clauses to fashion a lawless, limitless system of power, pork, and perquisites warned against by James Madison, the primary author of the Constitution: *"…it is evident that there is not a single power whatever, which may not have some reference to the common defense or the general welfare; nor a power of any magnitude which, in its exercise, does not involve or admit an application of money. The government, therefore, which possesses power in either one or other of these extents, is a government without the limitations formed by a particular enumeration of powers.*

"Consequently, the meaning and effect of this particular enumeration is destroyed by the exposition given to these general phrases… Congress is authorized to provide money for the common defense and general welfare. In both, is subjoined to this authority an enumeration of the cases to which their power shall extend…a question arises whether (any) particular measure be within the enumerated authorities vested in Congress. If it be, the money requisite for it may be applied to it; if it be not, no such application can be made.

"It is incumbent in this, as in every other exercise of power by the federal government, to prove from the Constitution, that it grants the particular power exercised.

"With respect to the words 'general welfare', I have always regarded them as qualified by the detail of powers connected with them. To take them in a literal and unlimited sense would be a metamorphosis of the Constitution into a character which there is a host of proofs was not contemplated by its creators."

Congress and presidents for many generations have violated the highest law in America in precisely this blank-check manner, at a cost of tens of trillions of dollars – and at the further cost of our liberty, privacy, and rights to property and peaceful self-government. When a government of, by, and for The People stands in perennial, collusive violation of the Constitution, We The People have constitutional authority to take enforcement action. The duty of constitutional law enforcement falls on We the People, not by resisting government's lawlessness with lawlessness of our own, but by having the courts of our States bring law enforcement power to bear as our right and duty under that Law.

With respect to compliance with his "Oath or Affirmation, to support this Constitution", no public official can be allowed to be the judge of his own case, as Presidents Jefferson and Madison observed.

The nefarious practice of executive orders is nowhere authorized in Article II of the Constitution. Numerous such executive fiats are demonstrable violations of the limited powers stipulated in Article II, yet We The People have had no voice in said imperial edicts issued by presidents. The same principle holds true for treaties signed by tyrannical presidents under the noses of the American people to our detriment, without popular review before being trundled through a complicit U.S. Senate.

Every public official's oath is made to We the People; the Constitution commands that the official be bound by that oath; thus We the People have the right to enforce that oath and the power to do so as well, for no right can exist without an effective remedy, including remedy via State courts.

With the Chinese virus hoax, Congress' corrupt, imperious practices to oust a sitting president then infested State, county, and municipal governments; as U.S. Supreme Court Justice Louis Brandeis suggested in his 1928 dissenting opinion in Olmsted v. U.S.: *"In a government of laws…Our government is the potent, the omnipresent teacher. For good or for ill, it teaches the whole people by its example. Crime is contagious. If the government becomes a lawbreaker, it breeds contempt for law…"*.

Congress has perennially refused to balance its federal budgets.

The flow of illegal aliens across our borders reached epidemic proportions long ago, yet Congress refused to allow President Trump to seal the border, instead arming a ticking time bomb against our culture and civil order; saddling Taxpayers with the cost of socialist programs for politicians' future political pawns. America was a melting pot Republic with a common language, currency, culture and work ethic; now it is polyglot warring factions seeking African-America, Mexican-America, Israeli-America, and Muslim America.

The U.S. Congress was intended to be populated by citizen-statesmen for limited terms so that no lifelong political oligarchy would rule over the citizens as is now the case, with members of Congress being wealthy, insular individuals with little affinity with, or empathy for, the average citizen. Members of Congress shamelessly enjoy fat pensions, insurance policies, private spas, limousines, private jets hidden in federal budgets, and much more – paid for by citizens who never enjoy such free luxuries.

The original intent of the Constitution's framers was to balance the Legislative branch with two bodies, the House of Representatives representing the interests of the People, and the Senate representing the interests of the States. Prior to

1913, the individual State legislatures appointed representatives to serve in the US Senate who were expected to act and vote in the interest of the State or were subject to immediate recall and replacement.

During the administration of Woodrow Wilson, Congress introduced the Seventeenth Amendment, which was ratified under questionable circumstances. The new amendment stripped away a critical power of the States to control D.C. by balancing the desires of the mob with cooler heads in their deliberative legislatures. Making both houses of Congress elected directly by the People opened the Senate to even greater corruption by moneyed interests and their lobbyists.

Many socialist accretions that have drained America's private sector wealth and inflated dependent populations, could never have passed if the sovereign States had retained direct control of the U.S. Senate as designed by the framers. Repealing the 17th Amendment will restore this critical check-and-balance mechanism as our founding fathers intended when they designed the U.S. Constitution.

Because the 13th Amendment disallows slavery or involuntary servitude, national conscription for military or other national service is illegal.

In the interests of a massive industry rather than national security, the U.S. Congress has refused to cut off funding for undeclared, unprovoked foreign attacks and invasions ordered or maintained by presidents who cannot prove they serve a national defense purpose. There will always be men in the world whose goal is plunder, to amass insane wealth; such chieftains buy and trade politicians as game pieces, world without end. They amass plunder using the U.S. military as free mercenaries.

The U.S. Constitution only authorizes Congress to use military power in declared war with a Navy, or with a Citizen Militia mustered for national purposes for a maximum of two years, or to use the Citizen Militia of the Several States, with officers and training provided by the States, "to execute the Laws of the Union, suppress Insurrections, and repel Invasions". No other federal armed forces are authorized by the Constitution.

Thus, it is illegal for full-time U.S. military ground forces to even exist, much less to plunder foreign resources or threaten foreign people who present no threat to us, under the guise of 'democracy', 'peacekeeping', 'war on terror', or 'protecting American interests abroad'.

The only difference that the United States military industry brings to conquered lands is replacing Arab family crests or banana republic dictators' logos with U.S.-based corporate logos. While this lawless plunder continues, We the People will continue to be regarded as enemies by citizens of the world.

The majority of Americans was once Christian; most still profess Christianity at least in name. The melting-pot culture that made America the envy of the world was not theocracy, but was demonstrably the ethic of Christ, not of Mormonism,

Judaism, or Islam. We The People refuse to have America become as Europe – another battleground for a 1,400-year old Islamic jihad.

The legislation labeled 'Legal Tender Act' beginning in 1862 and collusive rulings by the U.S. Supreme Court in 1871 and 1884 violated the U.S. Constitution's stipulations in Article I, Sections 8 and 10. By law, only Congress has the power only to coin gold and silver, and every State shall use only gold and silver coin as legal tender. All paper scrip – and the tens of trillions of dollars annually in derivative financial instruments – are illegal and immoral, yet enabled under the protection of Congress, whose members have overseen and acquiesced in a 150-year-old conspiracy to defraud, embezzle from, and place into servitude the citizens they pretend to serve and represent.

It is *illegal* for Congress to declare that paper shall be considered lawful money. It is *illegal* for Congress to grant a concession to a private cartel using the Federal Reserve brand to manufacture counterfeit (paper) money and to require the People and sovereign States to pay face value plus interest for the worthless scrip. Before Great Depression II falls on our heads, we declare *this will not stand*.

Congress has willfully allowed the Internal Revenue Service to perennially violate the federal tax laws, regulations, and its own operating manual, transforming Taxpayers by terrorist coercion into pack-mules to carry the financial burdens of Congress' demonstrable crimes. We refuse to allow Congress to burden future generations with an equally corrupt revenue-neutral 'fair tax', so-called, that would continue to amass over four times the revenues required to fund enumerated federal powers.

It is *illegal* for Congress to allow its servants, federal judges, to hold the entire population in 50 sovereign states hostage to the 1% sexual pervert lobby. In the Constitution, nowhere do We The People empower Congress or a federal court to hold the population hostage to an immoral minority by the imperial whim of five people in robes who on June 26, 2015 in their preposterous opinion, suggested that sexual perversion would now become 'marriage' in America. *This will not stand*.

Trillion-dollar tech corporations have occupied, captured, and dominate Town Square in every American community. Every major news outlet and social medium is working in lock-step towards Communist, environmental-anarchist goals inimical to our civilization and economy, while stratospherically enriching a tiny band of monopolist billionaires at Google, Facebook, Twitter, YouTube, Microsoft, Apple, Amazon and others who declare their hatred for conservative and Christian America. Year after year, Congress held pointless hearings and promised relief that never comes. Over 150 million Americans' lives remain occupied, dominated, and driven by godless globalists. *This will not stand*.

On a Sunday night in March 2010, the Democrat members of Congress conspired to transform the IRS into an American Gestapo – finally unmasking its terror organization to enforce its unconstitutional 'health care' scheme in which Barack

Hussein Obama was also complicit. Now with the GOP members of Congress fully on board with arrogant tyranny, history proves that if Congress is allowed to fully arrogate this lawless new power, it will never relinquish them. *This will not stand.*

It is illegal for Congress to allow illegal aliens to enter this country and be catered to by federal government — the exact opposite of enforcing immigration laws that every productive American expects to have enforced. Individual works of mercy and foreign missions are biblical outreach; unrestrained communism and open borders are not. The Obama administration and Congress held several hundred million productive Americans hostage on behalf of a militant, tactically shrewd lobby of a few thousand activists. Those who pay property taxes are forced to pay the education, food, clothing, medical, incarceration, and law enforcement bills of an illegal horde, invited in and catered to by a lawless, arrogant, dismissive Congress. *This will not stand.*

Now, the militant Islamist army is following the path opened by the abortionists, by militant sexual perverts, and by the illegal alien lobby. It is illegal for Congress to allow any federal judge to enforce, support, enable, or even allow any alien law-code — whether Islamic sharia or any other — to be recognized or enforced in place of the established civil and criminal laws of these sovereign States. *This will not stand.*

After our long failure to perform our citizen duties, bearing the cost of our abdication on every hand, We the People of these fifty united States intend to lawfully, peacefully begin enforcing the Constitution in each of the 3,141 counties of our 50 States against its violation by our U.S. congressmen and senators, effecting such law enforcement through local AmericaAgain! members singly and statewide in a process called TACTICAL CIVICS™ and using a mechanism called the AmericaAgain! Indictment Engine™.

We the People hereby announce our intention to draft, refine, and push through the passage of the following Legislative Action projects. As a plea-bargaining package offered to any member of Congress indicted by using the AmericaAgain! Indictment Engine™, or as an immunity package for those who have not yet been targeted, We The People will demand that members of the U.S. House of Representatives and the U.S. Senate agree in writing to enact the following:

1) The **Bring Congress Home Act**, or 'BCHA', stipulating: Whereas a general principle of constitutional law in these United States holds that no legislature can bind a subsequent one; and whereas the Apportionment Act of 1929 set a totally arbitrary 435-district limit to the U.S. House of Representatives in clear violation of the intention of Article I, Section 2, Clause 4 and also in clear contravention of the original first Article in the Bill of Rights as passed by the first Congress and sent to the States; and whereas a sufficient number of States have ratified that amendment and it has been recorded as the 28th Amendment to the U.S. Constitution; and whereas the expanded size of the U.S. House demanded by the

U.S. Constitution, in light of the benefits and cost savings of modern technology and the security risk of Congress operating from one location, therefore:

Section 1. No member of Congress shall have a private office or staff located in Washington D.C..

Section 2. All members of Congress shall serve a maximum of two terms.

Section 3. No district of the U.S. House of Representatives shall contain more than 50,000 people, as stipulated in the original First Amendment passed by Congress in 1789 and recently ratified by the State legislatures as the 28th Amendment.

Section 4. To remain properly accountable and accessible to the sovereigns People that (s)he represents, every member of the U.S. House of Representatives shall be provided with a single office located within his/her district, paid staff not exceeding two persons, reasonable office expenses, and the hardware, software, and encryption technology and services required to conduct the business of the U.S. House of Representatives, working from his/her own district.

Section 5. To remain properly accountable and accessible to the sovereign States that the U.S. Senate was originally de-signed to represent, every member of the U.S. Senate shall be provided with a single office located within close proximity to the State capitol, also with paid staff not exceeding six per-sons, reasonable office expenses, and the hardware, software, and encryption technology and services required to conduct the business of the U.S. Senate, working from his/her own State capitol pursuant to such time as the 17th Amendment shall be repealed.

Section 6. Public funds used by any member of Congress shall be limited to the member's salary – which shall in the case of a congressman, effective immediately, be 50% of present salary; office staff, space rent and expenses; self-operated vehicle lease payment, fuel and insurance; coach-class airfare for public business; and mail costs to communicate with his/her sovereigns. An annual audit of expenditures for each member of Congress and his/her staff and office operations shall be posted online on that member's public web page accessible to the public, no later than 60 days after the close of each congressional session.

Section 7. Beyond those listed in Section 6 above, any and all other publicly-funded expenditures inuring to the benefit of a member of Congress shall hereafter be considered illegal use of public funds, including but not limited to: pensions and insurance premiums (retroactive), foreign travel under the guise of legislative business, limousines or other special conveyances, spas, hairdressers, and club memberships.

2) The **Constitutional Courts Act**, stipulating:

Section 1. A consensus exists among the American public that the federal courts have been corrupted and are manipulated by powerful individuals and by lobbyists for industry and special interests, rendering moot the stipulated limitations placed by the People through the U.S. Constitution on its creature, federal government.

> *a. James Madison, Father of the Constitution, in his Virginia Resolution of 1798, and Thomas Jefferson, in his concurring Virginia Resolution, wrote that the States, as the creator parties to the U.S. Constitution, have the right and duty to judge when the U.S. Constitution has been violated by federal government; that the federal government cannot judge of its own infractions*

b. In Article III, Section 1 of the U.S. Constitution, the People grant to Congress the authority to create the inferior federal courts, thus the subject matter jurisdiction of the inferior federal courts is entirely within Congress' discretion.

c. In Article III, Section 2 of the U.S. Constitution, the People grant to Congress the authority to withhold subject matter jurisdiction even from the U.S. supreme Court, using "such Exceptions, and...such Regulations as the Congress shall make".

d. In Article VI, Section 2 of the U.S. Constitution, the People stipulate, "This Constitution...shall be the supreme Law of the Land; and the Judges in every State shall be bound thereby...", which binding includes enforcement as well as obedience.

e. Every federal legislator is now performing his federal duties full-time within his or her own district, which is the jurisdiction of his State Grand Jury and State Court.

f. Therefore, pursuant to the power granted by the People to Congress in U.S. Constitution Article III, Section 2, Clause 2, after the effective date hereof, no federal court shall have jurisdiction in any case in which a member of Congress is charged by his or her own State Grand Jury with violating, or conspiring to violate, the U.S. Constitution.

g. In no such case shall removal from state jurisdiction be available to the accused, whether pursuant to 28 USC 1441, or any subsequent federal law.

Section 2. The American People stipulated in Article I, Section 8 of the U.S. Constitution, that "The Congress shall have power...to constitute tribunals inferior to the supreme Court...", and in Article III, Section 1, that the federal courts are, "such inferior courts as the Congress may from time to time ordain and establish", and in Article III, Section 2, Clause 2, that the U.S. supreme Court, "shall have appellate jurisdiction...with such Exceptions, and under such Regulations as the Congress shall make".

In 1799 in Turner v. Bank of North America (1799), Justice Chase wrote, "The notion has frequently been entertained, that the federal courts derive their judicial power immediately from the Constitution; but the political truth is, that the disposal of the judicial power...belongs to Congress. If Congress has given the power to this Court, we possess it, not otherwise: and if Congress has not given the power to us or to any other Court, it still remains at the legislative disposal."

In Ex parte Bollman (1807), Chief Justice John Marshall wrote, "Courts which are created by written law, and whose jurisdiction is defined by written law, cannot transcend that jurisdiction".

The power of Congress to create inferior federal courts, necessarily implies, as written in U.S. v. Hudson & Goodwin (1812), "the power to limit jurisdiction of those Courts to particular objects".

The U.S. supreme Court held unanimously in Sheldon v. Sill (1850) that because the People in the Constitution did not create inferior federal courts but authorized Congress to create them, that Congress by necessity had power to define and limit their jurisdiction and to withhold jurisdiction of any of the enumerated cases and controversies.

The high court even acknowledged Congress' power to re-examine particular classes of questions previously ruled on by the U.S. supreme Court, as stated in The Francis Wright (1882): "(A)ctual jurisdiction under the [judicial] power is confined within such limits as Congress sees fit to prescribe…What those powers shall be, and to what extent they shall be exercised, are, and always have been, proper subjects of legislative control…Not only may whole classes of cases be kept out of the jurisdiction altogether, but particular classes of questions may be subjected to re-examination and review…".

In Lauf v. E.G. Shinner & Co (1938), the U.S. supreme Court declared, "There can be no question of the power of Congress thus to define and limit the jurisdiction of the inferior courts of the United States".

In Lockerty v. Phillips (1943), the U.S. supreme Court held that Congress has the power of, "withholding jurisdiction from them [federal courts] in the exact degrees and character which to Congress may seem proper for the public good".

Section 3. Therefore, Congress hereby excludes from federal court jurisdiction any and all cases involving:

> *a. Taking of human life, from point of conception;*
>
> *b. Sexual practices or the institution of marriage;*
>
> *c. Healthcare;*
>
> *d. Education;*
>
> *e. Official recognition or application of any foreign law or code within these united States or any of them; and*
>
> *f. Claims of United States control, possession, or juris-diction over any land outside of that granted by We the People (the sovereign People and States) as stipulated in Article I, Section 8, Clause 17, U.S. Constitution.*

Section 4. What constitutes due process in all courts within the united States or any of them shall be defined and determined exclusively from within the Bill of Rights and the American common law, in that order of precedence.

Section 5. In Article III, Section 1 of the U.S. Constitution, the People stipulate, "the judicial Power of the United States shall be vested in one supreme Court, and in such inferior Courts as the Congress may from time to time ordain and establish"; therefore within 12 months of the passage of this Act:

> a. *No 'administrative law' tribunal in these United States shall bind the citizen in any way;*
> b. *No administrative adjudicator shall be referred to as 'judge';*
> c. *No administrative tribunal shall be referred to, or refer to itself, as 'court'; and*
> d. *No administrative process or tribunal shall describe its processes in terms such as 'order', 'subpoena', 'warrant', or 'the record', which are reserved for constitutional judiciary.*

Section 6. Pursuant to provisions of Section 2(f) above and the proposed Return of Sovereign Lands Act, 24 months after enactment of this legislation and thereafter, it shall be a federal felony for any agency, agent, bureau, department, officer, contractor or other representative of the government of these United States of America to claim, own, maintain or operate a purported U.S. court or detention facility that is not located within the land or property stipulated in Article I, Section 8, Clause 17 of the U.S. Constitution.

Section 7. Because Federal Rules of Criminal Procedure Numbers 6 and 7 appear to create an unconstitutional barrier to the established prerogative power of the People when serving in their State Grand Jury, no federal judicial rules shall have any bearing or authority over any State Grand Jury. As U.S. Supreme Court Justice Antonin Scalia wrote in U.S. v. Williams (1992):

"(T)he Grand Jury is an institution separate from the courts, over whose functioning the courts do not preside…Rooted in long centuries of Anglo American history, the Grand Jury is mentioned in the Bill of Rights, but not in the body of the Constitution. It has not been textually assigned, therefore, to any of the branches described in the first three Articles. It is a constitutional fixture in its own right…

In fact, the whole theory of its function is that it belongs to no branch of the institutional government, serving as a kind of buffer or referee between the government and the People…The Grand Jury requires no authorization from its constituting court to initiate an investigation, nor does the prosecutor require leave of court to seek a Grand Jury indictment…[T]he Grand Jury generally operates without the interference of a presiding judge. It swears in its own witnesses, and deliberates in total secrecy."

Section 8. As stipulated in Article I, Section 8, Clause 15 of the U.S. Constitution, the several States retain the power to enforce this legislation by appropriate State legislation and duly authorized Citizen Militia enforcement action within their respective jurisdictions.

3) The **Non-Enumerated Powers Sunset Act,** stipulating:

Section 1. Congress hereby acknowledges as unconstitutional, any and all past enactment of legislation, 'positive law' Code sections and regulations, consent to treaties, or provision of federal funds applied to executive orders that confer on federal government any power not specifically enumerated in the U.S. Constitution or reasonably inferred from the powers enumerated, notwithstanding past creative interpretations applied by all three federal branches, to the terms 'interstate commerce', 'general welfare', and 'necessary and proper', and notwithstanding any and all 'positive law' Code sections drafted, finalized, promulgated, and/or enforced by federal employees who have no direct oversight by, or accountability to, the American People.

No federal 'positive law' regulation shall create a legal duty or liability for any citizen of these United States, unless and until the agency purporting to enforce such a regulation shall have established beyond reasonable doubt that said regulation is clearly and unambiguously authorized by the People in a specific section of the U.S. Constitution.

Congress hereby acknowledges that the government of these United States is a constitutional republic form of government under the Common Law as opposed to the positive law traditions of many foreign countries, notwithstanding the massive Deep State that has created an overwhelming burden of federal regulations produced by bureaucratic careerists at staggering cost to taxpayers.

Congress hereby further acknowledges that ultimate sovereignty in our republic is inherent in the American People rather than in a bureaucracy that propagates, promulgates and defends thousands of new 'positive law' regulations annually, which are too numerous and intentionally too complex for the average American to grasp or understand, much less to oversee or diminish.

The United States Code is the Code of Laws of the United States of America (also referred to as United States Code, U.S. Code, or U.S.C.) and is a compilation and codification of all the general and so-called 'permanent' federal laws of the republic. But no law in this republic can be repugnant to the specific words and spirit of the U.S. Constitution. Any federal law which is found to be in clear violation of, or repugnant to the plain language of the U.S. Constitution is and has been null and void since its enactment.

The U.S. Code does not include regulations issued by executive branch agencies, published in the Code of Federal Regulations (C.F.R.). Proposed and recently adopted regulations are posted in the Federal Register.

Congress shall make available online, at no cost to the user, the 51 titles of the United States Code as maintained by the U.S. House of Representatives Office of the Law Revision Counsel, and the cumulative supplements which are published annually.

Section 2. The Standing Committee to Defund Non-Enumerated Powers (SCDNEP) is hereby created in the U.S. House, to bind this body to obey the U.S. Constitution as actually written.

Section 3. Upon its formation, the SCDNEP shall appropriate adequate funding for a website and appurtenant support to serve and support the Citizens' Volunteer Research Service (CVRS) as described herein.

Section 4. In appropriating funds for CVRS website and support for citizen volunteers, Congress does not suggest that it, a federal servant, has authority to create such an oversight organ for the People themselves; only that Congress seeks hereby to provide for the People's oversight function to the extent that the People themselves require and employ it.

Section 5. Congress hereby acknowledges that the American People themselves, collectively, are sovereign in this and all other matters of federal government, as clearly and unambiguously stipulated in the Preamble, in Article I, Section 8 and especially in Amendment X of the U.S. Constitution, which sections only reiterate the People's original, God-given, organic, inherent, retained power to oversee all operations and budgets of their servants in federal government.

Congress hereby acknowledges that any CVRS Work Group or Supergroup casting its vote to de-fund and terminate any regulation issued by executive branch

agencies shall infer that the CVRS has determined that the regulation in question does usurp, undermine, or countermand the stipulations of the U.S. Constitution or the retained powers of the sovereign People as stipulated in Amendment X of the U.S. Constitution. Said regulation shall become null and void and of no effect, immediately upon said vote.

Section 7. Prior to being funded or observed for any future fiscal year, any federal budget request whether executive or legislative – whether submitted by an agency, bureau, department, office, power, program, code or regulatory body, service branch, or via executive order or treaty – shall be accompanied by a written demonstration that it falls within a specifically enumerated power in Article I Section 8 or Article II Section 2 of the U.S. Constitution or duly ratified Amendment thereto, or can be reasonably inferred by the American citizen of average intelligence to be a rational appurtenance thereto. Any budget request not so accompanied, shall cease to be funded at the end of the then-current fiscal year.

Section 8. Because the functions of federal government were enumerated so as to limit the reach and power of the federal servant, such that it should never be considered either the master or the provider of the People, any agency, bureau, department, office, power, program, code or regulation not specifically enumerated in the U.S. Constitution or being an unambiguously 'necessary and proper' adjunct to the powers enumerated, as can be reasonably inferred by the American citizen of average intelligence, unless proposed and ratified as a constitutional amendment adhering to Article V of the U.S. Constitution, shall be subject to CVRS review and closure.

Section 9. In light of the long history of federal legislative, executive and judicial malfeasance and treachery by stretching the 'interstate commerce', 'general welfare', and 'necessary and proper' clauses, no federal agency, bureau, department, office, power, program, statute, code or regulation shall be added to others in any omnibus bill or amendment. If not enumerated in Article I, Section 8 and requiring application of public funds, each proposed agency, bureau, department, office, power, program, statute, code or regulation shall be proposed as a discrete bill or constitutional amendment.

Section 10. To maintain the delineation between the jurisdiction of an authorizing committee and the House Appropriations Committee, House Rule XXI creates a point of order against unauthorized appropriations in general appropriations bills. While any appropriation in such a bill is out of order unless the expenditure is authorized by existing law, if the point of order is not raised or is waived and the bill is enacted, said unauthorized appropriation is treated as legitimate. This practice has been tantamount to embezzlement of public funds.

Language requiring or permitting government action carries an implicit authorization for money to be appropriated for that purpose. The 'authorization of appropriations' provision limits the authorization of a piece of legislation to the amount and/or to the fiscal years stated. Accordingly, any prior budget authorization appropriating "such sums as may be necessary", without specifying the amount, years, and specifically constitutional purpose for which such appropriations were authorized, shall receive no further funding after the date of enactment hereof.

Section 11. There is hereby authorized a national Citizens' Volunteer Research Service (CVRS) with five citizens per U.S. congressional district, comprising one CVRS Work Group, said citizens selected by each U.S. representative's staff at random from the legislator's congressional district tax and voter rolls.

No citizen selected at random to serve on a CVRS Work Group shall be compelled to serve. All CVRS members shall be volunteers, receiving no remuneration for their service to the public.

Section 12. As with a Grand Jury, all CVRS members selected shall remain anonymous, to protect the Members from lobbying pressure or threats, and from threats or retaliation by endangered government employees.

Section 13. The deliberations of each and every CVRS Work Group shall remain completely confidential within the Work Group. Divulging the name of a CVRS member or divulging in advance of publication on the 'More Constitutional Government' website, any decision of a Work Group to retain or de-fund a federal budget item – whether an agency, bureau, project, code section, regulation or project – shall be a felony.

Section 14. Each CVRS Work Group shall review individual federal codes, regulations and regulatory bodies and associated federal budget line items. Each CVRS Work Group shall review at one time only a single, discrete federal budget line item unless the powers and functions of the agencies, bureaus, programs, code sections or regulations entail several or many similar functions or areas of endeavor appearing to violate the U.S. Constitution, being neither explicitly nor implicitly authorized therein.

Section 15. In such cases, an entire federal agency, bureau or regulatory entity shall be reviewed and voted on for defunding and closure by a CVRS Supergroup, which shall consist of twelve (12) CVRS Work Groups located in twelve (12) states, with two Work Groups from each region (Northeast, South-east, Midwest, South Central, Southwest, Northwest).

Such draconian action by a 'mere' 60 citizens compares favorably to countless coercive actions impacting over 320 million citizens yet imposed by a single federal judge or at most by five justices of the U.S. supreme Court. As set out in the U.S. Constitution, the collective sovereignty of the American People is superior in authority to that of the People's servants, be they legislative, executive or judiciary, particularly when servants have violated the Constitution or occupy an office nowhere authorized by the People through that supreme Law.

Section 16. Each CVRS Work Group shall have 60 days to research, assess, and recommend de-funding and terminating a federal code section or regulation or its associated agency or office. At the conclusion of its deliberations, the CVRS Work Group shall submit the code section, regulation, agency, program or bureau selected for de-funding and termination, to the manager of the CVRS website, for posting.

Within 30 days after said posting, each recommended defunding and termination measure shall be voted on by each and every CVRS Work Group. Each Work Group shall cast one vote, representing the majority vote of that Work Group's members casting a vote on that item.

Section 17. Each Work Group's vote shall be the vote of the U.S. congressman who represents that district. No member of Congress shall influence, counter-mand, veto, or otherwise interfere with final decisions of a CVRS Work Group or Supergroup.

No member of Congress shall recruit, entice, hire, contract, coerce or otherwise obtain the services of any staff member, agent or intermediary to influence or otherwise interfere with a final decision of any CVRS Work Group or Supergroup.

Section 18. De-funding and termination of any federal code section or regulation shall occur within 180 days of a vote having been cast with a simple majority of all votes cast, in favor of de-funding and termination.

Each such vote shall be posted on the dedicated secure CVRS website server for public access within 72 hours after the vote is cast, on the CVRS 'More Constitutional Government' portal.

Section 19. Pursuant to this legislation, the SCDNEP shall provide adequate funding and staffing to maintain a comprehensive database of each and every federal agency, bureau, code and regulation under review including date of commencement of review and effective date for de-funding and termination..

Section 20. No member of Congress or staff of any member of Congress shall interfere with any CVRS Work Group, other than each legislator's staff randomly selecting from voter registration or tax rolls, the citizens to serve on a CVRS Work Group.

Section 21. A CVRS member must serve a minimum of 90 days, and may serve on a Work Group for four consecutive years. No CVRS member shall serve for more than eight years in aggregate, with a minimum of two years intervening between periods of service.

Work Group members shall provide 30 days' notice prior to resigning or retiring from service.

Every CVRS member rendered incapable of service due to death or disability shall be immediately replaced with the next name in the service queue in that district and said replacement shall be summoned to begin service within 10 calendar days.

Section 22. No person shall serve on a CVRS Work Group if (s)he is presently employed by any agency of government or has been so employed within the preceding three years.

Section 23. Any current or former CVRS member receiving a financial benefit of more than $100 by virtue of his/her positive decision to retain a federal code section, regulation, agency, bureau, program or project shall be guilty of a federal felony.

4) The **Clean Bill Act**, stipulating:

Section 1. No omnibus bill shall be permitted. All bills passing out of any committee in Congress shall treat only the subject found in the title of the bill, and shall not exceed 50 pages, single-sided, double-spaced, 12-point type.

Section 2. No committee shall add any amendment, rider, or earmark or authorize any agency, bureau, department, expenditure, office, power, program or regulation that cannot be demonstrated is directly entailed in the subject and title of the bill.

Section 3. All bills when filed shall list the names and contact information of every private-sector individual and entity who initiated and/or proposed or suggested elements of said legislation.

5) The **Secure Borders Act**, stipulating:

Section 1. Each citizen of these United States has an in-alienable right to defend his own life, liberty, and property.

Section 2. Attending that right is the duty stipulated in Article I, Section 8, Clause 15 of the U.S. Constitution, for Citizen Militia to "execute the Laws of the Union, suppress Insurrections, and repel Invasions".

Section 3. Congress hereby acknowledges each border State's legislature's special right and duty stipulated in Article I, Section 8, Clause 16, to appoint the officers and train the Militia of that State.

Section 4. To aid in its duty per Clause 15, Congress shall provide for immediately finish constructing a secure border barrier, with reasonable alternatives employed for riverine sections of the U.S.-Mexico border, and Congress shall waive environmental, regulatory, and bureaucratic requirements such that the border fence project shall avoid the time and cost overruns common to federal government projects.

Section 5. Congress shall provide for an increase in border federal troop strength, airborne assets, and electronic detection as to furnish a demonstrably effective impediment to illegal crossing by any means.

Section 6. Congress shall coordinate this effort with the legislatures and their duly authorized Citizen Militia (where applicable) of the sovereign States of California, Arizona, New Mexico, and Texas, and shall accept all reasonable aid and alliance with said legislatures along their own sovereign borders, to timely construct said wall and/or fence.

Section 7. Congress shall immediately discontinue and de-fund all agencies, bureaus, policies and programs that encourage, facilitate, or support illegal immigration.

Section 8. As the Islamic belief system is well established and self-described as a militant organization and an exclusive, invasive law-code, Congress will assure that any individual shall be barred from immigration into this republic who is reasonably believed to adhere to sharia law, regardless of whether the aspiring immigrant's domicile of origin is an officially Islamic state.

Section 9. As stipulated in Article I, Section 8, Clause 15 of the U.S. Constitution, the several States retain the power to enforce this legislation by appropriate State legislation and duly authorized Citizen Militia enforcement within their respective jurisdictions.

6) **Senate Joint Resolution 6** of the 111th Congress, ending the illegal alien 'anchor baby' practice.

7) The **Congressional Anti-Corruption Act**, stipulating:

Section 1. SEC insider trading rules shall apply to members of Congress. It shall be a federal crime for a member of Congress, directly or through proxies, trusts, or other entities, to purchase or sell stock in any company materially affected by legislation of which the member of Congress may be reasonably expected to have knowledge.

Section 2. No incumbent or former member of Congress may lobby Congress on behalf of any domestic interest for a period of five years after leaving Congress, or on behalf of any foreign interest, for life.

Section 3. For any member of Congress to require any member to raise money as a prerequisite to being considered for or offered a seat or leadership role on any committee of Congress, shall be a federal felony.

Section 4. As stipulated in Article I, Section 8, Clause 15 of the U.S. Constitution, the several States retain the power to enforce this legislation by appropriate State legislation and duly authorized Citizen Militia enforcement within their respective jurisdictions.

8) The **Citizens' Privacy and Liberty Act**, stipulating:

Section 1. The American people's own persons, houses, papers, telephone, email, and other communications, vehicles and effects shall be free from any and all government surveillance, collection, seizure, storage, or detainment unless preceded by issuance of a specific, bona fide judicial warrant issued upon probable cause, as stipulated in the Fourth Amendment to the U.S. Constitution.

Section 2. With the benefit of the doubt accruing to the citizen, any portion of the FISA, RFPA, USA Patriot Act, NDAA, and Intelligence Authorization Act of 2004 or any similar legislation presently in effect that violates the Fourth Amendment, are hereby repealed.

Section 3. Congress shall bear responsibility and accountability to the American People to assure that any operations of the FBI, NSA, CIA, or any other federal intelligence agency, <u>or any major U.S.-based technology provider</u> shall scrupulously refrain from infringing on the privacy, or on the freedom of speech and expression of any American citizen, whether residing in any of the 50 sovereign States or residing temporarily overseas.

Section 4. It shall be a federal felony for any individual, corporation, or federal entity to engage in any optical, electronic, airborne, or satellite surveillance, collection, seizure, storage, detainment, tracing, or tracking of any American citizen, his property, or his communications, whether by means of traditional devices and methods or by 'nanobots', mini-drones, sniffer aircraft, satellite, concealed cameras or sensors, or any other means, unless the citizen has requested such 'service', or until a judicial or Grand Jury warrant is issued upon probable cause, supported by oath or affirmation and particularly describing place, items, or data to be searched and persons or things to be seized.

Section 5. No visa of an American citizen seeking to return to one of the 50 sovereign States, shall be revoked without due process of law.

Section 6. As stipulated in Article I, Section 8, Clause 15 of the U.S. Constitution, the several States retain the power to enforce this legislation by appropriate State legislation and duly authorized Citizen Militia enforcement within their respective jurisdictions.

9) The **Religious Treason Act,** outlawing religious laws or seditious activities in the name of any foreign religion, state, or legal system operating within these United States, stipulating as follows:

Preamble. As explained in hundreds of passages in the Quran itself as well as in precise detail in the book <u>The Quranic Concept of War</u> by Pakistani General S.K. Malik, the belief system established by Mohammed in the 7th century is full theocracy; a system of law and government. Islam demands adherence by all, obedience by all Muslims, and payment of a dhimmi's tax by all non-Muslims.

As Europe reels under a new Muslim invasion, we are prudent to recall the words of U.S. supreme Court Justice Joseph Story, who wrote in his massive work on the Constitution, "The real object of the First Amendment was not to countenance, much less to advance Mohammedanism, or Judaism, or infidelity, by prostrating Christianity, but only to exclude all rivalry among Christian sects and to prevent any national ecclesiastical establishment."

Ending immigration of potential enemies of America and our Constitution is neither the establishment of religion or impeding the free exercise of religion; rather, it is within Congress' responsibility to support the U.S. Constitution and the security of the sovereign States of this republic.

Section 1. Because Islam is <u>a means of warfare against all rivals</u>, and given the common tactic known as taqiyya which instructs Muslims to deceive in the interest of furthering Mohammed's system of law and government, the United States shall not allow immigration of any foreign national who adheres to Islam.

Section 2. For the same reason, adherence or allegiance to Islam shall disqualify any American citizen from taking public office at school district, city, county, state or national level.

Section 3. It shall be a federal offense for any elected or appointed U.S. federal public servant to travel to a foreign country with such travel funded by a foreign government or by a foreign or domestic private foundation or lobbying organization on behalf of any foreign country, people, or religion.

Section 4. Every lobbying group for any foreign country or religious cause – specifically any lobbying organization for Israel or any Islamic state – is required to register within 180 days of passage of this legislation, under the Foreign Agents Registration Act of 1938.

Section 5. Every applicant for U.S. naturalization shall be required to swear under oath his or her full allegiance to these United States of America and their laws. Any reasonably suspected of adherence to Islam or any other faith that calls for or sanctions in its established doctrines forcible conversion, supplanting American Law, or substantive discrimination against other faiths, shall be required to make an unambiguous public, videotaped renunciation of that faith.

Section 6. It shall be a federal offense for any educational or religious institution, public or private, to promote or incite violence, war, or a foreign code of law on the basis of any religious teaching, tradition, law, or on any other basis than the liberty and security of these United States of America.

Section 7. All individuals including American nationals, immigrants, resident aliens, and foreign diplomats, and all institutions within these United States found in violation of this law shall receive a warning and fine for the first infraction. A second offense shall warrant forfeiture of the individual's U.S. visa, indictment for treason or sedition, and seizure of assets held within these United States.

Section 8. Upon the first instance in any of these United States of attempted murder by conventional explosive or mass attack (three or more victims) by any individual or group associated with, or on behalf of, a religious belief or legal system, using any potentially lethal object (firearm, knife or vehicle) there shall issue a nationwide <u>warning</u> of a ban on all gatherings in, or use of, any and all facilities affiliated with said religious belief system within these United States.

Section 9. Upon the second instance described in Section 8, there shall issue a <u>ban</u> throughout these United States on all gatherings in, or use of, any and all facilities affiliated with said religious system within these United States.

Section 10. Upon the third instance described in Section 8, all property and other assets held by or in favor of, said religious system within these United States shall be seized and where applicable destroyed, and willful adherence to said system of belief or law within these United States shall thereafter be classified as sedition and if sufficiently egregious, treason.

Section 11. Upon the first instance of an individual or group associated with a foreign religious or legal system, discharging in any of these United States a nuclear, chemical, or biological device capable of inflicting mass casualties: all U.S.-based land, buildings, training facilities, bank accounts, and other assets of said religious or legal system shall be seized and where applicable, destroyed.

Section 12. As stipulated in Article I, Section 8, Clause 15 of the U.S. Constitution, the several States retain the power to enforce this legislation by appropriate State legislation and duly authorized Citizen Militia enforcement within their respective jurisdictions.

10) The **Internet Liberty Act**, stipulating:

Section 1. It shall be a federal felony for any individual or group within federal government or within any major technology service provider who – unilaterally or with other individuals, groups, organizations, or governments – disables or censors any citizen's access to the Internet so that it becomes inaccessible to the average computer or other Internet device in these sovereign States.

Section 2. As stipulated in Article I, Section 8, Clause 15 of the U.S. Constitution, the several States retain the power to enforce this legislation by appropriate State legislation and duly authorized Citizen Militia enforcement within their respective jurisdictions.

11) The **Constitutional Supremacy Act**, assuring the sovereignty of the American People and States, stipulating:

Section 1. No provision of a treaty or agreement, public or secret, conflicting with this Constitution or not made in pursuance thereof, shall be the supreme Law of the Land or be of general force or effect.

Section 2. No provision of a treaty or other international agreement shall become effective as internal law in the United States until it is enacted through legislation in Congress acting within its constitutionally enumerated powers.

Section 3. No Continuity of Government (COG) order may contravene, suspend or violate the U.S. Constitution in any particular.

Section 4. Per Article III, Section 2, Clause 2 of the U.S. Constitution, Congress hereby stipulates as an Exception that no federal court shall have jurisdiction in any matter arising under this Act.

Section 5. Any vote regarding advice and consent to ratification of a treaty shall be determined by yeas and nays and names of all persons voting for and against shall be entered in the Journal of the Senate.

Section 6. It shall be a federal felony for any individual or group to engage in or to materially support actions that threaten the legal or financial sovereignty of any of the sovereign States of America without the knowledge and consent of the legislature of each and every State whose citizens would be affected, regardless whether such action may formally constitute treason.

Section 7. Within 12 months from passage of this Act, Congress shall cease all foreign aid of a military nature to any government, regime, entity, or individual.

Section 8. Within 24 months from passage of this Act, Congress shall cease all foreign aid of a non-military nature to any government, regime, entity, or individual. Said aid shall be immediately reduced by 33% for the first 12 months and by 66% for the second 12 months.

12) The **American Sovereignty Restoration Act** of 2017 (HR193) of the 115th Congress, and stipulating:

Section 1. This bill repeals the United Nations Participation Act of 1945 and other specified related laws.

Section 2. The President shall terminate U.S. membership in the United Nations (U.N.), including any organ, specialized agency, commission, or other formally affiliated body.

Section 3. The President shall close the U.S. Mission to the United Nations.

Section 4. The following shall hereafter be unlawful: a) Any funds for the U.S. assessed or voluntary contribution to the U.N.; b) Any authorization of funds for any U.S. contribution to any U.N. military or peacekeeping operation; c) Expenditure of funds to support the participation of U.S. Armed Forces as part of any U.N. military or peacekeeping operation; d) U.S. armed forces serving under U.N. com-mand; and d) diplomatic immunity for U.N. officers or employees.

13) The **Lawful Wars Act**, reiterating Congress' duty to declare wars, repealing the War Powers Resolution of 1973 and barring any administration from initiating foreign hostilities or mobilizing U.S. military in foreign lands without a Declaration of War; requiring Congress to assure that such mobilization or hostilities are necessary to defend against a demonstrable threat to these United States.

14) The **Federal Pork Sunset Act,** stipulating:

In Fiscal Year 2019, federal government doled out over $700 billion in illicit funds to the States, counties, and cities across our republic. The long tradition of such 'pork' projects with strings attached has perverted the citizen's view of his place atop the Constitution's hierarchy and allowed Washington D.C. organized crime to assume the role of benevolent master, with the sovereign States and cities as so many piglets at sow-teats. This criminogenic arrangement has rendered our local, county and State public servants willing to do whatever they must, to receive their share of funds (originating from the people themselves) from countless unaccountable, largely invisible federal agencies. This criminal activity must end.

Section 1. For three (3) fiscal years after passage of this Act, all revenues sent by federal government as grants to States and their subdivisions shall be remitted as a single block grant to each State, with no federal conditions attached, i.e., the States having liberty to determine all uses of said funds.

Section 2. Commencing on the first day of the fourth fiscal year after the date of passage of this Act, any federal grant to a State or subdivision thereof shall be a federal felony.

15) The **Minuteman Act**, pursuant to Congress's power to "provide for…arming…the Militia" contained in the U.S. Constitution, stipulating:

Section 1. The National Firearms Act of 1934, Omnibus Crime Control and Safe Streets Act of 1968, the Gun Control Act of 1968, the Firearm Owners Protection Act of 1986, and the Brady Handgun Violation Prevention Act of 1993 are hereby repealed.

Section 2. No statute, regulation, executive order, or other directive with the purported force of law of federal government, present or future, or that of any State or subdivision thereof, shall infringe on or burden the right of any citizen of, or legal resident alien in, any State who is eligible for membership in that State's Militia to purchase, own, possess, transport, or sell, whether interstate or intrastate, any firearm, ammunition, or related accoutrements suitable for service in a Militia as that term is used in the U.S. Constitution.

Section 3. No statute, regulation, executive order, or other directive with the purported force of law of federal government, present or future, shall infringe on or burden, except on the same terms as apply to any other business, the right of any person to engage in the commercial design, manufacture, repair, sale and distribution, or other trade or occupation involving firearms, ammunition, and Militia accoutrements.

Section 4. As stipulated in Article I, Section 8, Clause 15 of the U.S. Constitution, the several States retain the power to enforce this legislation by appropriate State legislation and duly authorized Citizen Militia enforcement within their respective jurisdictions and subdivisions.

16) The **Non-Conscription Act**, stipulating:

Section 1. Neither Congress nor any president or federal court has the power to conscript Americans of any age into involuntary national service or servitude of any kind.

Section 2. As stipulated in Article I, Section 8, Clause 15 of the U.S. Constitution, the several States retain the power to enforce this legislation by appropriate State legislation and duly authorized Citizen Militia enforcement within their respective jurisdictions.

17) The **Return of Sovereign Lands Act**, stipulating:

Section 1. Upon acceptance as a sovereign State of these United States, all lands and resources within said State become the sovereign property of the American People living within said State, and the individual right to private property is no more sacred than the collective right of sovereign property for every sovereign government on earth. The federal government has no lawful authority or claim of sovereignty over – or claim to minerals or other natural resources in, on or under – any land on earth, except as stipulated in Article I, Section 8, Clause 17 of the U.S. Constitution.

Section 2. No sale of any land or resource within any of the sovereign States shall be made by the U.S. government or any entity thereof on behalf of said government, effective immediately, except such surface land as stipulated in Article I, Section 8, Clause 17 of the U.S. Constitution.

Section 3. The United States government shall, within 24 months of the passage of this Act, relinquish all claims to, or jurisdiction in, all sovereign places other than those lands specifically stipulated in Article I, Section 8, Clause 17 of the U.S. Constitution as being within the exclusive legislative domain of Congress.

*Section 4. The federal government has no constitutional authority to **seize** private or State sovereign land, water, timber, oil, gas, minerals, or other natural resources in, on, or under such land in any State, for any reason, under any conditions.*

*Section 5. Other than purchases from the States for military installations, federal government has no constitutional authority to **accept** lands or resources via a State constitution or legislative act.*

Section 6. As to purchases from the sovereign States for military installations, federal government has constitutional authority to purchase lands in a State only with "Consent of the Legislature of the State in which the Same shall be". Said consent of the State Legislature must be accompanied by a majority-vote approval of the People of that State via single-issue referendum or plebiscite.

Section 7. All present federally claimed, held, or controlled lands and any minerals, water, forests and timber, or any other resource within each sovereign State shall revert within 24 months to full control and ownership of the State in which it is located, to be managed and controlled as the People of that State shall determine. The costs of transferring control of formerly federally-claimed lands and natural resources shall be borne by the State in which said lands and resources are located.

Section 8. All federal land-use regulations, national forest and park acts, and like federal controls, restrictions, and prohibitions that deprive private owners of the full use and enjoyment of their private properties pursuant to the laws of the several States, shall be repealed within 12 months of passage of this Act.

Section 9. As reparations for the past federal use and control of sovereign State lands, all federal government improvements, fixtures, facilities, equipment, vehicles and other appurtenances located within each sovereign State (except on military installations) shall become the property of that State, effective immediately. The legal transfer of all said public property located within each State shall be administered by the government of that State, and shall include executive, legislative and judicial branches and Citizen Militia as applicable.

Section 10. Congress shall provide to the sovereign People of the United States, within 12 months of passage of this Act, its detailed plan to relinquish control of all foreign military bases and to cease funding for, and operations of, all foreign land-based military and civil government operations, transferring foreign civil governance to the governments or people of those sovereign lands, within 36 months of the passage of this Act.

Section 11. Irrespective of any local independence movements within sovereign foreign lands outside the 48 contiguous and United States, all noncontiguous, foreign, and/or 'U.S. possession' claims shall revert to the full, un-fettered control of the peoples of those sovereign lands (including Hawaii and Alaska, neither of which People ever applied for statehood but were instead invaded and claimed by Washington D.C.) at their own expense and with no additional expense borne by American citizens after 24 months from passage of this Act.

18) The **Lawful United States Money and Banking Act** which will contain elements of, but be more comprehensive than H.R. 459, 833, 1094, 1095, 1098, 1496 and 2768 and SB 202, stipulating:

Section 1. The American people have delegated the power to 'coin Money' only to Congress, and have delegated to Congress only the power to 'coin' Money.

Section 2. Congress lacks any authority to delegate or to fail, neglect, or refuse to exercise this power.

Section 3. The Legal Tender Act of 1862, the Federal Re-serve Act of 1913, and all subsequent amendments of those acts, have been unconstitutional since their enactment.

Section 4. The special privileges now attaching to Federal Reserve Notes— that such notes shall be redeemed in lawful money by the United States Department of the Treasury, shall be receivable for all taxes and other public dues, and shall be legal tender for all debts, public and private—have since enactment been in violation of our Supreme Law.

Section 5. As remedies for these violations of the Constitution, Congress shall establish as an alternative to the Federal Reserve System and notes, a system of official money consisting solely of gold and silver, with silver coins valued in 'dollars' at the prevailing exchange rate between silver and gold in the free market.

Section 6. This new, lawful U.S. money shall be produced through immediate free coinage of whatever gold and silver may be brought to the United States Mints; including sale of the existing national gold stocks, replaced by silver stock if the gold-silver ratio suggests silver as preferable for the initial coinage.

Section 7. Said reserves and coinage and/or fully-convertible paper or electronic receipts for physical gold and silver, shall be substituted for Federal Reserve Notes as rapidly as maintenance of stability throughout America's economy will permit, in all financial transactions of the general government.

Section 8. The Federal Reserve Act of 1913 (as amended) shall be further amended such that: a) after the effective date of such legislation, the Federal Reserve System shall have no official relationship to the general government, and b) Federal Reserve regional banks shall obtain new charters from the States consistent with the laws thereof or cease doing business as of the date on which the Secretary of the Treasury shall certify that all financial transactions of federal government are being conducted solely in gold and silver or fully-convertible paper or electronic receipts for physical gold and silver.

Section 9. The States have always enjoyed the right as sovereign governments and a duty pursuant to Article I, Section 10 of the Constitution to employ gold and silver coin or fully-convertible paper or electronic receipts for physical gold and silver, to the exclusion of any other currency as the medium of exchange in their functions. Neither Congress, nor the president, nor any court, nor any international or supra-national body, nor any private parties have any authority to require a State to employ anything other than gold and silver coin or fully-convertible paper or electronic receipts for physical gold and silver, for such purposes.

Section 10. The practice of fractional reserve banking is to be ended within 12 months of passage of this legislation, and all American financial institutions shall be required to maintain in their vaults 100% reserves against loans made. Any financial institution accepting deposits, that is unable to pay on demand all such deposits in gold and/or silver or fully-convertible paper or electronic receipts for physical gold and silver, the directors, officers, shareholders, partners, trustees, or other owners and managers of said institution shall be personally liable (their own personal assets subject to seizure) to satisfy unpaid deposit balances under the laws of the State in which the demand for payment of such balances is made.

Section 11. It shall be a federal felony for any person to enact or enforce any tax or financial burden on: a) any exchange of one form of United States money for another form of money thereof, notwithstanding that the nominal value of one form may be different than the nominal value of the other form involved in the transaction; or b) the movement of privately-owned United States money by any private citizen, to or from the United States to or from any other domicile that said private citizen may desire, provided said funds are not being demonstrably used in, or do not demonstrably result from, illegal activity.

Section 12. This legislation shall apply to Federal Reserve Notes, base-metallic and debased silver coinage, and all paper currencies of the United States until the date on which the Secretary of the Treasury shall certify that all federal financial transactions are being conducted solely in gold and silver or fully-convertible paper or electronic receipts for physical gold and silver, and thereafter only as Congress deems necessary.

19) The **Intelligent Republic Act**, a reform law based loosely on the Smart Nation Act, sponsored by Congressman Rob Simmons (R-CT), must provide for orderly dismantling of all secret intelligence operations of federal government as recommended by former CIA officers Kevin Shipp and Robert Steele.

The National Security Act of 1947 created the CIA and the National Security Council, which is accountable only to presidents. *Congress, which represents the People and the States, allowed itself no oversight of the NSC.* That criminal act of legislation never defined or limited what the CIA can do or cannot do, but also clearly cannot and must not authorize, allow, or fund covert operations closed to congressional oversight.

Even if the House Permanent Select Committee on Intelligence and the Senate Select Committee on Intelligence attempted to de-fund the most egregious crimes of this criminal agency, the CIA makes this impossible. First, it makes all of its budget line items and appropriations classified, keeping its operations secret from Congress thus making it impossible to de-fund the agency in part.

Second, the CIA maintains blackmail dossiers on all members of Congress so that no legislator would dare reduce that criminal organization's programs or funding. Thus, this criminal operation as well as the deeply corrupt FBI, must be dismantled, outlawed, and de-funded *in full*.

With illicit funding generated by foreign drug operations, these criminal agencies give themselves vast, unconstitutional powers over the American People and even over American elections and those of foreign countries.

Secret agencies unaccountable to the American people are unconstitutional and have increasingly destructive impact on American security, liberty, and public morale. It is clearly unconstitutional for federal government to create foreign operating agencies, fund private offshore contractors, or create alliances with foreign countries, whether for intelligence or supposed 'defense'. Such corrupt traditions violate the Constitution by usurping the authority of Congress and the Militia.

The Constitution stipulates that the Citizen Militia shall *"execute the Laws of the Union, suppress Insurrections, and repel Invasions"*. Thus, all networks, cells, and offices for intelligence in the American republic *must* operate under the local aegis of the Citizen Militia and are ultimately the duty and authority of the American People themselves. Each unit of Citizen Militia, according to the Constitution, is to follow *"the discipline prescribed by Congress"*, with officers appointed by and training, equipment, logistics supplied by its State legislature.

~~~

We The People reserve the right to revise and extend the list of federal government arrogations, violations, and usurpations brought to our attention for remediation by AmericaAgain! members via our State courts and through reform legislation.

Notwithstanding the long tradition of congressional corruption and arrogation warned against by James Madison, the numerous retained powers of We the People includes power to allow *no implication beyond the powers specifically enumerated* to our federal servant; for our benefit, not theirs. As members of AmericaAgain! and its TACTICAL CIVICS™ chapter network, we resolve to enforce the Law of the Land under Amendment X; the People and States retain all powers not specifically enumerated to federal government.

For many generations, Washington D.C. has arrogated to itself powers nowhere granted to federal government by the sovereign People or States. We The People shall now put the shoe on the other foot, exercising our almost limitless retained powers as clearly stipulated in Amendment X, but only to enforce the U.S. Constitution and its limitations on our federal servants. We intend to thus tighten the chains of the Constitution via our Indictment Engine™ and the Grand Juries of our States to criminally indict members of Congress and State legislatures whose violation of the supreme law and our liberty are found to coincide with felonies in their State criminal statutes.

We shall bring our members of Congress home from doing the bidding of powerful individuals in party machines behind the scenes – to now work beside us and under our watchful eyes in their own home districts which shall now be smaller and more difficult for powerful interests to corrupt.

Violations of State criminal statutes are exclusive original and appellate jurisdiction of the courts of the State in which the parties reside. No State being a party to these actions, nothing in the Constitution or federal law can be construed to allow federal courts to steal jurisdiction and exonerate such perpetrators.

AmericaAgain!, through its TACTICAL CIVICS™ chapter network, seeks to rekindle the lawful, pre-constitutional Grand Juries and Militias in each County, for we share the founders' concerns about government – now including many State governments – seeking to disarm the People, their sovereign and violating the U.S. Constitution and their state constitutions with impunity. It is the duty of all citizens, as codified in the Fourth, Fifth, and Sixth Amendments to the U.S. Constitution, to serve in their county Grand Jury to check and superintend their servants in county and municipal government, and any other servant, whether in state or federal office who lives and works in the county, to investigate any credible complaint or presentment of potential criminal behavior by said officers.

And it is also the duty of all citizens who are physically and mentally fit for the duty, to be armed and trained to fulfill the Citizen Militia functions in Article I, Section 8, Clause 15 of the Constitution. Per Clause 16, it is the duty of the States to provide officers and training for Citizen Militias, yet no State legislature has yet fully performed such duty. Until the State legislatures do so, it is the People's express and retained power as well as our God-given right, to have our County governments fill the void, or even to defend ourselves.

We seek to be better stewards of the natural resources that God has entrusted to us – rather than allowing our government in our name, to help corporations plunder resources of foreign countries.

This organization is explicitly, unashamedly Christian. It will *perpetually* hold to, support, and defend the Christian doctrine of the Apostle's Creed, and will require of all national leadership and regional trustees, an oath or affirmation of that statement of faith. Although this be a perpetual trust, should it ever fail to glorify Jesus Christ and defend the faith and norms attached thereto, *it shall be dissolved.*

In our membership and operations we seek no theocracy; but the American civilization was founded as a Christian – not Atheist, Jewish, Muslim, Hindu, Buddhist, Catholic or Mormon – commonwealth. None of those beliefs, or any other, has produced equally efficacious or humane law, economics, or social practices. Although some Founding Fathers were not orthodox Christians, the vast majority were. A survey of America's original colonial documents of government, law, economics, and social life demonstrates that America is founded on Christianity and no other belief system. A survey of the history of atheism, 1947 political Judaism, Islam, Hinduism, Buddhism, Catholicism, and Mormonism have no such historical record of accomplishments. Yet we only exclude Muslims because that is a system of government and law at war with ours; it is not merely a 'religion'.

In building, reinforcing, promoting, refining and organizing our TACTICAL CIVICS™ chapter network, we refuse to operate in any unlawful, seditious, riotous, rebellious, paranoid, or terrorist manner. We also refuse to allow this tactical mission of We the People to be co-opted, overseen, or infested by politicians, lobbyists, or operatives from any government or political party, foreign or domestic. We will organize and operate locally as free citizens in the privacy of our homes, businesses, and churches – or in public parks and any venue that suits us as owners and residents of such places – expecting to have no government infiltration, or coercion as is common to tyrant regimes.

Should our member of congress, state legislator, or governor refuse to cease violating the law; should he prevaricate and bloviate as politicians do, or conspire anew with like-minded scoundrels and oligarchs who purchased his first allegiance – we will seek his criminal conviction in State Court; the longest possible State Penitentiary term; and as actual and punitive damages for massive fraud and conspiracy, we will seek to have our State Court seize all assets held under any structure, in any jurisdiction, inuring to his benefit or that of his family or descendants.

To any state or county prosecutor, district attorney, judge, constable, sheriff or other public servant who refuses to oversee justice as your oath of office demands, We The People will see that your complicity in potential high crimes is included in a separate felony presentment to your Grand Jury, jointly deployed with our community or county Militia.

No defendant in Congress can plead ignorance of the U.S. Constitution or ignorance of federal laws over which he is responsible – even those for which he voted without reading. Ignorance of the law is no defense for public servants who swear an oath to support the U.S. Constitution, only to violate it daily, as was done in the 'COVID-19' scheme of 2020.

We the People will offer immunity from indictment to a member of Congress only if that defendant, in writing with notarized witnesses from among our membership, agrees to withdraw support for or cease acquiescence in the crime(s) for which we seek his indictment; sponsor or co-sponsor legislation outlined above, drafted by citizens; and refrain from supporting any amendment thereto.

AmericaAgain! and its TACTICAL CIVICS™ chapter network is an effort conceived by free, productive citizens of these sovereign States of America who believe that by God's grace, a diligent minority can restore liberty, property, rule of law, honest elections, and the collective sovereignty of We the People that we guaranteed ourselves in the U.S. Constitution.

Each public servant leaves a public record in history. Their response to their sovereigns now enforcing the Constitution will demonstrate either their repentant fidelity or their ignominious corruption.

We give thanks to God in the name of Jesus Christ His Son, and ask His blessing on this formerly godly republic, that we may be AmericaAgain!

We The People of the fifty United States of America

National Day of Thanksgiving

Original, November 22, 2012   (Rev 112- Nov 22, 2021)

Appendix G
Tactical Civics™ Declaration

The charter members of TACTICAL CIVICS™ are, for the first time in mankind's history, forging a responsible, repentant Remnant into an educated, organized, lawful, peaceful force of Popular Constitutionalism, and helping our Congress to become history's first distributed legislature. *That is no small feat.*

What Obama and the Dragon Brought

Hatched in the Lincoln administration, we began witnessing the kicking, screaming, clawing, biting death of 150-year-old American Communism when Hussein Obama removed Communism's mask and the Chinese dragon took resident Biden's invitation and removed its mask as well. Now, the CCP is helping to transform Washington DC into a brazen, arrogant, clinically insane Communist stronghold. *This is the attempted overthrow of America.*

More than 100 million normal, productive Americans in the heartland will never stand for this. As the criminal, ruthless 10-by-10-mile city state on the Potomac finally shows the world its true colors, it is awakening the American Heartland. Until TACTICAL CIVICS™, We The People did not know what to do about it. *Most still don't.*

What America's Going to Do About It

But now, we in the repentant remnant *do* know what to do...

First, we are turning off Washington DC; watching and listening to organized crime as it sinks into its final pathetic years as a world power. We're increasingly tuning it out. For us normal folks, watching this idiocy in the federal, state, county, local, and school district palaces is like sitting in an insane asylum. We're outta there, and taking our money, too (more on that, below).

Second, We The People are walking away from Google, Facebook, Twitter, all mainstream media, Hollywood, and any tech company that decides to de-platform or ban us. Fantastic; you're dead to us, too. We'll find alternatives. *You won't.*

Third, We The People will pay no more attention to the sociopath political machines of Atlanta, Baltimore, Chicago, Dallas, Detroit, Houston, Los Angeles, Phoenix, Minneapolis, New York City, Philadelphia, and a couple of dozen other feral hellholes. In America's 31,000 small towns and all the rural homesteads in between, we intend to take control back, and *not* by the rigged game called politics. We're going to live our lives as normal, God-fearing, God-glorifying Americans. We refuse to give another minute to the sick values of God-hating, collapsing urban sewers. Hey, big cities: that's why your real estate values and tax bases are plummeting. Get a clue.

Fourth, We The People are restoring our Grand Jury and constitutional Militia in every one of the 3,141 counties, boroughs, and parishes in these sovereign States.

Fifth, We The People working on the app development team at TACTICAL CIVICS™ plan to develop, refine, and launch the Indictment Engine™ mobile app to scan every proposed state or federal bill before it becomes legislation, and if it violates the Constitution, generate felony presentments to be sent to the Grand Jury of the counties of every sponsor and co-sponsor (conspirator and co-conspirator of the attempted felony) in each perpetrator's State Judicial District.

Sixth, We The People intend to force 27 more State legislatures to ratify the original First Right in the Bill of Rights, requiring that no US congressional district exceed 50,000 persons; the only subject on which George Washington felt strongly enough about to address during the four-month constitutional convention in 1787. America's 31,000 small towns and millions of rural Americans will have representation in the U.S. House and Electoral College for the first time in a century.

Seventh, We The People intend to then bring Congress home to work under *our* watchful eye, as they obviously have not 'checked and balanced' one another in generations. In Article I, Section 8, Clause 17, we grant that Congress shall have 'exclusive legislative jurisdiction' in that 10-by-10-mile plot of land on the Potomac. So once we bring them home and have normal American statesmen filling those seats, we will take control of the agencies and bureaucracies that fill that ruthless, criminal city-state that plunders and threatens the whole earth, beginning with its own sovereigns, enriching the few thousand wealthiest and most ruthless humans on earth.

Eighth, through 6600+ Citizens Volunteer Research Service (CVRS) teams created by our Non-Enumerated Powers Sunset Act (NEPSA), We The People will review, red-line, de-fund, and outlaw ('sunset') every agency, bureau, department, office, program, and regulation that We The People did not *specifically* authorize in our Constitution and have no need for. This review will be *at the People's sole discretion,* with each member of the U.S. House *required* to sign off to his/her CVRS team's decisions. When a majority of CVRS teams has red-lined an agency, program, or regulatory line item, it is de-funded, shut down, and outlawed. *Period.*

We The People are serious about organized crime. Any congressman found to have interfered with or attempted to change any CVRS team's decision will have committed a felony, as will be stipulated in NEPSA and similar State statutes.

Ninth, We The People intend to immediately de-fund the US Department of Education (Indoctrination) and assure that no public, private, or religious school shall have any nexus with federal government, except as stipulated in our proposed *Religious Treason Act,* outlawing religious laws or seditious activities in the name of any foreign religion, state, or legal system operating within these United States, stipulating,

"As explained in hundreds of passages in the Quran itself as well as in precise detail in the book The Quranic Concept of War by Pakistani General S.K. Malik, the belief system established by Mohammed in the 7th century is theocracy; a system of law and government. Islam demands adherence by all, obedience by all Muslims, and payment of a dhimmi's tax by all non-Muslims".

Any such 'school' is seditious and destructive to America's rule of law. We The People are shutting down jihad.

Tenth, We The People intend to start keeping what we earn. As explained in the book, *A Tax Honesty Primer,* without a dollar of individual income taxes, corporate tax revenues, federal excises, imposts, and import duties are *more* than sufficient to fund what We The People authorize government to do.

Note on Parental Choice in Child-Rearing

We will support other efforts that are not included in our formal mission's trust deed; especially every state reform law providing parental school choice vouchers, beginning with tax credits and equal to 100% of state per-pupil expenditure, no strings attached, for each student who is homeschooled or enrolled in a private school. Liberating American minds from the propaganda and counter-factual American history programmed into us for the past century is vitally important.

Note on Private Property in this Republic

The same is true of ending *ad valorem* property taxes in this Republic. The rapacious state legislatures in their palaces, in the name of bureaucrats have *outlawed* private property in America, in favor of wasteful, bloated pork programs and bureaucratic empires over which the owners of homes, farms, and shops have no control or voice, yet by which predators and parasites (and their collections lawyers) are held hostage for life, as the people of every Communist country. This practice of a monarch holding the People hostage for life to the crown began with William the Conqueror in 1066 A.D. and was exported to the American colonies by King James, along with chattel and indentured slavery.

It is time for this cruel, despotic practice of feudalism to end in this Republic! When an American has paid in full for a piece of property, that property should be the free, clear property of its owner, with no level of government having its hooks – and its collections lawyers' and sheriffs' hooks – in that private property. It has always been a fundamental tenet of American self-government that the People be truly self-governing; that a grasping, communistic majority cannot seize the property of the minority against the minority's will or hold that minority in lifelong servitude to cover ever-growing expenses of lawless bureaucracies.

This practice has led to an increasing number of Americans opting for entire careers in the cancerous, lawless, limitless 'public sector', which at this point is far closer to Karl Marx's system than to that of our Founding Fathers.

Preparing For Your Chapter

We The People are now rising up and reporting for duty in our own counties from coast to coast, to create and maintain a 3,141-county *permanent* law enforcement against organized crime and corrupt arrogations from our federal, state, county, city, and school district palaces. *Enough is enough!*

There are 19 reform laws in the AmericaAgain! Declaration that TACTICAL CIVICS™ members will be pushing in decades to come. But no population has ever done anything like this before. Yes, it's just what's in our Constitution. Yes, the Internet and social media makes it a no-brainer. But by God's grace and the counsel of the Holy Spirit over more than a decade in the lives of 44 volunteers, TACTICAL CIVICS™ is the first mission to finally put all the pieces together.

Now, every corrupt careerist in all levels of government is thinking like *the cantina scene in A Bug's Life* when Hopper tells the other grasshoppers that their lives of leisure are over. The sleeping giant is waking up, and our mission is the point of the spear: lawful, peaceful, full-spectrum, and long-term.

So far, we are like infants in a crib, just figuring out our shapes, colors, and letters. So until you know the materials, don't hold your first formal meeting. But as soon as you do the Chapter Builder Boot Camp, you can gather with one or two or a handful of new acquaintances to show them the new way of life that lies ahead for the responsible remnant.

We cannot adequately stress that your first task is: join your County Chapter, follow the step-by-step instructions, and *learn the mission.*

Your First Chapter Meeting

Each chapter leader should watch our video *Introducing Tactical Civics™,* then play it for your new members to begin your first formal county chapter meeting, then discuss it. If you have time, show the PowerPoint presentation. Or you can do that at your second meeting, then discuss that.

When you join our mission, you will have three field handbooks.

Chapter Leader's Field Handbook Volume 1 walks you through every step:

- Holding your first meeting (press release, blogger resources to announce it)
- When, where, and how to run regular meetings
- How to prepare your county for your annual Tactical Civics™ gala event
- How to recruit responsible, concerned citizens
- How to spot and quickly eject moles, *agents provocateurs*, and showboats

- How to work with area constitutional Militia unit(s), or help others start one

- How to recruit Tactical Civics™ Affiliates in local small businesses

- How to work with area churches

- How to train/brief county residents in their Grand Jury duty and authority

- And much more...

Field Handbook Volume 2 introduces you to the Grand Jury; things you never knew will inspire and liberate you as political parties were never able to do. Teaches you how to get a Grand Jury page added to your county government's website where citizens can volunteer for Grand Jury and submit confidential presentments (reports or complaints of potentially criminal activity in the county). Presents our model County Grand Jury Ordinance and teaches you how to get it enacted in your county.

Field Handbook Volume 3 is the definitive operations book in America today on constitutional Militia: what it is, how to restore it, and how to operate your local or county unit. Presents our model County Militia Ordinance and teaches you how to get it enacted in your county.

[Note: while our members may wish to join Militia, Tactical Civics™ is not Militia; we only support and aid local constitutional Militia.] Even for existing armed groups who believe they're 'militia', this book will be liberating to every man humble enough to return to the Founding Fathers' plan.

For those who want a preliminary explanation of constitutional Militia or want to begin a county unit, read our book, *Time to Start Over, America*. It explains in simple terms why it's absurd for a person to claim they're for the Constitution but don't like Militia: if you're against Militia then you're against the Constitution. *Militia is the only way to enforce the Constitution,* authorized in that law.

Regarding Militia

We advise you in advance: *the Alpha Male private militant group leader will almost never be a good fit because he thinks the unit belongs to him. The easiest test of such men is, challenge them to get our Militia Ordinance passed in your county governmental board's public meeting, at the same meeting just after we get our Grand Jury Ordinance passed. If they refuse or drag their feet in getting the County Militia Ordinance passed, you can bet that they have no interest in properly executed, constitutional Militia and will eventually destroy the unit or at least waste a great deal of time before splitting off.*

We recommend to Militia leaders that if you must start with a clean sheet, do it. But be sure to recruit men who are tough, smart men of their word, who will show up for training and muster; who are godly, rational, and respectful. We call our program American Militia 2.0™ because too many 'militia' groups are like false flag Antifa cells hidden among honorable American men who want to do their duty.

Regarding Pastors

'Men of God' need to start acting the part. We have several pastors in our number; all the same kind of man. They don't march to the tune of a religious franchise, and they don't lead a flock for a salary, car, house, and benefits.

America's careerist pastors are even more stiff-necked than 'threeper' Alpha Males. That's why George Barna reported over a decade ago in his book *Revolution,* that 25 million Christians had walked away from church buildings and back to Jesus. The number is surely much larger now. On both sides of the Atlantic, men in frocks have a great deal to repent.

The local church can be every bit as vital as the local gun dealer, shooting range, or Militia unit. Repairing these ruins without pastors makes no sense. Our 7-week Crash course is a book called *Mission to America,* and is perfect for church small groups. The book *Tactical Civics™ For Church Leaders* was written specifically for American pastors to stop avoiding our civic duties while making the excuse, "we don't do politics". *Our Romans 13 duty over the Constitution and rule of law is <u>not</u> politics!*

What a Massive Job Ahead!

Well, yes. That is true.

And what a zoo all around us, predators and parasites threatening to outnumber the honest and productive if we, like Europeans, continue to avoid our duties.

Tactical Civics™ is full-spectrum, long-term, and looks extremely difficult. But those who go through our Training Center step by step will learn that this mission is designed for the newbie; we break this new way of life down into simple steps and individual study units and action projects. It will be much easier for the next generation, and even easier for the one after that.

But for now, we repeat the old aphorism...

People who say that it cannot be done should not interrupt those who are doing it.

Copyright 2021 AmericaAgain! Trust

Revision 4 (2 February 2022)

About the Author

David M. Zuniga is a graduate of the University of Texas (BS, Architectural Engineering) and was for 28 years a professional architectural engineer designing schools, churches, industrial, and commercial buildings and their structural, plumbing, HVAC, electrical, and site civil systems. He has also been a cattleman, custom homebuilder, commercial contractor, SCUBA instructor, cross-culture church planter, missionary pilot, land surveyor, and subdivision designer and developer.

Having founded four classical Christian K-12 schools in three states, he designed their curricula including Latin, Logic, Rhetoric, and the Great Books of Western Civilization.

Shocked at the government fraud of 9/11, beginning in 2006 he spent 14 months in monastic seclusion, prayer and study of 110 key books. He wrote the first draft of the *AmericaAgain! Declaration* and refined the document with the help of many fine Americans including constitutionalist radio show host Mike Church and constitutional scholar and author Edwin Vieira Jr.

Establishing AmericaAgain! Trust with his brother Oscar in 2009, David wrote his first book *This Bloodless Liberty* in 2010 to convey his vision. In 2015 he published *Fear The People,* introducing a full-spectrum action plan to restore popular sovereignty and rule of law. In 2018, he began writing the 5-volume Tactical Civics™ series to break down this new way of life into brief books for action, and he has now published over a dozen books.

With his co-founders, in January 2021 David helped launch the TACTICAL CIVICS™ Training Center and a year later, Americans had already launched about 250 county chapters.

David has been a guest on Infowars Nightly News and is a recurring guest on radio shows across the republic. His published articles have appeared on many blogs, forums and alternative media.

David has two children and six grandchildren. They live in the Hill Country of Texas where they serve no king but King Jesus.

NOTES

Made in United States
Orlando, FL
08 September 2022